"The Lord Jesus shall be revealed from heaven..."
2 Thess. 1:7

THINKING THROUGH
THESSALONIANS

BIBLE STUDY TEXTBOOK

THINKING THROUGH THESSALONIANS

A New

- Commentary
- Workbook
- Teaching Manual

Wilbur Fields

College Press, Joplin, Missouri

Dedicated

To My Father

Whose holy life and hard work
will surely be remembered in heaven.

ACKNOWLEDGEMENTS

1. To Robert E. Huffman, Midland, Ohio, for art work illustrating the chapter topics.
2. To Seth Wilson, Dean of Ozark Bible College, Joplin, Mo., for permission to print his articles—"The Coming Judge" and "A Secret Rapture Considered."
3. To Don DeWelt, editor of College Press, Joplin, Mo., for much assistance. Also for a quotation from his booklet, *You And Me and God.*
4. To R. C. Foster, Cincinnati, Ohio, for permission to use his book, THE FINAL WEEK. (Copyright 1962)
5. To University of Chicago Press, for permission to quote THE BIBLE, AN AMERICAN TRANSLATION, By J. Powis Smith and Edgar J. Goodspeed. Copyright 1935.
6. To Oxford University Press and Cambridge University Press for use of a few quotations from THE NEW ENGLISH BIBLE. (Copyright 1961)
7. To Loizeaux Brothers, Bible Truth Depot, New York 10, N.Y., for use of a few quotations from *Addresses On The First and Second Epistles of Thessalonians,* By H. A. Ironside. Copyright 1947.
8. To Harper and Brothers Publishers, New York, N.Y., for use of a few quotations from *The New Testament, A New Translation,* By James Moffatt. Copyright 1922, 1935.
9. To the Macmillan Company, New York, N.Y., for use of a few quotations from *The New Testament in Modern English,* By J. B. Phillips. Copyright 1958.
10. To Thomas Nelson and Sons, New York, N.Y., for use of a few quotations from the *Revised Standard Version* of the New Testament. Copyright, 1946.
11. To the Lockman Foundation, La Habra, Calif., for use of certain references from the *Amplified New Testament.* Copyright 1958.
12. To the many other people and books that have been helpful in the preparation of this book. Wherever possible, we have tried to give credit where credit is due.
13. To the Lord God whose answers to prayers made this book possible.

Preface

HELP FOR YOU—FIVE LAYERS DEEP!

To help you to know and understand God's word, this book offers five layers of help.

(1) *"Thinking Through Thessalonians"*—At the beginning of the study of each chapter is a group of questions called "Thinking Through Thessalonians." These are designed to help the person who has little or no knowledge of the Bible text to get acquainted with it. All the blanks in these sections can be filled in with no help but a common King James Bible.

(2) *Outlines*—Outlines of both of the Thessalonian letters, and all of the chapters are given.

(3) *Translation and Paraphrase*—A translation from Nestle's Greek New Testament is given. This is as accurate and literal as we can make it. With the translation we have included a paraphrase, other words to make the meaning of the verses as clear and complete as possible. The words in parentheses are the paraphrase. Usually reading the translation and paraphrase alone will make Paul's thoughts quite clear.

(4) *Notes*—Notes on every verse are given. Most notes are practical comments on the message of the verses. Some notes are technical, but wherever possible, we have tried to make all of them understandable to the general reader.

(5) *"Did You Learn?"*—The study of each chapter concludes with a section of review questions entitled "Did You Learn?" (The Introductory Sections also have questions of this type.)

Besides these five layers of help, there are some useful Introductory Sections at the beginning of both epistles, and some special studies in the back of the book.

CONTENTS

CONTENTS

— Special Studies —

Introductory Section I
CAN YOU ANSWER THESE QUESTIONS?

1. What made the Thessalonian church a church to be thankful for? (I Thess. 1:2-7)
2. What will happen to the dead when Jesus comes back? (I Thess. 4:14-17)
3. The shortest verse in the Bible is actually in I Thessalonians. Where is it?
4. Would God actually cause anyone to believe a lie? (II Thess. 2:11-12)
5. Was Captain John Smith the first man to say, "If any man will not work, neither let him eat"?

These, and many other equally interesting questions, will be answered in your study of THINKING THROUGH THESSALONIANS.

Introductory Section II
A. CHAPTER TOPICS OF I THESSALONIANS

(By all means *memorize these chapter topics.* If you only remember these, you will have gained a fair idea of what is in every chapter of the whole epistle.)

Chapter 1—Paul's Thanks for the Thessalonians.
Chapter 2—Paul's good record among the Thessalonians.
Chapter 3—Paul's current dealings with the Thessalonians.
Chapter 4—(Two topics)
 (1) The walk of the Christian.
 (2) The dead in Christ and the Lord's coming.
Chapter 5—(Two topics)
 (1) Times and seasons of the Lord's coming.
 (2) Practical exhortations.

B. OUTLINE OF I THESSALONIANS

(You should memorize *now* the headings of Part One and Part Two of the outline, and the Scripture limitations of these parts. Notice also that both parts close with a prayer. You will not need to memorize the sub-points in each part now. These will be taken up as each chapter is studied. More complete outlines of each chapter are given at the beginning of the notes on each chapter.)

Greeting; 1:1
PART ONE—Paul's relations with the Thessalonians, past and present; Chapters 1,2,3.

11

I. Paul's thanks for the Thessalonians; 1:2-10
  A. When Paul expressed thanks; 1:2-3
  B. Things for which Paul expressed thanks; 1:4-10
    1. Their election; 1:4-6
    2. Their ensample; 1:7-10
II. Paul's good record among the Thessalonians; 2:1-16
  A. Paul's work among them; 2:1-12
  B. Thanks for the way they received the word; 2:13-16
III. Paul's current dealings with the Thessalonians; 2:17-3:10
  A. Paul's desire for personal visit hindered; 2:17-20
  B. Timothy sent; 3:1-5
  C. Joy upon Timothy's return; 3:6-10
  Concluding prayer; 3:11-13
PART TWO—Exhortations and teachings; Chapters 4 and 5.
  I. The walk of the Christians; 4:1-12
  II. The Lord's coming; 4:13-5:11
  A. The dead in Christ and the Lord's coming; 4:13-18.
  B. Times and seasons of the Lord's coming; 5:1-11
    1. Comes as a thief; 5:1-3
    2. Will not come to Christians as a thief; 5:4-11
III. Practical exhortations; 5:12-22
  Concluding prayer, commands, and benediction; 5:23-28

Introductory Section III

THE LORD'S COMING
IN THE THESSALONIAN EPISTLES

(Memorize the facts written in italics.)

1. The Lord's second coming is mentioned so many times in the Thessalonian epistles, that we can accurately say that *His second coming is the theme of both of the epistles*. It is mentioned in every chapter of both epistles.

2. *About one out of every eight verses in I Thessalonians refers to the Lord's coming.* I Thessalonians has a total of 89 verses. Eleven of these verses mention or refer to the Lord's coming. These verses are 1:10; 2:19; 3:13; 4:13-18; 5:1-4, 23.

3. *About three out of every eight verses in II Thessalonians refer to the Lord's coming.* II Thessalonians has a total of 47 verses. Eighteen of these refer to or mention the Lord's coming. Verses referring to His coming are 1:6-10; 2:1-12; 3:5.

4. "Often today we are told that the second advent is a doctrine with which generally Christians are not to be occupied. Many

12

ministers never preach on it at all; many have no clear convictions regarding it. In the classrooms of theological seminaries this doctrine often becomes just a theme for academic discussion. But to Paul it was a tremendously important and exceedingly practical truth which needed emphasis because of its bearing on the hearts and lives of God's beloved people." (H. A. Ironside, *Addresses On the First and Second Epistles of Thessalonians,* p. 11)

5. What do the chapters of the Thessalonian epistles tell us about the Lord's coming?

> First Thessalonians—
>> Chapter 1—We wait for His coming.
>> Chapter 2—The souls we have won will then be our crown.
>> Chapter 3—We shall be perfectly holy then.
>> Chapter 4—The dead in Christ will rise first, and then we shall all be caught up together to meet the Lord.
>> Chapter 5—The day of the Lord comes as a thief, but Christians will not be overtaken by that day.
>
> Second Thessalonians—
>> Chapter 1—It will be a time of retribution.
>> Chapter 2—A falling away and the man of sin must come first.
>> Chapter 3—May the Lord direct your hearts into the patient waiting for Christ.

Introductory Section IV

FACTS ABOUT I THESSALONIANS

(Memorize all facts in italics.)

1. *It is the first and oldest epistle of Paul that we have* preserved for us. It may seem rather strange that the first epistle written by Paul should be placed near the end of the collection of Paul's epistles as they are arranged in the New Testament.

2. *It was written during Paul's second missionary journey. I and II Thessalonians are the only letters of Paul we have that were written during the second missionary trip.*

3. *It was written about 53 A.D.* Faucett's Bible Dictionary says it was written either in the autumn of 52 or the winter of 53, at the start of his one and a half year stay in Corinth.

4. *It was written from Corinth.* It was NOT written from Athens, as an unauthorized addition at the end of the King James says.

Introductory Section V

DID PAUL REALLY WRITE I THESSALONIANS?

Yes, beyond question.

The epistle is referred to by Ignatius (about 110 A.D.), and by Polycarp (70-156 A.D.). It is quoted by Irenaeus (130-190 A.D.), by Clement of Alexandria (about 195 A.D.), by Origen (about 225 A.D.), and others. Tertullian (about 200 A.D.) quotes it twenty times. These people were Christian writers in the early history of the church.

I Thessalonians is listed in the Muratorian Canon (after 150 A.D.), in that of Marcion (about 140 A.D.), and Laodicea (A.D. 364). These are ancient lists of the books that were accepted as being inspired and part of the New Testament Scriptures.

Even critics who do not fear to assert that Paul did not write Ephesians can find no question about I Thessalonians.

Introductory Section VI

THESSALONICA, THE PROUD CITY

(Thessalonica is pronounced Thess-uh-low-NYE-kuh.)

(We think all of the material in this section is interesting. We hope you will find it so also. But we confess that some of it is not of great importance in getting acquainted with the Thessalonian epistles of Paul. Therefore, we are printing in *italics* certain facts that *are* especially important. It is likely that questions will be asked about these facts in the "Did You Learn?" questions that follow section VII.)

1. Ancient Thessalonica reminds us of our modern cities like San Francisco or Los Angeles-seacoast cities, bustling, commercial, proud of their past and present.

2. *Thessalonica was located in* the province of *Macedonia*, northern *Greece*. Macedonia has no geographical boundaries on a modern map. Parts of ancient Macedonia lie in Greece, Bulgaria, and Yugoslavia. But in the fourth century B.C. Macedonia was the ruling country of a great empire under Philip of Macedon and his son Alexander the Great.

3. *Thessalonica lies on the seacoast* of the Thermaic Gulf (now called the Gulf of Salonika), a part of the Aegean Sea. It rises from the end of the basin at the head of the gulf, climbs the slopes behind the gulf, and presents a striking appearance from the sea.

14

4. The original name of Thessalonica was Therma, a Greek word meaning "hot places," being named for the warm mineral springs in the neighborhood. Cassander, one of the generals of Alexander the Great, changed its name to Thessalonica, the name of his wife, who was the daughter of Philip of Macedon and step-sister to Alexander.

5. After the battle of Pydna (164 B.C.), Thessalonica fell to Rome and was made capital of the second region of Macedonia. When the four regions of Macedonia were united into one province, Thessalonica became virtually THE metropolis of Macedonia. It was the capital of the entire province, and the residence of the provincial governor.

6. Augustus Caesar rewarded the loyalty of Thessalonica to him during the second civil war (42 A.D.) by making it a free city, with a popular assembly (Gr., ekklesia), and "rulers of the city" (called in Greek, "politarchs." This word is used in Acts 17:8). The political title "politarchs" is still to be read on an arch spanning the main street, from which we learn that there were seven politarchs.

7. In Paul's time Macedonia was not an imperial province requiring the presence of troops, but a senatorial province with the garrison removed. Perhaps this accounts for the fact that the people in Philippi and Thessalonica were so eager to declare that they were "Romans" and under "Caesar." See Acts 16:21; 17:7.

8. *The great Roman road called the Egnatian Road* (Via Egnatia) *ran through Thessalonica.* Indeed the main street of modern Thessalonica is the old Egnatian Road. This was the overland military highway from the city of Rome to the countries at the eastern end of the Mediterranean. From Thessalonica this road pass on through Apollonia, Amphipolis, Philippi, Neapolis, and on eastward. All of these places are mentioned in the book of Acts in telling about Paul's travels. It was about 100 miles from Philippi to Thessalonica on this road.

9. *Thessalonica was blessed with the best natural harbor in Macedonia.* The Romans esablished there a naval station and docks, and its importance as a seaport was thereby increased. The harbor of Thessalonica connected it commercially with Asia Minor and other more distant places.

10. *The excellent harbor and highway connections of Thessalonica made it ideal as a center from which the gospel could be sounded forth,* not only in Macedonia and Achaia (southern

Greece), but in every place. (Achaia is pronounced A-KAY-yuh.)

11. *Thessalonica was home of some religions that practiced sexual orgies*. It was the home of two recognized mystery religions, the religion of Dionysius, the dying and rising God, and Orpheus, hero of a related and somewhat reformed Dionysiac cult. Both of them were fertility cults, expressing themselves in phallic symbols and sexual symbols, in wild orgies, and extravagant ecstasies. Along with these there was also a primitive cult of Cabiri (Kabeiroi), which was of similar character. Furthermore, at the time Paul lived, emperor worship was practiced in Macedonia. These facts explain why Paul wrote such commands as I Thess 4:3-6: "This is the will of God———that ye should abstain from fornication."

12. In Paul's time Thessalonica had a mixed population of Greeks, Romans, and Jews, the first being the most numerous. Perhaps the Jews were drawn to Thessalonica by the opportunities for commerce there. There was a synagogue in Thessalonica, whereas Paul found none in Philippi. As many as 10,000 Jews have dwelt in Thessalonica in modern times.

13. Thessalonica was the mainstay of Eastern Christianity during the Gothic invasion in the fourth century A.D. It was called the "Orthodox City." It continued to be a bulwark of the Christian faith in the East for centuries.

14. Thessalonica was taken by the Saracens (Mohammedans) in 904, by the Crusaders in 1185, and the Turks in 1430. They held it till 1913 when the treaty of Bucharest gave it to Greece.

15. Thessalonica is still a flourishing city. Its modern name is Salonika. It is one of the only two really large cities in Greece, and has grown rapidly in recent years. 1951 population, 217,049. 1961 population, 373,635. (The other large city is Athens, which, with its port of Piraeus, had a 1961 population of 1,852,709.) Thessalonica was severely damaged in World War II.

16. Modern Salonika is described as a "maze of crooked and cobbled alleys, flanked by the bare walls and stout doors of small houses. Spires of Christian churches (Greek Orthodox) and minarets of Mohammedan mosques rise against the sky. Everywhere one sees Turkish costumes, and the peasant dress of Greece, Albania, and Bulgaria." (From *Compton's Pictured Encyclopedia*, art. "Salonika". F. E. Compton & Co., Chicago, Ill., Copyright 1960).

Introductory Section VII

PAUL'S WORK AMONG THE THESSALONIANS

This is an important section. Paul's work among the Thessalonians forms the background of many verses in the Thessalonian epistles. You will not be able to understand the Thessalonian epistles without knowing this background, which is largely told in Acts chapter 17. We are again printing in *italics* certain facts which are especially important for you to learn. Anything in italics will almost certainly be found in the questions that follow this section.

1. Paul was scourged and *imprisoned at Philippi*. I Thess. 2:1-2; Acts 16:19-40.

2. *Paul went* with Silas and Timothy *from Philippi to Thessalonica* (about 100 miles). Acts 17:1. (See if you can find both Philippi and Thessalonica on the map inside the cover of this book.)

3. Paul was bold to speak in Thessalonica, even after his experiences in Philippi. I Thess. 2:2.

4. In Thessalonica *Paul labored* early and late *to support himself*. I Thess. 2:9; II Thess. 3:8. (However, Paul did receive some help from the Philippian church while he was in Thessalonica. See Phil. 4:6.)

5. *In Thessalonica Paul preached* on *three Sabbath days* (3 weeks) in the synagogue of the Jews. Acts 17:1-3.

6. Some Jews believed. Acts 17:4.

7. *A great multitude of* devout *Greeks* and chief women *believed*. Acts 17:4. Paul's remarks in the Thessalonian epistles make it evident that the Thessalonian church was predominantly Gentile. I Thess. 1:9.

8. The converts received the word with joy of the Holy Spirit. I Thess. 1:5.

9. It would appear that Paul remained in Thessalonica longer than the three weeks he preached in the synagogue. The reference to the large number of Gentile believers who turned from idols to serve the living God (I Thess. 1:9; Acts 17:4) suggests that some time elapsed between his last service in the synagogue and the riot stirred up by the Jews. Also the evidence of organization and leaders in the Thessalonian church suggests that Paul was in Thessalonica longer than three or four weeks. I Thess. 5:12-13. Ramsay thinks that the period

17

must be extended seven or eight months. Others say only a few weeks. The time cannot be determined precisely. But it was not long enough to have solidly established the church.

10. In Thessalonica Paul evidently lodged in the house of Jason. Acts 17:5-7. Perhaps he held services there after quitting the synagogue. Jason may have been his kinsman. Romans 16:21.

11. Thessalonian Christians besides Jason (Acts 17:9) were Gaius (Acts 19:29), Aristarchus, and Secundus (Acts 20:4; 27:2), and possibly Demas (II Tim. 4:10). Aristarchus was his companion in travel, and shared his perils at Ephesus, and his shipwreck, and was his fellow-prisoner and fellow-laborer at Rome. (Acts 27:2; 19:29; Col. 4:10; Philemon 24).

12. *The Jews stirred up a riot against Paul* in Thessalonica. They apprehended Jason, but Paul escaped. Acts 17:5-9.

The Jews accused Paul and the Christians of doing things contrary to the decrees of Caesar, and of saying that there was another king, Jesus. Acts 17:7. Paul had indeed preached about the "kingdom" of God. I Thess 2:12. The Jews perverted his words about the kingdom so as to have an accusation against him. It is an "undesigned coincidence" between the story in Acts and this epistle that the very charges against Paul and Jason (which are told in Acts) concerned this very matter of the kingdom (which is mentioned in the epistle).

13. *Paul* and Silas *fled* by night *to Berea*. Acts 17:10. Timothy must have joined them there afterwards. Acts 17:14.

14. After Paul left Thessalonica, the Thessalonians became missionaries themselves, and spread abroad the word of the Lord. Their experiences with the gospel become known in Macedonia and Achaia and every place. I Thess. 1:8.

15. Paul taught in Berea, but soon had to flee from there because of the Jews who came from Thessalonica. Acts 17:10-14; I Thess. 2:15-16.

16. *Paul went on from Berea to Athens*. Silas and Timothy remained at Berea, but Paul sent for them. *Timothy came on to him at Athens*. Acts 17:15; I Thess. 3:1-2.

17. Paul attempted twice, at either Berea or Athens, to get back to Thessalonica, but he was prevented from doing so. His anxiety over the young converts became very great. I Thess. 2:18; 3:10.

18. Not being able to return himself, *Paul sent Timothy back to Thessalonica from Athens* to see how the Thessalonian Christians were getting along. I Thess. 3:1-2.

18

19. After *Paul* sent Timothy to Thessalonica, he *left Athens and went* on *to Corinth.* Acts 18:1.

20. We cannot tell exactly where Silas stayed after the time Paul left Berea. He may have remained in that vicinity. But when Paul sent Timothy to Thessalonica, Silas rejoined Timothy somewhere, and *both Silas and Timothy came* from Macedonia *to Paul in Corinth.* Acts 18:5.

21. *Timothy brought Paul good news* of the faith and love *of the Thessalonians,* and that they had good remembrance of him. I Thess. 3:6.

22. However *Timothy* also seems to have *had a report of some defects* still *among the Thessalonians:*

   (1) *They had not forsaken wholly the sensuality that characterized them as pagans.*

   (2) *They had not forsaken the idleness* of some of their heathen countrymen. Some were not working to support themselves. I Thess. 4:3-5, 11.

   (3) Also, because of a misunderstanding about the Lord's second coming, some of them were sorrowing. Paul had taught them to wait for the Lord Jesus from heaven. I Thess. 1:10. But as time passed and some of their number died, *they became grieved,* apparently *fearing that these dead would not share the blessings of the Lord's return.* I Thess. 4:13-18.

23. As we read the epistle, we get the impression that either by a verbal inquiry through Timothy, or in a note which the Thessalonians had written, that they had asked Paul about certain matters:

   (1) Concerning brotherly love. I Thess. 4:9.

   (2) Concerning the dead Christians. I Thess. 4:13.

   (3) Concerning the times and seasons of the Lord's coming. I Thess. 5:1.

24. *It also appears that some accusations had been made* in Thessalonica *against Paul* after his departure. In First Thessalonians (especially in the second chapter) Paul defends his record among the Thessalonians quite vigorously. He defends himself against charges of flattery, mercenary motives, and impurity. He calls both the Thessalonians and God himself to witness that their lives were above reproach. I Thess. 2:3-10. It would have been surprising if the Jews had not made all manner of accusations against Paul after he left Thessalonica.

25. *Paul wrote and sent the first epistle to the Thessalonians im-*

mediately upon the return of Timothy to him with the report about the Thessalonians. I Thess. 3:6.

26. We can more or less sum up the first epistle of Paul to the Thessalonians as including the following:
    (1) Thanksgiving for their fidelity.
    (2) A defense of Paul's record among them.
    (3) Instructions on matters about which they were ignorant, especially the Lord's second coming.
    (4) Warnings about sinful attitudes still in some of them.

27. Paul visited Thessalonica later on his third missionary trip. Acts 20:1-2.

28. Paul probably visited Thessalonica when he came through Macedonia after his first imprisonment in Rome, in accordance with his hope to visit the Philippians (also in Macedonia). I Tim. 1:3; Phil. 2:24.

DID YOU LEARN?

(Questions over the Introductory Sections)

(No questions over Section I)

(Questions over Section II, CHAPTER TOPICS AND OUTLINE)
1. Write out from memory all the chapter topics of I Thessalonians. Check your answers with the list given.
2. What is the title of Part One of I Thessalonians?
3. What chapters are in Part One?
4. What is the title of Part Two of I Thessalonians?
5. What chapters are in Part Two?
6. With what does each part of I Thessalonians close?

(Questions over Section III, THE LORD'S COMING IN THE THESSALONIAN EPISTLES)
1. What could we say was the theme of both the Thessalonian epistles? Why?
2. Approximately what portion of the verses in I Thessalonians is devoted to this topic?
3. Approximately what portion of the verses in II Thessalonians is devoted to this topic?

(Questions over Section IV, FACTS ABOUT I THESSALONIANS)
1. Who is the author of I Thessalonians?
2. What is the first and oldest epistle of Paul that we have?

3. During what missionary trip was I Thessalonians written?

4. What other letters were written by Paul during the same missionary trip?

5. In what year was I Thessalonians written?

6. From what city was I Thessalonians written?

(No questions over Section V)

(Questions over Section VI, THESSALONICA, THE PROUD CITY)

1. In what modern country was Thessalonica located?

2. What was the name of the ancient province where Thessalonica was located?

3. Does Thessalonica lie on the plains, seacoast, or the hill country?

4. What famous road ran through Thessalonica?

5. What natural feature made Thessalonica a great seaport?

6. What made Thessalonica an ideal center from which the gospel could be sounded forth?

7. What was the character of some of the mystery religions practiced in Thessalonica?

(Questions over Section VII, PAUL'S WORK AMONG THE THESSALONIANS)

1. In what city was Paul imprisoned before he came to Thessalonica?

2. How was Paul supported in Thessalonica?

3. On how many Sabbath days did Paul speak in the synagogue in Thessalonica?

4. How did the Greeks receive Paul's preaching?

5. What happened that caused Paul to leave Thessalonica?

6. Where did Paul go from Thessalonica?

7. Where did he go after that?

8. Whom did Paul send to Thessalonica when he could not return himself?

9. After Paul sent (whom?) _____ to Thessalonica, Paul left (what city?) _____, and went to (what city?) _____.

10. In what city did Silas and the man Paul sent to Thessalonica rejoin Paul?

11. Was the report about the Thessalonians good or bad?

12. What were two defects in the Thessalonian Christians?
13. What misunderstanding about the Lord's coming grieved some of the Thessalonians?
14. What does Paul's defense of his record among the Thessalonians make it appear had happened in Thessalonica after he left?
15. How long was it after Paul received the report about the Thessalonians before he sent the first epistle to the Thessalonians?

MEMORY WORK

The following passages should be committed to memory. But you can learn the verses suggested from each chapter as you study that chapter. The verses to be committed to memory are also given in the "Thinking Through Thessalonians" questions at the start of each chapter.

I Thess.—1:9-10; 2:13; 3:12-13; 4:13-17; 5:1-2, 23.
II Thess.—1:6-9; 2:3, 13; 3:1,3,10.

I THESSALONIANS, CHAPTER ONE

Chapter Topic:

Paul's Thanks for the Thessalonians

"We give thanks to God always for you all, making mention of you in our prayers." I Thess. 1:2

I THESSALONIANS,
CHAPTER ONE

(Use your King James Bible to fill out these questions.)

1. What three men joined in sending the first epistle to the Thessalonians? 1:1

   _____; _____; _____

   _____.

2. The church of the Thessalonians is said to be "in" two people. Who are they? 1:1

   _____; _____

   _____.

3. What two things does Paul request to "be unto" the Thessalonians? 1:1

   _____; _____.

4. How often did Paul give thanks for the Thessalonians? 1:2

   _____.

5. In what did Paul make mention of the Thessalonians? 1:2

   _____.

6. What three things did Paul remember about the Thessalonians? 1:3

   _____; _____

   _____; _____

   _____.

7. In whose sight did the Thessalonians work and labor? 1:3

   _____.

8. By what title did Paul address the Thessalonians? 1:4 _____

   _____ _____.

9. What did Paul know about the Thessalonians? 1:4 _____

   _____.

10. What had come unto the Thessalonians? 1:5 _____

    _____.

11. In what four ways had the gospel come unto the Thessalonians? 1:5 _____; _____; _____

    _____; _____.

12. The Thessalonians knew that the gospel had come to them in much assurance, because they knew "what _____ of _____" Paul and his helpers had been while they were among them." 1:5.

13. For whose sake had Paul behaved as he did among the Thessalonians? 1:5 _____.

14. Paul said that the Thessalonians had become "followers of _____ and of the _____." 1:6

15. In what had the Thessalonians received the word? 1:6 _____ _____.

16. Do you think that the afflictions experienced by the Thessalonian Christians were an exceptional experience for Christians? (Compare Acts 14:22). Yes or No. (Circle which).

17. What brought joy to the Thessalonians? 1:6 _____ _____.

18. What had the Thessalonians been to other believers? 1:7 _____ _____.

19. In what two places had the Thessalonians become ensamples? 1:7 _____; _____.

20. What had sounded forth from the Thessalonians? 1:8 _____ _____.

21. Not only in Macedonia and Achaia, but also in _____, the faith of the Thessalonians had been spread abroad. 1:8

22. Because the Thessalonians had spread abroad their faith, what did Paul not need to do? 1:8 _____ _____.

23. How did Paul feel about the Thessalonians spreading abroad their faith so greatly? 1:8,2-3. _____.

24. Fill in these blanks from 1:9: "For they (the people) shew (or report) of us _____ _____ of _____ _____ _____ we had unto you."

25. To whom did the Thessalonians turn? 1:9. _____.

26. From what did the Thessalonians turn? 1:10. _____.

27. How did Paul describe God? 1:9. _____ _____.

28. What two things did the Thessalonians turn to God to do? _____ ____. 1:9 _____ _____. 1:10

29. Did the Thessalonians expect Christ to come again? 1:10. Yes or No. (Circle which)

30. Who is the Son, for whom the Thessalonians were waiting? 1:10. _____.

31. What has God done for the Son? 1:10. _____ _____.

32. What is coming on the world? 1:10. _____.

33. Who delivers us from this? 1:10. _____.

34. Memorize I Thess. 1:9-10.

I THESSALONIANS, CHAPTER ONE

Chapter Topic, *"Paul's Thanks for the Thessalonians"*

Outline

Greeting; 1:1
    1. From Paul, Silvanus, and Timothy.
    2. Grace and peace to them.
A. When Paul expressed thanks; 1:2-3
    1. Always; 1:2a
    2. In prayer; 1:2b-3
        a. Remembering their work of faith.
        b. Remembering their labor of love.
        c. Remembering their patience of hope.
B. Things for which Paul expressed thanks; 1:4-10
    1. *Their election*; 1:4-6
        a. Their election known by Paul; 1:4
        b. How their election was known by Paul; 1:5-6
            (1) By the way the gospel came to them; 1:5
                (a) Not in word only.
                (b) In power.
                (c) In the Holy Ghost.
                (d) In much assurance—This demonstrated by Paul's manner among them.
            (2) By the way they received the gospel; 1:6
                (a) They became followers of Paul and the Lord.
                (b) In much affliction.
                (c) With joy of the Holy Ghost.
    2. *Their ensample*; 1:7-10
        a. They became ensamples to all believers; 1:7
        b. They sounded forth the word; 1:8-10
            (1) Where? Macedonia, Achaia, and every place. 1:8
            (2) Result—Paul needed not to speak anything;
        c. What others reported about the Thessalonians; 1:9-10
            (1) What manner of entering in Paul had among them; 1:9
            (2) How they turned from idols; 1:9-10
                (a) To serve God; 1:9
                (b) To wait for Jesus from heaven; 1:10

THOUGHTS FROM THE OUTLINE
Of I Thessalonians, chapter one

There were two things in the Christian experience of the Thessalonians that made Paul thankful—their election and their ensample. These same two things in every Christian's experience ought to cause every gospel preacher to give thanks.

But sad to say, these words mean very little to the average church member.

"Election" means "choice." So the *election* of the Thessalonians was the way God chose them to be His children. Or, to express it in another way, it was the way they became Christians and were saved.

Any time a person is saved, he will have a thrilling story to tell. Many half-converted church members of modern times cannot give a thrilling testimony of their election, because they are not "elect."

"*Ensample*" means "example" or "pattern." Not only should our conversion (or election) be a thrilling story, but our service for Christ after conversion should also be an inspiration and a challenge to all who know about it. It was such in the case of the Thessalonians.

Text (1:1)

1 Paul, and Silvanus, and Timothy, unto the church of the Thessalonians in God the Father and the Lord Jesus Christ; Grace to you and peace.

Translation and Paraphrase

1. Paul, and Silvanus (who is also called Silas), and Timothy (send greetings) to the congregation of Thessalonians (who are) in God (our) Father, (in his family, favor, and fellowship,) and (in) the Lord Jesus, the anointed one. (May the) favor (of God) and peace (come) to you.

Notes (1:1)

1. While three men, Paul, Silvanus, and Timothy, sent this epistle (or letter), it is plain that Paul is the main writer. This is evident by such verses as I Thess. 3:1, 5, 6.
2. The very names of Paul, Silvanus, and Timothy stir up mental pictures of heroic courage and hard service. These men had the faith, the determination, and the vision of victory that we need. They did the Lord's will, not fearing the consequences, even as we must do it in our generation.

27

3. Paul does not assert his apostleship at the beginning of this letter, as he does in some of his later ones. See Rom. 1:1; Gal. 1:1; I Cor. 1:1; etc. The Thessalonians had no question about the genuineness of Paul's apostleship, and the false brethren who tried to force the Gentiles to keep the law of Moses had not, at that time, done so much to undermine Paul's authority as they later did.

4. All three of these men (Paul, Silvanus, Timothy) had been in Thessalonica together, and were well known there. It is worthy of note that although Paul had greater gifts and knowledge than Silvanus or Timothy, he had no feelings of superiority and assumes no titles of preeminence. He places their names on an equal with his own at the beginning of this letter.

5. Silvanus is the man who is uniformly called Silas in the book of Acts. In the epistles he is always called Silvanus. He was a Jew by race. Acts 16:20. He was a Roman citizen. Acts 16:37. He was a prophet. Acts 15:32. Silas and Judas bore the letter from the conference in Jerusalem to the churches in Syria and Cilicia. Acts 15:22-23, 27. Paul chose Silas as his helper on his second missionary trip after the dispute with Barnabas. Acts 15:37-40. References to Silas during Paul's second missionary trip are Acts 16:19, 25, 29; 17:4, 10, 14, 15. Silas was with Paul in Corinth at the time when Paul sent this first letter to the Thessalonians. Acts 18:5. He was also with Paul there when Paul sent the second Thessalonian letter a few months later. II Thess. 1:1. Most interpreters think that the Silvanus mentioned in I Peter 5:12 is the same Silvanus who was with Paul on his second missionary trip.

6. Timotheus is the same man who is usually called Timothy. Timotheus is just the Latin spelling of his name. Timothy grew up in Lystra. He joined Paul and Silas there during the early part of Paul's second missionary trip. Acts 16:1-4. He continued with Paul during his third trip, and in Rome, and afterwards. He was a loyal constant, beloved, and effective helper to Paul.

7. The long title, "church of the Thessalonians *which is* in God the Father and *in* the Lord Jesus Christ," is not a name for the church, but rather a description of it. The term *church* (Gr., *ekklesia*) simply means "a called-out assembly," and the Thessalonians were familiar with the term. (See Introductory Section Vi, paragraph 6.) But the "assembly" to which Paul was writing was not a civil or political or earthly assembly, but the assembly which was "in God the Father and the Lord Jesus Christ." The fact that they were in God the Father made them

separate from the idolatrous Gentiles. The fact that they were in the Lord Jesus Christ separated them from the unbelieving Jews.

8. The words in *italics* in the Bible text throughout the Bible in the King James and American Standard versions do NOT indicate that these words are to be specially emphasized. Rather, the italics indicate that these words are not in the Greek New Testament (and you know that the New Testament was written in Greek), but have been supplied into the English translation to make it smoother and more readable. Sometimes these words in italics are helpful, and sometimes they are not. This verse would be just as clear without them.

9. The Thessalonian church was "in God—and in the Lord Jesus Christ." This description of the church in Thessalonica emphasizes the new relationships of the Thessalonian disciples. A similar description is given of the churches in Judea. Gal. 1:22.

  The fact that Paul speaks about God being *our Father* in this verse shows the kinship which Paul felt with the Thessalonian Christians. We are all brothers in Christ, because God is our common father.

10. The phrase "in the Lord Jesus Christ," used in this verse, is a favorite of Paul. The phrase "in Christ," and similar ones, often is found in his writings. Note II Cor. 5:17: If any man be *in Christ,* he is a new creature." See also Rom. 16:7, and others. To be "in Christ," is to be in his church, in his favor, in his fellowship, and actually in his very person. See Ephesians 5:30.

  Note—The term "LORD" from Acts 2:36 onward refers to Jesus. God is the Father. Jesus is Lord. Acts 10:36.

11. The word "Christ" means "the anointed one." We have rendered it that way in our translation. The Greek word *Christ* means the same as the Hebrew word *Messiah,* and in English, both mean "the anointed one." In the Old Testament times kings, priests, etc., were installed into their offices by "anointing," that is, by pouring sweet oil upon their heads. See I Sam. 16:13. Jesus, our anointed one (or Christ), was anointed with the Holy Spirit. See Acts 10:38; Heb. 1:9; Matt. 3:16.

12. This letter, like every one of Paul's epistles except Hebrews, begins with a request for "grace" to be with them. See Rom. 1:7; I Cor. 1:3; etc. "Grace" means "favor," especially "unmerited favor." Christians are saved by grace. Ephesians 2:8. They need God's grace to sustain them after they are saved. Hebrews 4:16.

The word "Grace" was often used by the Greeks as a form of greeting. But they could not use it with the rich connotation of God's favor that Christians do.

13. Paul's request that they might have "Peace" is a Hebrew greeting. ("Shalom!") See Luke 10:5. This was a meaningful request to these brethren who were suffering persecutions. I Thess. 1:6; II Thess. 1:4-6.

14. The words "from God our Father, and the Lord Jesus Christ" are omitted by the American Stan. Version, Nestle's Gr. N.T., Westcott and Hort's Gr. N.T., the Latin version, and others. They are found in the Sinaitic and Alexandrian manuscripts of the N.T. and some later ones. But it is probably correct to omit them, and we have done so in our translation.

Text (1:2)

2 We give thanks to God always for you all, making mention *of you* in our prayers;

Translation and Paraphrase

2. We are giving thanks unto God always for all of you (Thessalonians), making mention (of you) in our prayers (for you are that dear unto us).

Notes (1:2)

1. Here in I Thessalonians, as in almost all his letters, Paul begins with a giving of thanks. Compare Romans 1:8; I Cor. 1:4; etc. Even when he had to scold people in his epistles, Paul usually began with an expression of thanks. We ought to imitate this way of thinking and speaking when we deal with our brethren. We so often scold publicly, but seldom praise publicly. What other institution so greatly deserves public thanks as the church?

2. Paul says, "We give thanks," because Silas and Timothy joined with him in the greeting. But, of course, Paul was the main author of the epistle.

3. "Give thanks" is in the present tense, which indicates continuous action. Therefore we have rendered it "giving thanks" in our translation. Paul considered giving thanks a privilege and duty that needed to be repeated often.

4. The word "mention" (Gr. *mneia*) can also mean "remembrance" or "memory." Like Paul, we should not forget our brethren when we go away from them. God hears our prayers for them at a distance, as well as near. Paul prayed for them, mentioning them by name before God.

5. Paul often spoke about bearing people up in prayer. He was busy teaching and writing. But he devoted much time to prayer, praying for people by name. See Romans 1:9; Phil. 1:3-4; etc. This was essential for Paul. It is also essential for us. Paul even prayed for the Colossians and Laodiceans whom he had never seen face to face. Col. 2:1.

Text (1:3)

3 remembering without ceasing your work of faith and labor of love and patience of hope in our Lord Jesus Christ, before our God and Father;

Translation and Paraphrase

3. (In our prayers it is our practice to be) recalling unceasingly the work (that you have done because) of (your) faith, and the toil (that is a fruit) of (your) love, and the steadfastness of the hope (that you have held) in our Lord Jesus Christ (that He will save us, establish us, and return for us. These things you have done, being conscious of the fact that even here in this life we are) in the presence of God (who is) even our Father.

Notes (1:3)

1. Faith, hope, and love are the three great virtues that abide with us always. I Cor. 13:13. But these virtues, to be genuine, must be backed up by works. The thing that made Paul so thankful about the Thessalonians was that their faith, hope, and love had indeed been put to work.

   J. B. Phillips translation of this verse is very much to the point: "Your faith has meant solid achievement, your love has meant hard work, and the hope that you have in the Lord Jesus Christ means sheer dogged endurance in the life that you live—"

   The man of faith, hope, and love is not a sentimentalist who lounges about, but one who works and labors for what he believes in, hopes for, and loves. Our faith must work. Faith without works is dead. James 2:26. Faith worketh by love. Gal. 5:6.

2. The word "labour" (Gr., *kopos*) means fatiguing toil, intense labor united with trouble. It is a very strong word. Only love could lead us to labor willingly in such a manner. Love leads us to attempt labor from which we would ordinarily shrink in dismay. Love leads us to do good without having any feeling of superiority because we have done it, or resentment because it has been imposed upon us.

3. The word "patience" in the New Testament usually means "steadfastness," or "endurance," or "constancy." Thus "patience of hope," means hope which is held steadfastly. The person who clings to his hope in the Lord when storm after storm and battle after battle sweeps over him, leaving him empty-handed and hurt, has shown "patience of hope."

   As Christians we need such "patience of hope." For often by our standards of counting time, God seems to be in no hurry, and we can become impatient when our hope is delayed in coming. James 5:7. God promised Abraham a son, but it was twenty-five years before a son was born. God promised Abraham a homeland. But Abraham's life on earth ended before he received his home. Hebrews 11:8-10. Let us have the same patience of hope that Abraham had.

4. The hope of the Thessalonians was primarily a hope in the return of Christ. They had been taught to await the return of Christ, and we also should have the same glorious hope. I Thess. 1:10. It is utter foolishness to set our hopes upon making this world a perfect place, and a place where we can have satisfaction. We are to set our hope perfectly upon the grace that is to be brought to us at the revelation of Jesus Christ. I Peter 1:13. Our hope extends beyond death, and the end of the world. Our hearts should not be gloomy with regret and disillusionment, but eager with the expectation of the coming Christ. Do you share that hope?

Text (1:4)

4 knowing, brethren beloved of God, your election,

Translation and Paraphrase

4. (Furthermore, our thankfulness comes in) knowing, my brethren beloved by God, that God has chosen you (as His very own because you have received His Son Jesus).

Notes (1:4)

1. Paul was thankful for the *election* of the Thessalonians. What does *election* mean? It means a *choosing* or a *choice*. It means that God had chosen them as His people.

2. How did God make this choice? Upon what basis did He make it? Did He make it by whim, or partiality, or "sovereign grace"? To ask that question is almost to answer it. Of course not. God does not desire that any person should perish. I Tim. 2:4; II Pet. 3:9. Therefore God certainly does not arbitrarily select some to be saved and some to be damned.

3. God has chosen us *in Christ*. Ephesians 1:4. God has now chosen Christians as His people, because they have chosen Christ, God's Son. The grounds of the choice lie in Christ and His merits, and not in our own merits or God's partiality. All Christians are "elect." I Pet. 2:9: "Ye are a chosen nation." The American Standard Version renders this: "Ye are an *elect* race."

4. Paul asserts that he KNEW that the Thessalonians were chosen of God. How could Paul have known that they were elect, if "election" were the result of some arbitrary choice in the mind of God? He could not have done so, for no man can read God's mind. But since election does not rest upon an arbitrary choice by God, Paul could know that they were elect, and he tells in verses 5 and 6 how he knew it.

   He knew their election because of these two reasons: (1) The way the gospel came to them; (2) The way they received the gospel. (Review the outline of chapter 1 for more details.)

5. The Thessalonians became Christians and were chosen (or elected) by God in the same way that you and I are saved and become Christians. These are the steps that they followed, and which we must also follow:

   (1) They *believed* on the Lord Jesus. Acts 16:31.
   (2) They *repented*. Acts 17:30. To repent means to change the mind, and decide to serve Christ, instead of doing as we ourselves prefer.
   (3) They made a *confession*. We must confess with our mouths that we believe in the Lord Jesus Christ. Romans 10:9-10; Acts 8:36-37.
   (4) They were *baptized*. Acts 2:38; Mark 16:16. We are baptized in water. Acts 10:47. We are buried with Christ in baptism. Romans 6:4. This is pictured in the act, as we are completely covered, buried, immersed, in the water.

By doing these things we take Jesus as our Lord and savior. We become God's elect (chosen), even as the Thessalonians became the elect of God.

6. God's election (or choosing) is never independent of man's response. In olden times the nation of Israel was chosen. But it was later cast off for unbelief. Matthew 8:11-12; Rom. 11:20. Of course, those who believed were not cast off.

   Even so, we who have been chosen by God are urged to give diligence to make our calling and election sure. II Peter 1:10. Without faith, we shall be cut off like unbelieving Israel. Rom. 11:21.

7. Paul addressed the Thessalonians as "brethren." We should use this word when speaking to, or about, our fellow Christians.

8. In the Greek New Testament, the phrase, "of God," follows "brethren beloved," and not "election." So the correct translation of this verse would be, "Knowing, brethren beloved of God, your election." This is the rendering given in the American Standard version and in our translation. The title, "brethren beloved of the Lord," is also found in II Thess. 2:13.

Text (1:5)

5 how that our gospel came not unto you in word only, but also in power, and in the Holy Spirit, and *in* much assurance; even as ye know what manner of men we showed ourselves toward you for your sake.

Translation and Paraphrase

5. (We have assurance of your election) because our gospel (the good news which we preached) came not unto you as a spoken message only, but also with (miracle-working) power, and with the (evident presence of the) Holy Spirit, and with much full assurance(such as can exist only when men know they speak a true and powerful message. We preached unto you with assurance like that,) even as ye know what sort of men we were (while we were) among you (laboring as we did) for your sakes.

Notes (1:5)

1. Paul declares that the gospel which he preached came to the Thessalonians in four different ways:
   (1) In word, but not in word only.
   (2) In power.
   (3) In the Holy Spirit.
   (4) In much assurance.

2. The way the gospel had come to the Thessalonians, and the

34

way they received it, are set forth by Paul as proofs of their election. Sometimes people wonder if they are truly saved and accepted by God. If they have heard the gospel proclaimed truly, and have received it, they can know that their "election" is a reality.

3. The word "gospel" means "good news." Rotherham renders the phrase, "our gospel," as "our glad-message."

   The gospel concerns the facts of the death, burial, and resurrection of Jesus, with all the blessings brought by these events. I Cor. 15:1-4. You should by all means remember that the gospel concerns these three things.

   The gospel has commands that must be obeyed. This is indicated by the fact that men must "obey" the gospel. II Thess. 1:8.

4. While Paul calls his message "our gospel," it is the same message as is elsewhere called "the gospel of God" (I Thess. 2:2), and "the gospel of Christ" (I Thess. 3:2). Paul calls it "our gospel" because he believed it, was saved by it, and preached it. But it did not originate in his mind. It was revealed to him by God. Gal. 1:11-12.

5. The gospel which Paul preached is the ONLY gospel that can save us from our sins. We must strive for THE faith of the gospel. (Phil. 1:27). For there is only one faith. (Eph. 4:5). We preach not "a" faith, but *the* faith. The gospel is by its very nature intolerant. It is kind, but intolerant. We must recognize it as THE truth of God, and preach it with full assurance, as Paul did. We cannot yield an inch when it comes to standing for the gospel.

6. Paul's preaching in Thessalonica went forth to them "in word," that is, as a spoken message. Paul in Thessalonica, reasoned with the Jews out of the Scriptures. He opened the Scriptures and alleged from them that the Christ had to suffer and rise again, and that Jesus was the Christ. Acts 17:2-3.

   In our generation we cannot deliver God's message without using God's words. Modern attempts to deny that the message of God can be communicated in words are foolishness. If every man has to discover for himself what the will of God for him is, then we shall all live and die in uncertainty.

7. The gospel also came to the Thessalonians in "power." This probably refers to miracles which Paul worked in Thessalonica. Compare Hebrews 2:4. It is true that the account in Acts 17:1-9 of Paul's work in Thessalonica does not mention him doing any miracles. However, Romans 15:19 says, "Through

many signs and wonders, by the *power* of the Spirit of God; so that from Jerusalem and round about to Illyricum, I have fully preached the gospel of Christ." See also I Cor. 2:4. It is very probable that Paul demonstrated "power" by doing miracles in Thessalonica as he did elsewhere.

8. Also the gospel came to them "in the Holy Spirit." This probably refers to the fact that Paul had supernatural guidance by the Holy Spirit in his preaching in Thessalonica.

Can we claim to preach "in the Holy Spirit"? We certainly do not claim direct guidance by the Holy Spirit as Paul experienced it. Nonetheless, what gospel preacher even today has not at times digressed from his prepared messages, and made extemporaneous remarks that he had not planned to make, and found afterwards that the unplanned remarks were exactly what some person present needed to hear? Surely the Holy Spirit must have guided the preacher to say these words, and brought them to his remembrance at the proper time.

Also we could stand up and say religious words to people forever without bringing conviction to them. Only as the Holy Spirit takes the words which we preach and uses them to bring conviction to people's hearts, will we be able to win them. See John 17:8. So in a very real manner we still preach "in the Holy Spirit."

9. Finally, Paul preached "in much assurance." May God help us to have the same assurance. The assurance we have inwardly will be exhibited outwardly by every word we say and every deed we do. Weak convictions produce weak actions. Assurance produces ardent actions.

On the other hand, we might have inward assurance, but because we were too reserved or formal or naturally hesitant, we might speak in a very conversational, and apparently unconcerned manner, which would give people the impression that we did not have real assurance. God help us to preach fervently, and to lift up our voice with strength, and cry aloud. Paul says that his manner of life proved that his gospel had come to the Thessalonians "with much assurance." Let us have the same urgency in our speech and actions that Paul had, so that men will know we preach the gospel "with much assurance."

Text (1:6)

6 And ye became imitators of us, and of the Lord, having received the word in much affliction, with joy of the Holy Spirit;

Translation and Paraphrase

6. And you (having become the chosen people of God because you received the word,) became imitators of us (who preached unto you) and of the Lord (Jesus himself. For even as we, and the Lord himself, have suffered joyfully because of the word which was given to us to deliver, you also) having received the word with much affliction (from the Jews, and yet) with (the) joy that comes from the Holy Spirit (have shared our experiences.):

Notes (1:6)

1. The Thessalonians had become "imitators" of Paul and of the Lord. "Imitators" is a better translation than "followers" in this verse.
2. The Lord Jesus, Paul, and the Thessalonians had all shared these three experiences:
   (1) Each received the word of God.
   (2) Each experienced much affliction.
   (3) Each had joy in their affliction.
3. The Lord Jesus received the *word* from his Father to deliver to the world. John 7:16; 8:28. For doing this he endured *affliction*. And yet for the *joy* set before him, he endured the cross despising the shame. Heb. 12:2.
4. Likewise Paul the apostle received the *gospel* by revelation from Jesus Christ. Gal. 1:11-12. When Paul declared this message, he encountered *suffering* in every place. Yet he *rejoiced* in his sufferings. Col. 1:24.
5. Thus also the Thessalonians received the *word* from Paul. They soon found themselves in much *affliction*. But they endured with *joy*. Thus they became imitators of Paul and of the Lord himself. Some of the afflictions of the Thessalonians are described in Acts 17:5-9.
6. The word *affliction* (Gr., *thlipsis*) means "a pressing, a pressing together, pressure, oppression, affliction, distress, straits." (Thayer)
7. "Joy of the Holy Spirit," I take (as an ablative of source) to mean "joy that comes from the Holy Spirit." See Gal. 5:22; Acts 13:52; Acts 8:8, 39. All Christians have experienced this joy when they were first saved. Alas, some have permitted the joy to fade away afterwards.
8. There was a quality in Paul's life which inspired people to follow and imitate him. Paul could boldly say, "Be ye followers of me, even as I also am of Christ." I Cor. 11:1. People just

could not ignore him. They were either warmly for him, or violently against him. We should pray that we shall be people like Paul, who will inspire others to imitate us in their struggle for perfection.

Text (1:7)

7 so that ye became an ensample to all that believe in Macedonia and in Achaia.

Translation and Paraphrase

7. (But your sufferings with joy have resulted in much good, so much so) that you have become an example to all (of those) who believe (both) in Macedonia (northern Greece) and in Achaia (southern Greece).

Notes (1:7)

1. Much good resulted from the troubles of the Thessalonians. Soon Christians from all over Greece were looking to the Thessalonians as an example.
2. The word "ensample" is an obsolete word in modern English. It means practically the same thing as "example." This is well indicated by the fact that there are two Greek words that are translated "ensample" (*tupos* and *hupodeigma*), but that these same words are also translated "example" in other references. The word used here is *tupos*. (We get our word "type" from this word.) Technically, it means a pattern in conformity to which a thing must be made. The image left on a coin by stamping it is called a "type." Children are said to be "types" of their parents. So these Thessalonians were clearly stamped and typed as children of God.
3. For information as to the location of Macedonia, see the map inside the cover, and Introductory Section VI, par. 2.
4. Achaia was the great Roman province in southern Greece, of which Corinth was capital. Athens was also in Achaia.
5. Probably travellers going in and out of Corinth (where Paul was) from Macedonia reported to Paul how they had heard about the Thessalonian Christians.

Text (1:8)

8 For from you hath sounded forth the word of the Lord, not only in Macedonia and Achaia, but in every place your faith to God-ward is gone forth; so that we need not to speak anything.

Translation and Paraphrase

8. (You have become an example,) for from you has sounded forth the message of the Lord, not just in Macedonia and Achaia, but into every place (where we have come, the report of) your faith has (already) gone out, so that we have no need to tell (people) anything (about it. They tell us what they have heard from you).

Notes (1:8)

1. Here was a preacher's dream come true! His converts had picked up the work where he had to leave it, and had spread abroad the word of the Lord so effectively that he had no need to say anything more in that area.

   However, we must note in all frankness that these zealous converts were not perfect in their understanding or manner of life. I Thess. 3:10. But they had done an outstanding job. They are an ensample to us.

2. The Thessalonians were like the Romans, of whom Paul said, "Your faith is spoken of throughout the whole world." Rom. 1:8. The reputation of any church, however big or small, good or bad, soon becomes known far and wide. People will know us for what we are and do. How wonderful it is for a church to be known for its faith, evangelistic zeal, and missionary efforts!

3. Paul says that the faith of the Thessalonians had been spread abroad in "every place." Probably we need to understand this as referring to the provinces and countries near to Macedonia.

4. The Thessalonian church—A Church to Be Thankful For.
   (1) Thankful for their conversion experience; 1:4, 6.
   (2) Thankful for their steadfastness; 1:3.
   (3) Thankful for their work; 1:3.
   (4) Thankful for their testimony; 1:8-9.
   (5) Thankful for their hope; 1:10.

Text (1:9)

9 For they themselves report concerning us what manner of entering in we had unto you; and how ye turned unto God from idols, to serve a living and true God,

Translation and Paraphrase

9. For they themselves (the people in every place) report (to us when we talk to them,) concerning us (telling us about) what (a wonderful) sort of entering in we had unto you (when we came to Thessalonica to preach), and how that you (so completely) turned to God from idols, (determined) to serve (yes, even be slaves of) a living and true God.

Notes (1:9)

1. News about a genuine conversion is quickly known far and wide. Paul found himself hearing reports from many people about how the Thessalonians had turned to God. As travellers came into Corinth from various places, many of them told how they had heard about the Thessalonians, and how Paul had had such a successful entry into Thessalonica, and how that so many of them had turned from idols to the true and living God. The Thessalonians had really placed their light on a candlestick for all to see. Matthew 5:51. They were a church to be thankful for.

2. The discussion of the manner of Paul's entering in unto the Thessalonians is taken up in detail beginning at 2:1. The word translated *entrance* in 2:1 (*eisodos*) is the same word translated here as "entering in."

3. Acts 14:15 gives an example of how Paul urged the Gentiles to turn from idols: "We ... preach unto you that ye should turn from these vanities unto the living God." It will not do to put up a picture of Christ on an idol shelf along with the statue of Buddha. People must turn FROM idols to serve God acceptably.

4. The verb "turned" is in the aorist tense, indicating completed, punctilliar, point action. They did not half turn. They turned once for all from idols.

5. They turned from idols "to serve" the living God. The verb translated "serve" (*douleuo*) means "to be slaves (or bond-servants) of." Paul frequently referred to himself as the "servant" or "slave" of Christ. See Romans 1:1. The unavoidable truth is that ALL people are going to be bondservants of someone, either of sin, or of the Lord. Romans 6:16; John 8:34. However, sin is so deceptive that men can be slaves to it, and think they are completely free and emancipated. This is the devil's method of enslaving people.

6. The expression, "living and true God," is a Hebrew way of describing God, and is gloriously correct. Jesus himself spoke of His Father in a similar manner when He said, "That they might know thee, the only true God, and Jesus Christ whom thou has sent." John 17:3.

7. The fact that the Thessalonians had so generally turned from idols shows that it was predominantly a Gentile church, as Acts 17:4 also indicates.

8. It is a fact that a person becomes like what he worships. The idol worshippers reflect on their faces the likeness (often the sadness) of their gods. The worshippers of the living God show by radiant joy that their God is REAL. "They looked unto him, and were radiant; and their faces shall never be confounded." Ps. 34:5; American Standard Ver.

Text (1:10)

10 and to wait for his Son from heaven, whom he raised from the dead, even Jesus, who delivereth us from the wrath to come.

Translation and Paraphrase

10. And (how you turned from idols with a new hope, that has caused you) to look confidently for his (God's) son (to come) from heaven, (the very son) whom He raised up from the dead, (even) Jesus, who is delivering us from the wrath (of God's judgment) that is coming (upon this whole world).

Notes (1:10)

1. The Thessalonians turned to God to do two things:
   (1) To serve the living and true God; 1:9.
   (2) To wait for Jesus to come from heaven; 1:10.
2. The verb "wait" indeed means "to wait," but has the added sense of patience and trust. We should thus be waiting for the return of our Lord Jesus. Our Lord has promised most definitely that He will return. He cautioned us to be watching always. The apostles always taught their converts to watch for His return. Matthew 24:44; Titus 2:13. "Looking for that blessed hope, and the glorious appearing of the great God and our Savior Jesus Christ."
3. Some interpreters have said that Paul taught the people of his generation to expect the Lord to come within their lifetime. Then in the course of time, as the Lord delayed His coming, Paul changed his doctrine. If that were true, it would prove that Paul was NOT giving inspired teachings when he first told the people to wait for the Lord's return. We reject any such interpretation of Paul's teachings. Paul himself has given us abundant proof that he spoke by revelation of Jesus Christ, and not from men. See Paul's defense of his ministry in Galations 1:11-2:9. We believe that when correctly understood Paul's teachings about the Lord's return (and any other matter) are true and beyond challenge.

4. Even while Paul was with the Thessalonians, he told them that some things would have to happen first before the Lord's coming. See II Thess. 2:5. Paul taught the same thing that Jesus himself taught, namely that the Lord MIGHT come at any time. Paul never said that Christ would definitely come within anyone's lifetime, including his own. We challenge anyone to produce a verse from Paul's writings that indicates that Paul said that Christ was going to come within his lifetime. Even today the teaching that Christ will surely come some time, and may come any time, is the true teaching. We must be watching always for the Lord's coming. The Lord says that He will come just when we think He is not coming. Matthew 24:44.

5. We are sometimes told that waiting on the second coming tends to throttle Christian service. Supposedly, people become dreamers. But just the opposite is true. Those who believe the Lord is coming, and maybe very soon, are out winning souls, going to new foreign mission fields, translating the Scriptures into new languages that have never had the word of God, and broadcasting on the radio. They may not be in Washington, D.C., lobbying for a socialistic system of government and economics, but they will be doing what the Lord told them to do—preaching, baptizing, teaching. The socialistic schemers are not doing anything but running the country into bankruptcy and making its money worthless, even when they are doing it in the name of religion. Those who believe the Lord is coming again will be working to turn men to righteousness.

6. The fact that God raised Jesus from the dead guarantees that Christ will return, and that there will be a judgment. Acts 17:31; I Cor. 15:12; I Thess. 4:14.

7. The word "delivered" is actually a present tense, indicating continuous action (and we have indicated this in our translation). Jesus *is delivering* us. Some interpreters feel that this present tense form is timeless, and refers to a single act of deliverance which Jesus will do for us at a given time in the future. We prefer to think of our deliverance as continual. For Jesus delivers us from evil every day. Matt. 6:13. What we are now doing determines whether or not we shall escape in the day of God's wrath. I am thankful that Jesus is now delivering us from the sins that would cause God's wrath to fall upon us in the day of wrath. Romans 5:9: "Much more, then, being now

justified by his blood, we shall be saved from *wrath* through him." We are being delivered now from the future wrath that would come upon us for our present sins.

8. The *wrath to come* is not a popular subject, but it is coming, regardless of men's unwilingness to face it. John the baptist said, "Who hath warned you to flee from the *wrath* to come?" Matt. 3:7. Rev. 6:17 tells you of a fearful time when even kings will try to hide themselves, "For the great day of his *wrath* is come, and who shall be able to stand?" God's wrath is described as a winepress, with the earth cast into it, and the earth, like grapes in a winepress, was stomped down, and blood came out of the winepress. Rev. 14:19-20. God has seven great vials (or bowls) of wrath to pour out on the earth. Rev. 15:7. Compare Rom. 2:5.

Some people speculate that the wrath of God will be poured out during a period of tribulation after Christ has once come and taken the Christians out of the earth, leaving the sinners behind. It seems more probable to us that the wrath of God is to be poured out upon the nations in a series of wars and disasters before Christ comes, and then the terrors of the judgment and hell will consummate His righteous wrath against those who have flouted His laws and despised His mercy. (See Special Study II on page 242, "A Secret Rapture Considered.") But however the wrath may come, the sure thing is that it IS coming, and that Jesus is delivering the saints from it.

9. The wrath to come. (I Thess. 1:10).
 (1) A sure thing. John 3:36; Rom. 1:18; Eph. 5:6.
 (2) A sure thing. Rom. 2:5-6; 9:22; I Thess. 2:16; II Thess. 2:10, 12.
 (3) A terrible thing. Rev. 14:10, 11, 19, 20.
 (4) An escapable thing. I Thess. 1:10; 5-9; Rom. 5:9.

DID YOU LEARN?

(Questions over I Thessalonians, chapter one)

(These questions are over the outline and the notes on chapter one. The Scripture references direct you to the notes on particular verses where the answer to each question is given. Try to answer these questions without consulting your Bible or the notes.)

1. What is the topic of chapter one?
2. For what two things in the experience of the Thessalonians was Paul thankful? (See outline)

3. What three men joined in sending I Thessalonians? (1:1)
4. Who was the main writer of I Thessalonians? (1:1)
5. What is Silvanus called in the book of Acts? (1:1)
6. Why does Paul not assert him apostleship at the start of I Thessalonians as he does in other letters? (1:1)
7. What does the word "church" mean? (1:1)
8. The Thessalonian church was "in" what two people? (1:1)
9. Why are some words in your Bible printed in italics? (1:1)
10. What does Paul request for his readers at the beginning of all his epistles (except one)? (1:1)
11. What does the word "Christ" mean? (1:1)
12. With what does Paul begin most of his letters, including I Thessalonians? (1:2)
13. What three things did Paul remember in prayer about the Thessalonians? (1:3)
14. What does "patience" mean in the phrase "patience of hope"? (1:3)
15. In what did the Thessalonians primarily hope? (1:3, 10)
16. What does "election" mean? (1:4)
17. By what two means did Paul know their election had actually taken place? (1:4-5)
18. What are the four things we must do to be saved (and "elected")? (1:4)
19. Whom has God now chosen as His people? (1:4)
20. Why does Paul call the gospel "our gospel"? (1:5)
21. Did the gospel come to the Thessalonians in word only? (1:5)
22. What did Paul mean when he said that his gospel came to the Thessalonians in "power"? (1:5)
23. How did Paul's gospel come "in the Holy Spirit"? (1:5)
24. What was it that proved that the gospel came to the Thessalonians "in much assurance"? (1:5)
25. What is a better translation of the word "followers"? (1:6)
26. Of what two people had the Thessalonians become followers? (1:6)
27. What three experiences had the Thessalonians shared with those of whom they were followers? (1:6)
28. What does the phrase "joy of the Holy Ghost" mean? (1:6)
29. What does "ensample" mean? (1:7)
30. To whom were the Thessalonians ensamples? (1:7)
31. Where was Macedonia? (Introductory Section IV)
32. Where was Achaia? (1:7)

33. In what three places (or areas) had the word of the Lord sounded forth from the Thessalonians? (1:8)

34. What effect had the words spoken by the Thessalonians had on what Paul needed to do? (1:8)

35. Concerning what did Paul get reports from people in every place? (1:9)

36. Where does Paul take up in detail the discussion of his "entering in" unto the Thessalonians? (1:9)

37. Was the Thessalonian church primarily Jewish or Gentile? Give a reason for your answer. (1:9)

38. What does "serve" mean in the phrase "to serve the living and true God"? (1:9)

39. What two things had the Thessalonians turned to God to do? (1:10)

40. What is the correct tense and form of the word "delivered"? (1:10)

41. From what does Jesus deliver us? (1:10)

42. Write out from memory I Thess. 1:9-10. Verse 9 begins, "For they themselves shew ... "

I THESSALONIANS, CHAPTER TWO

Chapter Topic:

Paul's Good Record
Among The Thessalonians

"We were bold in our God to speak unto you the gospel of God."
I Thess. 2:2

THINKING THROUGH THESSALONIANS
I Thessalonians, chapter two (2:1-16)

Chapter Topic—"Paul's Good Record Among the Thessalonians"

1. Paul's entrance in unto the Thessalonians to preach was not
   _____ _____. 2:1

2. In what city had Paul suffered before coming to Thessalonica?
   2:2. _____.

3. In spite of past sufferings, Paul was _____ in God to
   speak the gospel in Thessalonica. 2:2.

4. In Thessalonica, Paul spoke the gospel of God with much
   _____. 2:2.

5. Paul's preaching and exhortation was not based on three things.
   What were these? 2:3. _____;
   _____; _____.

6. With what was Paul allowed to be put in trust? 2:4.
   _____.

7. Whom did Paul seek to please? 2:4. _____.

8. What does God do to our hearts? 2:4. _____.

9. What two things did Paul NOT use in his ministry at Thessalonica? 2:5.
   _____;
   _____
   _____.

10. Who was witness that Paul did not use a cloke over covetous-
    ness? 2:5. _____.

11. What did Paul NOT seek from the Thessalonians? 2:6.
    _____.

12. What did Paul have authority, as an apostle of Christ, to be?
    2:6. _____.

13. Among the Thessalonians, Paul had been _____. 2:7.

14. To the Thessalonians Paul had been like a _____
    cherishing her own children. 2:7.

15. What two things was Paul willing to have imparted to the
    Thessalonians? 2:8. _____;
    _____.

16. Paul was willing to do this, because the Thessalonians were
    _____ unto him. 2:8.

17. What two things could the Thessalonians remember about
    Paul? 2:9. _____; _____.

18. What did Paul do day and night in Thessalonica? 2:9.
    _____.

19. Paul labored, because he would not be
_____ unto any of the people. 2:9.

20. What two peoples were witnesses to Paul's conduct among the Thessalonians? 2:10. _____;
_____.

21. In what three ways had Paul behaved among the Thessalonians?
2:10. _____; _____;
_____.

22. Paul had _____, and _____ and
_____, as a _____ doth his own
_____. 2:11.

23. For what purpose had Paul thus exhorted them? 2:12.
_____

_____.

24. Unto what has God called us? 2:12.
_____

_____.

25. The Thessalonians received the word of God, "not as the
_____ of _____, but as the _____ of
_____. 2:13.

26. Paul says, "The word of God (which)
_____   _____

in you that believe." 2:13.

27. The Thessalonians became followers of the
_____ of _____ which (were) in
_____. 2:14.

28. The churches of God in Judea were "in" whom? 2:14.
_____.

29. Of whom had the Thessalonians suffered things? 2:14.
_____.

30. Of whom had the churches of God in Judea suffered? 2:14.
_____.

31. What did the Jews do to the Lord Jesus? 2:15.
_____.

32. What did the Jews do to the prophets? 2:15.
_____.

33. What had the Jews done to Paul? 2:15.
_____.

34. Did the Jews please God? Yes or No. (Circle which)

35. The Jews "are _____ to all men." 2:15.

36. What did the Jews forbid Paul to do? 2:16.

_____

_____.

49

37. What did the Jews fill up? 2:16. _____
38. What was come upon the Jews? 2:16. _____.
39. Memorize I Thess. 2:13.

(The remaining "Thinking Through Thessalonians" questions on chapter two are treated as part of chapter three.)

I THESSALONIANS, CHAPTER TWO (2:1-16)*

Chapter Topic: *"Paul's Good Record Among the Thessalonians"*
Outline

II. Paul's good record among the Thessalonians; 2:1-16.
  A. Paul's work among them; 2:1-12.
    1. Not in vain; 2:1.
    2. Bold; 2:2.
    3. Sincere; 2:3.
      a. Not of deceit.
      b. Not of uncleanness.
      c. Not of guile.
    4. Only what God allowed; 2:4.
    5. Used no flattering words; 2:5.
    6. Used no cloke of covetousness.
    7. Sought no glory; 2:6.
    8. Gentle; 2:7.
    9. Self-supporting; 2:8-9.
      a. Why; 2:8.
      b. How; 2:9.
    10. Backed up by a holy life; 2:10.
    11. An exhorting ministry; 2:11-12.
      a. As a father does his children; 2:11.
      b. That they would walk worthy of God; 2:12.
  B. Thanks for the way they received the word; 2:13-16.
    1. As the word of God; 2:13.
    2. They became followers of the churches in Judea; 2:14-16.
      a. Thessalonians suffered of their countrymen; 2:14a
      b. Judeans suffered of the Jews; 2:14b-16.
        (1) The Jews killed Jesus; 2:15.
        (2) The Jews killed the prophets.
        (3) The Jews persecuted Paul.

---

* We have placed 2:17-20 with chapter three.

(4) The Jews please not God.
(5) The Jews are contrary to all men.
(6) The Jews forbade Paul to speak to the Gentiles; 2:16.
    (a) They fill up their sins always.
    (b) Wrath is come upon them.

THOUGHTS FROM THE OUTLINE
Of I Thessalonians, chapter two

Paul's work among the Thessalonians should be a pattern for every preacher or other Christian worker. We should ask ourselves, "Has our work been like Paul's—not in vain, bold, sincere? Have we used flattering words, covetousness, or sought glory of men?"

Then the way the Thessalonians received the word which Paul preached is a pattern to every one who hears the word. They (1) received the word as the word of God, not the word of men, and (2) they became followers (or imitators) of the Judean churches which had suffered for their faith. The Thessalonians did not shun the full consequences of obeying the gospel. Can we in this generation assume that we are privileged to receive the blessings of Christ without sacrifice or suffering, when Christians in other ages and places have endured so much?

Text (2:1)

1 For yourselves, brethren, know our entering in unto you, that it hath not been found vain:

Translation and Paraphrase

1. For you yourselves, brethren, (saw and) know that our entering in unto you (when we came to Thessalonica to preach) was not fruitless (or useless).

Notes (2:1)

1. Letting in a fresh breeze of truth will usually soon blow out a room full of poisonous lies. After Paul left Thessalonica, some people, most likely Jews, had apparently accused him of being a flatterer, a deceiver, immoral, and money hungry. I Thess. 2:3, 5.

2. Therefore in this second chapter Paul takes up the matter of his good record among the Thessalonians. (This is the chapter topic.) Paul thoroughly demolishes all the insinuations against him. This really was not very hard to do. For, as he reminds the Thessalonians, they themselves knew all about what he had done among them.

3. The type of "entrance" which Paul had unto the Thessalonians was a vindication of Paul himself and all he stood for. His record of accomplishment and conduct was good enough to silence any malicious accusers.

4. In our outline, we have called the section 2:1-12 "Paul's work Among Them." It seems to be an elaboration of Paul's statement in 1:5, "Ye know what manner of men we were among you."

5. In 2:1, Paul picks up the thought of 1:9, where he had mentioned what "matter of *entering in* we had unto you." The word translated *entrance* here in 2:1 is the same word that is translated *entering in* in 1:9.

6. Paul's visit to the Thessalonians had most certainly NOT been "in vain." "In vain" (Gr., *kenos*) means "empty, vain, devoid of truth, fruitless, without effect." (Thayer) The fact that Paul left a flourishing church there was proof that his visit was not in vain. The Thessalonians themselves could vouch for that fact.

Text (2:2)

2 but having suffered before and been shamefully treated, as ye know, at Philippi, we waxed bold in our God to speak unto you the gospel of God in much conflict.

Translation and Paraphrase

2. On the contrary, even though we had suffered previously (in many places), and had been treated insultingly at Philippi (just before we came to Thessalonica), as you know, we were bold (and free) in our God to speak unto you the gospel of God (even though we did so) in much anguish of mind.

Notes (2:2)

1. This verse emphasizes that Paul's work among the Thessalonians was BOLD. Boldness is the first great need of Christian workers. It takes much boldness to go knock on a stranger's door, seeking an opportunity to talk about Christ. It takes boldness to teach God's word in a place where people do not want what you are teaching. If a person has already endured opposition in other places, the boldness is doubly tested, because of fears created by past difficulties. The early Christians prayed for boldness. Acts 4:29. Paul asked for prayer that he might speak boldly. Ephesians 6:19-20; Philippians 1:20. Did you ever pray that God would give you boldness? Some people are bold to practice evil, but we need to be bold to declare the whole counsel of God.

2. Before Paul ever came to Thessalonica, he had been rejected at several towns during his first missionary trip. See Acts, chapters 13 and 14. He had been stoned at Lystra. Acts 14:19. Truly he had "suffered before."

3. Then at Philippi, the city he visited immediately before preaching in Thessalonica, he was treated most shamefully. The expression "shamefully entreated" (Gr., *hubridzo*) means "to treat one insolently and shamefully," emphasizing the attitude of the abusers. This accurately describes the treatment Paul received at Philippi. There he was (1) arrested illegally after healing a girl; (2) put through a mock trial; (3) scourged unlawfully; (4) severely imprisoned. Read Acts 16:11-40 for details.

4. In the light of Paul's previous experiences, it would have been understandable if he had been fearful and hesitant in Thessalonica. His work might have been "in vain" (or fruitless) because of fears generated by past experiences. BUT that was not the case. (The word *but* used in this verse (Gr., *alla*) indicates a strong contrast between the possibility of his work being in vain, and what it actually was.) Paul's boldness in preaching in Thessalonica is described in Acts 17:1-5.

5. Paul was bold "in our God" to speak. If it had not been for the help and fellowship of God, Paul could never have done what he did. It was only by God's help that Paul went in triumph from place to place. II Cor. 2:14. It is likewise only by God's help that we can do His work.

6. The phrase "the gospel of God," is frequently used by Paul and other writers in the N.T. See I Thess. 2:8, 9; Rom. 1:1; 15:16; II Cor. 11:7; Mark 1:14; I Pet. 4:17. The phrase, "gospel of Christ," is also quite common. See I Thess. 3:2; Phil. 1:27.

7. Paul may have been bold in preaching in Thessalonica, but he was far from insensible to the mental anguish, and the possible physical pain also. He declares that he spoke the gospel "with much contention." The word translated "contention" (*agonia*) is the word from which we get our English word "agony." It refers to severe mental struggles and emotions, agony, anguish. Any sincere preacher often preaches in agony, fearing he will not say the words he ought to say, or fearing he will say things he should not say, and sometimes fearing how people will receive what he says. The acute suffering in Paul's mind shows how far he was from being a Stoic. Suffering is real. But, thank God, it has its rewards, both in the development of our personalities, and in heaven.

Text (2:3)

3 For our exhortation is not of error, nor of uncleanness, nor in guile:

Translation and Paraphrase

3. For (you see) the message which we urge you to accept is not (something that springs) from misleading error (which we hold), nor from (any sexual) uncleanness (such as the Gentile religions often practice), nor from (any) hidden scheme (by which we seek to trap you).

Notes (2:3)

1. When a man knows he is telling the truth, he will speak confidently, and have a ring of reliability in his tone. Paul was willing to endure all the troubles he experienced in Thessalonica, because he knew that his message was true, pure, and without concealed secrets.

2. The word "exhortation" (Gr., *paraklesis,* from *parakaleo*) has a double significance. It includes the idea of rousing the slothful, and also of comforting the sorrowful. (McGarvey)

3. Paul's exhortation was not "of deceit." "Deceit" means "error" or "wandering," or "straying about." It refers to error that is not merely the result of ignorance, but of evil intentions. The false brethren who taught the Gentile Christians to keep the law of Moses were guilty of such deceit as this.

4. "Uncleanness" refers to sexual indulgence and impurity. Note I Thess. 4:4, 7; Rom. 1:24; Colossians 3:5. The prophetess Jezebel taught people to commit fornication. Rev. 2:20. But Paul neither practiced nor taught such things. Some of the mystery religions in Thessalonica practiced moral uncleanness. See Introductory Section VI, par. 11.) Paul's exhortation was not of that species.

5. "Guile" comes from a Greek word, *dolos,* meaning "bait," hence a lure or snare. The word therefore indicates craft or deceit by which people may be trapped. It refers to any hidden purposes or motives, especially bad ones. The minister of Christ must not have any secret motives or requirements that he plans to spring on his disciples.

6. "The ministerial work must be managed purely for God and the salvation of the people, and not for any private ends of our own. This is our sincerity in it. A wrong end makes all the work bad from us, however good in itself." (Richard Baxter)

Text (2:4)

4 but even as we have been approved of God to be intrusted with the gospel, so we speak; not as pleasing men, but God who proveth our hearts.

Translation and Paraphrase

4. Instead (of our message being rooted in such wicked motives as we have just mentioned, we govern ourselves by this standard, namely that) just as we have been tested (and approved) by God to be entrusted with the good news, in (just) that manner we speak, not as (those who are) seeking to please men, but (seeking to please) God, who (constantly) tests our hearts (to see if we are sincere).

Notes (2:4)

1. To put this verse briefly, it says, "We did and said only what God approved us to say." Paul did not preach anything motivated by deceit, uncleanness, or guile (2:3), but only what God approved him to say.
2. God told Jonah the prophet to preach unto Nineveh "the preaching *that I bid thee.*" (Jonah 3:2) God approved Jonah to preach only a certain message. Likewise God gave Paul a certain message to deliver. Paul delivered what he was supposed to, and nothing else. It is always a temptation to inject our own feelings, opinions, and hobbies into our preaching. We do well in our preaching not to go beyond what is written. (I Cor. 4:6; American Stan. Vers.). Speak where the Scriptures speak, and leave our own opinions out.
3. The word translated "allowed" actually means "approved," particularly that which is approved by testing. People test metals like gold by melting them over fire. If no impurities come to the top, then the gold is said to be "tested" or "approved," or "tried by fire." God likewise tests and approves us. No greater honor could come to us than to be approved by God to be entrusted with the gospel.

   "To be put in trust with the gospel is the highest conceivable responsibility; the sense of it is enough to exclude every base motive and deceitful practice." (Findlay)
4. There are two words in this verse that are translations of the same word. The King James version does not make this apparent. (Our translation indicates it.) The words are "allowed" and "trieth."

55

(1) "Allowed" (Gr., *dedokimasmetha*) means "tested" or "approved."

(2) "Trieth" (*dokimadzonti*) means "tests."

God tests us for our ability and sincerity. If we measure up to His requirements, we are declared to be "tested" and "approved" to do whatever God sees fit.

5. Many Scriptures teach us that God tests and tries human hearts, so as to know their innermost secrets. "The refining pot is for silver, and the furnace for gold, but Jehovah trieth the hearts." (Prov. 17:3; Amer. Stan. vers.) See also Jeremiah 11:20; I Cor. 4:5; Rom. 2:16.

6. God's testing of our hearts is a continual thing. The verb "trieth" is in the present tense, indicating continuous action. God must continually test our hearts, for sin can creep into them at any time and change them from good to evil.

7. It was always a joy to Paul to think that he had not only been forgiven for his fierce unbelieving past, but even entrusted with preaching the gospel he had once opposed. I Tim. 1:12: "I thank Christ Jesus our Lord, who hath enabled me, for that he counted me faithful, putting me into the ministry." See also I Tim. 1:11; Eph. 3:2-3, 7-8.

8. Since God had given Paul the gospel, Paul tried to please *God*, rather than men. There is much in the gospel that is distasteful to the natural man—its humiliating exposure of our sin and helplessness, its demands for our acceptance of God's will, the fact that it claims to be the only unchangeable truth, and the severity of its judgments upon those who reject. A preacher can become popular by saying only what the people want to hear. See Isa. 30:9-10; II Tim. 4:3-4. Paul would not do this, and we dare not do it either. Remember, God is testing our hearts continually!

9. In one way, however, Paul did seek to please men. See I Cor. 9:19-22, especially 22b: "I am become all things to all men, that I might by all means save some." If Paul could gain the good will of people without compromising God's message, he certainly did so, even if that meant extra effort and discomfort to him. When he was among Jews, he ate Jewish food and lived like a Jew insofar as doing so did not violate the gospel. Thus also he did among Gentiles. By doing this, he was able to win more people.

Text (2:5)

5 For neither at any time were we found using words of flattery, as ye know, nor a cloak of covetousness, God is witness;

Translation and Paraphrase

5. (We avoided other wrong doings besides men-pleasing while we were with you;) for neither were we at any time found using flattering speech, as you (well) know; neither (did we use any) pretext (to cover a motive) of covetousness, God is (our) witness (that we are telling the truth about that).

Notes (2:5)

1. God had preserved for us in this verse (and paragraph) a record of how an inspired apostle went about preaching in a city where the gospel had never before been heard. We must imitate his methods and motives.
2. "As to his *outward* conduct (that it was without flattery) Paul calls the Thessalonians to witness; as to his *inward* desires (that they were without covetousness) he calls God to witness." (McGarvey)
3. Flattering words are often very powerful, and can bring about some spectacular results. Such words will win the favor of the majority of people. Absolom stole the hearts of the people of Israel by flattery. II Samuel 15:2-6. But flattery is dangerous to use, and its effects are not lasting. It should be avoided. Good-will gained through flattery will not stand the tests that brotherly love produced by conversion will stand. "He that rebuketh a man afterwards shall find more favor than he that flattereth with his tongue." Prov. 28:23. See also Prov. 29:5; 26:28; 6:24.
4. The word "cloke" means "a pretext," or "pretense," or "show." Jesus said that the scribes "for a pretense (cloke) make long prayers." Mark 12:40. Their long prayers covered up their desire for the praise of men.

   Thus a "cloke of covetousness" would be a pretended manner such as a person would use to cover up the fact that he wanted money. Covetous men have often used such a pretense. "And through covetousness shall they with feigned words make merchandise of you." II Peter 2:3. Paul did not put a cloke over covetousness, for he had none to hide.
5. Paul did not use his ministry as a pretext for making money. Acts 20:33. "I have coveted no man's silver, or gold, or apparel." The world of the Greeks was full of teachers and philos-

ophers who travelled about lecturing and disputing, seeking to live by their wits. Notice Acts 13:6-12; 19:13-20. Paul was that kind of a man, and he was careful to conduct himself so that he could not possibly be accused of being one. Preachers must be supported, according to God's command, but if money becomes their motive, they have missed the path altogether.

6. It might almost appear that Paul used an oath when he called upon God to witness that he had not been covetous among the Thessalonians. However, inasmuch as Paul was an inspired man, it would be presumptious of us to judge him. See I Cor. 2:15. Paul had the mind of Christ perfectly. I Cor. 2:16. What he said here was, therefore, befitting before God.

But for ourselves, we should avoid saying, "By God," that anything is true or not true. Let your "Yes" mean "Yes," and your "No" mean "No." Whatsoever is more than these cometh of the evil one. Matt. 4:37. Paul's words were acceptable by God. But we cannot know with the certainty of Paul when such a statement would be an oath, and when we would be stating a harmless fact. Therefore, "Swear not at all." Matt. 5:34.

Text (2:6)

6 nor seeking glory of men, neither from you nor from others, when we might have claimed authority as apostles of Christ.

Translation and Paraphrase

6. Neither (were we ever found) seeking glory from men, neither from you, nor from (any) others, though we have authority to be burdensome (and demand that you support us) as apostles of Christ.

Notes (2:6)

1. How hard men will strain to get glory and honor in this world! They will lie to get it. They will embezzle money so they can appear greater than they truly are. They will run down other people so that they themselves can appear better by contrast. But Paul did not even seek glory when he could have legitimately claimed it.

2. What is this *glory* which Paul did not seek? The word naturally suggests honor and praise. Paul did not seek that type of glory. In this verse he denies the motive of ambition, as he denied the motive of covetousness in verse five.

Jesus said that He did not receive "glory" from men. John
5:41. But those who opposed Jesus sought honor (glory) one
of another. John 5:44. "He that speaketh of himself seeketh
his own glory: but he that seeketh his glory that sent him, the
same is true, and no unrighteousness is in him." John 7:18.
Paul was that type of a man. He sought no glory from men,
only from God.

3. However, the word "glory" has another meaning, which is suggested by the context. (By "context" we mean the verses that
go immediately before and after this verse.)The context suggests that the glory which Paul shunned was the *financial gain*
that he might have obtained from his office and work.

4. Thus the two meanings of "glory" are:
    (1) Honor and praise.
    (2) Financial rewards and support.

5. Paul had every right to demand financial support from his converts, even if that required making himself burdensome to them.
I Cor. 9:6-14. But Paul supported himself by his own labors,
and did not collect support from them. This he did to impress
upon them the sincerity of his intentions and message.

6. There are three negatives (in verses 5 and 6), each introduced
by the Gr. conjunction *oute,* which we should notice:
    (1) "Neither . . . used we flattering words."
    (2) "Nor a cloke of covetousness."
    (3) "Nor . . . sought we glory."
    Can you make these same emphatic denials in describing your
service to Christ?

Text (2:7)

**7 But we were gentle in the midst of you, as when a nurse cherisheth
her own children:**

Translation and Paraphrase

7. But (instead of seeking glory) we were gentle (while we were)
in the midst of you. (Indeed we treated you so) that it was as
if a nurse were cherishing her own children.

Notes (2:7)

1. A man seeking his own glory would have been domineering and
demanding. But Paul was gentle among the Thessalonians.

2. He treated them as a nurse would cherish and protect her own
children. The word *own* should be in the translation before the

59

word *children*. A nurse, even a devoted one, would probably be more loving and attentive to her own children, than to the children of strangers. Paul considered the Thessalonians to be as dear and close to him as a nurse's own children would be to her.

3. Gentleness is never weak. Gentleness is the strong self-sacrificing spirit which makes heroes and martyrs. Abraham Lincoln was gentle. Jesus was gentle. But how strong He was! The Lord's servant must be gentle and not strive. II Timothy 2:24. The real power of a man is seen not in how violent he can get, but in what he can endure with gentleness.

4. There is some uncertainty about one word in this verse. Some New Testament manuscripts have "gentle" (Gr., *epioi*), as our common King James version has, and some have "babes" (*nepioi*). By dropping the first letter of the word for "babes" we get the word for "gentle." The American Standard Version margin says, "Most of the ancient authorities read "babes." (That seems an overly strong statement to us.) Westcott and Hort's Greek N.T. has "babes" in the text. Nestle's Greek N.T. (which we are following) has "gentle" in the text, and "babes" in the margin.

To us it seems that the word "babes" would make little sense in this verse. (Why should Paul say, "We were babes among you"?) Furthermore, it does not have overwhelming manuscript support. Its chief support is the Latin text and the Vatican manuscript. We feel that the King James version is correct in adopting the reading, "gentle."

Text (2:8)

8 even so, being affectionately desirous of you, we were well pleased to impart unto you, not the gospel of God only, but also our own souls, because ye were become very dear to us.

Translation and Paraphrase

9. Even so (in the same manner as the nurse cherishing her own children, we,) yearning after you (greatly as we did,) were well-pleased to impart unto you not only the good news of God, but even our own lives, because ye were (that) beloved unto us.

Notes (2:8)

1. Paul's feelings toward the Thessalonians overflowed with love so deep and genuine that it led him to make many great sacrifices for them. He worked day and night to support himself while with them.

The true minister of Christ does not count the cost to him of helping people to know Christ. Anything he can give he will give.

2. Paul was like Jesus, who came not to be ministered unto but to minister. Matt. 20:28.

3. II Cor. 12:15—"And I will very gladly spend and be spent for you; though the more abundantly I love you, the less I be loved."

4. Concerning the "gospel of God," see notes on I Thess. 2:2, paragraph 6.

5. Paul's self-sacrificing sincerity is also seen in Romans 9:1-3, where Paul says that he could wish himself accursed from Christ for the sake of his brethren in the flesh, the Israelites, if that would help save them.

Text (2:9)

9 For ye remember, brethren, our labor and travail: working night and day, that we might not burden any of you, we preached unto you the gospel of God.

Translation and Paraphrase

9. For you remember, brethren, our toil and hard labor, (how that by) working night and day so that we would not be burdensome to any of you, we preached unto you the good news of God (without charging you a cent).

Notes (2:9)

1. This information about Paul's manual labor in Thessalonica is not given in the book of Acts. But Acts records how Paul worked similarly in Corinth. See Acts 18:3; II Cor. 11:9; I Cor. 4:12. See also notes on I Thess. 2:6, paragraphs 5 and 6.

2. Paul's laboring in Thessalonica (2:9) set an example for the "labor of love" by the Thessalonians. I Thess. 1:3.

3. Paul's labor in Thessalonica also set an example for those who were inclined to be idle. See II Thess. 3:8-9.

4. What are the literal meanings of the words translated "labour" and "travail"?

    (1) "Labour" (Gr., *kopos*) means "intense labor, united with trouble, toil. It gives prominence to the fatigue involved." (Thayer)

    (2) "Travail" (Gr., *mochthos*) means hard and difficult labor, and it gives prominence to the hardship involved. It does not mean birth-pains. This is another word. See I Thess. 5:3.

5. We probably should understand the phrase, "labouring night and day," to mean that Paul began work even before daylight and worked on after dark in the evening.
6. Can we honestly say that we have the sincerity and dedication of Paul? May God help us to have the earnestness and the spirit of joyful self-sacrificing that possessed him. If we had more of his disposition, we might have more of his results.
7. Regarding the expression, "gospel of God," see notes on I Thess. 2:2, par. 6.

Text (2:10)

10 Ye are witnesses, and God *also*, how holily and righteously and unblamably we behaved ourselves toward you that believe:

Translation and Paraphrase

10. You (yourselves are) witnesses, and God (also), how holily (toward God), and righteousnessly (toward men), and unblameably (toward all) we behaved (ourselves) toward (you,) the believing ones.

Notes (2:10)

1. Paul saw in his hard physical labor a sacredness. The holy man sees in life's duties a sacredness, and in life's sacred acts a duty.
2. Paul's insistence upon the righteousness of his conduct almost compels us to think that he was answering some accusations and criticisms that had been thrown at him.
3. "Holily" means "undefiled by sin, pure." It expresses a relationship between our activities and God.
4. "Justly" means "in a just or righteous manner; in harmony with what is right." It expresses a relationship between our activities and men.
5. "Unblameably" (Gr., *amemptos*) means "deserving no criticism, not subject to blame." The same Greek word is used in I Thess. 5:23, where it is translated "blameless."

Text (2:11-12)

11 as ye know how we *dealt with* each one of you, as a father with his own children, exhorting you, and encouraging *you*, and testifying, 12 to the end that ye should walk worthily of God, who calleth you into his own kingdom and glory.

Translation and Paraphrase

11. (We truly behaved unblameably toward you,) even as ye know how that (we dealt with) each one of you as a father (would

deal with) his own children, exhorting you, and encouraging, and testifying (to you).

12. That you would be walking (that is, conducting yourselves) worthily of God, who calls you into his kingdom and (his) glory.

Notes (2:11-12)

1. During the short time Paul was with the Thessalonians, he exhorted "every one" of them, meaning each one individually. This in itself is an astounding accomplishment. (How did he ever have time to do manual labor in addition to all of this personal exhorting?) Concerning the meaning of the word "exhort" or "exhortation," see notes on I Thess. 2:3, paragraph 2.

2. Paul not only "exhorted" them, but also "comforted" them. The ministry of comforting and consoling people is most needful. This world has an abundance of things that cause grief, fear, and sorrow, and a scarcity of comforting. Real comforting means very much to people.

3. Paul had behaved toward them as a father would behave toward his own children. (The word *own* is important, and should be in the translation, as also in 2:7.) Any father worthy of his position would instruct his children in the right way to live, and urge them to do it. Paul had done that very thing to the Thessalonian disciples.

   Paul did not have the Thessalonians addressing him as "Father Paul," in the fashion of the Roman Catholic clergy. (Remember, Jesus said, "Call no *man* your father upon the earth." Matthew 23:9.) But even so, Paul was a spiritual father to the Thessalonians in every sense that a man can be. I Corinthians 4:15: "For though ye have ten thousand instructors in Christ, yet have ye not many fathers: for in Christ Jesus I have begotten you through the gospel."

4. Paul urged them that they walk *worthy of God*. The word, "worthy," means "of equal weight." We must imagine a set of balances, with God in one side. On the other side of the balances, we must place our "walk" (or manner of life), and it must be "worthy" (of equal weight) of God. This may seem impossible. Whether it is impossible or not, it is certainly difficult. Paul had to exhort and testify repeatedly to the Thessalonians to get them to do this.

Probably we ought not to say that it would be impossible to be *worthy* of God, since Paul taught us to walk *worthy* of God not only here, but in other places as well. Vol. 1:10: "That ye might walk worthy of the Lord." See also Ephesians 4:1; Phil. 1:27 (in American Standard version); II Thess. 1:5. (Also see notes on II Thess. 1:11, paragraph 4.)

5. For specific instructions about how we "ought to walk" (or live), see I Thess. 4:1-12, the section entitled, "The walk of the Christian."

6. How sublime and dignified a Christian's character may become! It is actually possible to walk *worthy* of God. Paul's good record among the Thessalonians was crowned by his efforts to stimulate his converts to the noblest possible way of living.

7. Notice that we are called unto (or into) God's *kingdom* and glory. The kingdom of God is "visible as the church on earth." (B. W. Johnson.) There are many Scripture verses that indicate that the kingdom of Christ has already been established on earth, and is practically synonymous with the church. Here are a few:

> Col. 1:13—"God hath translated us into the kingdom of his dear Son."
>
> Matt. 16:18-19—"I will build my church . . . and I will give unto thee the keys of the kingdom of heaven."
>
> Rev. 1:9—"I John . . . am your brother, and companion . . . in the kingdom . . . of Jesus Christ."
>
> Hebrews 12:28—"Ye are come . . . to the general assembly and church. . . . Wherefore having received a kingdom that cannot be shaken . . . "
>
> (See also the *Special Study* on page 250, "The Throne of His Father David.")

8. Of course the kingdom of God will extend into the future life in a more glorious form. II Tim. 4:18; II Pet. 1:11.

9. The glory of God which we share includes such future promises as the resurrection of the dead, transformed bodies, the new heaven and earth, and other glories.

STUDY SUGGESTIONS

1. At this point in your study of I Thessalonians, we urge you to turn back to the outline of chapter two, and review the points in this section, 2:1-12, which is called "Paul's work among them."

2. Also it would be well for you at this time to turn ahead to the "Did You Learn?" questions, following the notes on 2:16. You should now be able to answer questions 1 to 29.

Text (2:13)

13 And for this cause we also thank God without ceasing, that, when ye received from us the word of the message, *even the word* of God, ye accepted *it* not *as* the word of men, but, as it is in truth, the word of God, which also worketh in you that believe.

Translation and Paraphrase

13. And we also thank God unceasingly for this (cause, namely) that when ye received (the) message which ye heard from us, (even the message) of God, you (welcomed and) received it not as a message from men, but as (what) it truly is, (the) message of God, which (is not just another dead philosophy, but is a living word that) also works actively in you that believe (it).

Notes (2:13)

1. Any man who has a burning conviction that the apostles of Christ taught the words of Almighty God would rejoice to see people receive the apostles' teachings as the word of God.

2. Paul was so pleased that the Thessalonians had received his message as the word of God, that he thanked God for this "without ceasing."

3. Paul knew perfectly well where his gospel came from, "I certify you, brethren, that the gospel which was preached by me is not after men." Galations 1:11. When the Thessalonians received his gospel as coming from God, as he KNEW it had come, he was most thankful.

4. This verse should forever establish the fact that we cannot have a faith like the apostles had, and then deny the miracles and prophecies and other things which the apostles taught.

   Modern interpreters try to make the Bible acceptable to unbelievers by "demythologizing" it. Thus they reject such things as miracles and prophecies as being myths. Let us say right now that we do not believe that the Bible has myths in it. It is a combination of God's actual words, with the true history of His dealings with men.

   We accept the testimony of the honest men who penned the Bible, that Jesus actually was born of a virgin, and actually walked on the water, and actually died for our sins, and rose

65

bodily from the tomb, and is coming again. A believer has no part with an unbeliever. See II Cor. 6:15; II John 9-11.

5. This verse (2:13) begins the second section of chapter two, a section giving Paul's thanks for the way they received the word. The section covers 2:13-16. See outline of chapter two. The section is somewhat of an elaboration of Paul's statement in 1:6: "Ye became followers of us, and of the Lord, having received the word in much affliction."

6. To "receive" the word, of God as the Thessalonians received it, carries the idea of welcoming it as well as just taking it. (The Gr. verb *dechomai* has that connotation.) The teachable attitude of the Thessalonian Christians was in sharp contrast to that of the Jews, who not only refused to be taught themselves, but would not let Paul teach anyone else.

7. As if it were not a sufficient privilege for the Thessalonians to have received the word of God for its own sake, Paul adds further food to heaven's table of blessings, by saying that "the word of God is *working* within you."

The word of God is not some dead philosophy or speculation, but is living ("quick") and active. Hebrews 4:12. It is like good seed which springs up when it is planted. Luke 8:11. The word of God does not return void (and fruitless) unto God, but it is like rain that comes down from heaven and causes grass and flowers to grow out of the ground. The word of God accomplishes whatever God sends it worth to do. Isaiah 55:10-11.

The word of God, because it is living and working, causes sinners to be born again and saved. We are "born again," not of corruptible seed, but of incorruptible, by the word of God." I Peter 1:23.

Then, after being born again, the word of God continues to work within us. (The middle voice of the verb *energeo* indicates that the word of God is self-operative, and self-sustaining.) God is at work within Christians, working through His word and His Spirit, causing them both to will (or desire) and to work (accomplish) His good pleasure. Philippians 2:13. We have power from heaven energizing within us:

8. Something is working in YOU:
   (1) Is it the spirit that now works in the sons of disobedience? Ephesians 2:2.
   (2) Or is it the word of God? I Thess. 2:13.

Text (2:14)

14 For ye, brethren, became imitators of the churches of God which are in Judaea in Christ Jesus: for ye also suffered the same things of your own countrymen, even as they did of the Jews;

Translation and Paraphrase

14. (It is obvious that you truly received the gospel as the word of God,) for you became imitators, brethren, of the churches of God which are in (the land of) Judea in Christ Jesus, because you also suffered the same things from your own people as they also (did) from the Jews.

Notes (2:14)

1. There is no more painful hurt that a person can endure than for his own friends and relatives to turn against him because he has received Jesus Christ as his Lord. The unkindest cut of all is one from the sword of our own people, those with whom we have pleasant memories and blood kinship.
2. The Thessalonians endured such anguish when the Jews set their whole city on an uproar against the Christians. Acts 17:5-9.
3. But this very experience, and others like it that followed, marked them as truly one with the children of God everywhere. For by their sufferings, they became followers (or, more accurately, "imitators," as in I Thess. 1:6) of the Christians in Judea.
4. Judea was the main homeland of the Jews, with Jerusalem being its capital. It was there that the church of Christ was started. Churches were soon in existence in many of the villages of Judea. Paul calls these churches, "the churches of God which in Judea are in Christ Jesus." Note that you cannot be "of God" and not be also "in Christ Jesus." (These churches were also called the "churches of Judaea which were in Christ." Gal. 1:22.)
5. The churches in Judea soon suffered persecution. Stephen was killed. Acts 7:59-60. A great persecution followed his death. Acts 8:1, 3. Many of the Hebrew Christians lost their homes and property. Hebrews 10:32-34. The unbelieving Jews tried to exterminate the followers of Christ, just as they had sought to kill Christ himself.
6. Paul could well have written the same words to the Thessalonians that he wrote to the Philippians: "For unto you it is given in the behalf of Christ, not only to believe on him, but also to suffer for his sake." Phil. 1:29.

Text (2:15-16)

15 who both killed the Lord Jesus and the prophets, and drove out us, and please not God, and are contrary to all men; 16 forbidding us to speak to the Gentiles that they may be saved; to fill up their sins always; but the wrath is come upon them to the uppermost.

Translation and Paraphrase

15. (These Jews are the people) who both killed the Lord Jesus and the prophets, and have persecuted (and pursued) us, and (they) please not God, and are antagonistic to all men.

16. preventing us (if they possibly can) from speaking to the Gentiles so that they could be saved. (All of this wickedness is working) unto the (result, that they, like the Amorites of old, are) filling full their (cup of) sins always. But (God has not overlooked this wickedness any more than He overlooked the iniquity of the Amorites.) Rather, the wrath (of God) has come upon them to the (bitter) end.

Notes (2:15-16)

1. Facts about the Jews.
   (1) They killed the Lord Jesus.
   (2) They killed the prophets.
   (3) They persecuted and pursued Paul.
   (4) They please not God.
   (5) They are contrary to all men.
   (6) They forbade Paul to speak to the Gentiles.

2. This list of charges which Paul lays upon the Jews would be enough in modern times to raise scrams of "Anti-Semitism!" from coast to coast. Nonetheless, everything which Paul said about them was true.

3. They killed the Lord Jesus. We have observed in recent times a lot of propaganda trying to get people to stop blaming the Jews for killing Jesus. But the fact remains that Pilate, the Roman governor who sentenced Jesus to die, did not want to do so. See John 19:6, 12. Only the mob pressure from the Jews prevailed upon him to do it.

   The Jews had tried to kill Jesus several times previously, before He finally was crucified. See John 8:59; 10:31; Luke 4:29.

   Just fifty days after Jesus died, right in Jerusalem where He was killed, the apostle Peter said publicly to the Jews, "YOU have taken (Jesus) and by wicked hands have crucified and slain." Acts 2:23. No Jew there could deny that Peter spoke the truth about their deed.

4. The Jews killed their prophets. Jesus himself laid this charge upon them. "O Jerusalem, Jerusalem, thou that killest the prophets, and stonest them which are sent unto thee." Matt. 23:37. See also Matt. 23:29-35; Acts 7:52.

The Jews during their history had turned against Moses. They persecuted Jeremiah. Amos was told to leave and prophesy no more. Amos 7:12. Micaiah was imprisoned. I Kings 22:24-28. Hanani imprisoned. II Chron. 16:7-10. Zechariah slain. II Chronicles 24:20-22. This list could go on and on.

5. The Jews had persecuted Paul, almost from the moment he had become a Christian. To list all the places where Paul had been hounded and persecuted by the Jews would be to list every place he ever visited—Damascus, Jerusalem, Antioch of Pisidia, Lystra, etc. Shortly before this letter was written, Paul had had to leave Berea, because Jews had come all the way from Thessalonica to run Paul out of town. See Acts 17:10-13.

This was such an unreasonable thing for them to do, sort of a "dog in the manger" attitude. But, "there is no limit to what religious prejudice will really do when men's eyes become blinded." (Ironside, ADDRESSES, p. 28.)

6. The Jews please not God. Probably of all the charges made by Paul against the Jews, this one would be the most hotly disputed. But as proof that Paul was right when he said, "The Jews please not God," let us remind you that God's prophets which He sent to the Jews confirm Paul's judgment:

   (1) John the baptist called them a "generation of vipers." Matt. 3:7.

   (2) Isaiah called them a "sinful nation, a people laden with iniquity, a seed of evildoers, children that are corrupters." Isa. 1:4.

   (3) Jeremiah said that they were all grievous revolters, walking with slanders. Jer. 6:28.

   (4) Malachi declared God's judgment, that "from the days of your fathers ye are gone away from mine ordinances." Malachi 3:7.

Jesus said to his apostles, "Whosoever killeth you shall think that he offereth service to God." John 16:2. The mistaken zeal of men like Saul of Tarsus led them even to commit murder in God's name. This certainly did NOT please God.

Now we must in all fairness interject, that there have always been many devout, gracious, open-hearted Jews, men like their father Abraham. Paul himself acknowledged this, for he himself was a Jew. Romans 11:5. Many Jews honestly considered what Jesus said and did, and many became Christians. But many closed their minds, and became violent against Christ and His followers. In doing that, they did NOT please God.

7. The Jews are contrary to all men. "Contrary" (Gr., *enantios*) means "opposite, antagonistic, etc."

The Jews of Paul's time delighted in hatching all manner of sedition, private conspiracy, and rebellion. Tacitus, the Roman historian, brands them as "the enemies of all men." The great Jewish doctor of the law, Gamaliel, himself tells of two violent rebellions of the Jews. Acts 5:36-37.

The Jews despised the Gentiles as unclean. They would not enter the house of Pilate the Roman governor. John 18:29. The apostle Peter said to Cornelius, "Ye know how that it is an unlawful thing for a man that is a Jew to keep company or come unto one of another nation." Acts 10:28.

We admit that it is plain evident history that Gentiles (and even professed Christians) have been cruel to the Jews throughout the centuries. But the Jews have themselves been guilty of everything that they have suffered from others. Gentiles and Jews alike are guilty before God.

8. The Jews forbade Paul to speak to the Gentiles. Nothing roused the Jews to more fury than for Paul to go to the Gentiles with the gospel of Christ.

Paul, in telling about his conversation and life before the Jews in Jerusalem, said, "And He (Jesus) said unto me, Depart; for I will send thee far hence unto the Gentiles. And they gave him audience *unto this word,* and then lifted up their voice, and said, Away with such a fellow from the earth: for it is not fit that he should live. And as they cried out, and cast off their clothes, and threw dust into the air. . . ." Acts 22:21-23.

It was always the same story wherever Paul went. The Jews tried to prevent him from teaching the Gentiles. In Lystra the Jews from Antioch and Iconium persuaded the people (Gentiles) to stone Paul. Acts 14:19; 17:13.

9. The result of all these wicked acts by the Jews, was that "they fill up their sins always." This expression appears to be a reference to what God had long before said about the wicked Am-

orites in the land of Canaan: "The iniquity of the Amorites is not yet full." Gen. 15:16. At a later date God indicated that their iniquity was full, and that their own land would vomit them out. Lev. 18:24-28.

To say that the Jews resembled the heathen Amorites, whom they conquered in the time of Joshua, was perhaps a crowning insult, but not an exaggeration.

10. As a result of the iniquity of the Jews, wrath was come upon them to the uttermost, or "unto the end." This does not mean that wrath would continue upon them to the end of the world. For Paul himself prophesied that the Israelites would return to God before that time. Romans 11:25-26. Rather, "wrath unto the uttermost" means wrath that fully expends itself.

God's wrath against the Jews was particularly demonstrated at the destruction of Jerusalem in 70 A.D. Already at the time when Paul wrote this epistle, the great rebellion of the Jews against the Romans was taking form. When the rebellion finally came in 66 A.D., it led to a bloody war, in which the walls, temple, and much of the rest of Jerusalem were demolished and burned down. 97,000 people were carried away captive into slavery, and eleven hundred thousand (1,100,000) perished, many by starvation and killing one another. Josephus, the Jewish historian, tells us about this in *Wars of the Jews*, VI, ix, 4.

Paul was certainly correct when he said that wrath was come upon them to the uttermost.

11. This statement about "wrath upon them to the uttermost" leaves some overly sensitive people shuddering with dislike and unbelief. Some interpreters even assert that this statement must be a "later interpolation" into the text. (So Moffatt, Interpreter's Bible, etc.) There is no proof whatsoever of such an opinion. It is just the reaction of the "natural mind" of man to God's judgment. Naturally, men do not like to accept what God says about such things as hell, the blood of Jesus, God's wrath, and the judgment. See I Cor. 2:14. But surely we must accept anything that God says. The Thessalonians did. I Thess. 2:13.

STUDY SUGGESTIONS

1. You have now come to the closing verses of the second part of chapter two. We urge you to review the outline of chapter 2.

2. Also you should now try to answer the remaining questions in the section that follows. Questions over the second section of chapter two are questions 30 to 45.

DID YOU LEARN?

(Questions over I Thessalonians, chapter two)

1. What is the topic of chapter two (2:1-16)?
2. What is the first main point of the outline of this chapter? (Point A)
3. What are its Scripture limitations?
4. What did the Thessalonians themselves know about Paul's entrance unto them? (2:1)
5. What Scripture verse and word does the "entrance" of 2:1 refer back to?
6. Where had Paul suffered immediately before he came to Thessalonica? (2:2)
7. In spite of Paul's previous sufferings, how did he speak in Thessalonica? (2:2)
8. What are the two ideas (or the double significance) in the word "exhortation"? (2:3)
9. Paul denies that his exhortation was prompted by three things. What were they? (2:3)
10. To what does "uncleanness" refer? (2:3)
11. What does the word "guile" mean? (2:3)
12. Paul spoke the gospel, as he was allowed by whom? (2:4)
13. What does the word "allowed" in 2:4 actually mean?
14. What two words in 2:4 are translations of the same word?
15. Whom did Paul seek to please, and whom did he not seek to please? (2:4)
16. What does God do to our hearts? (2:4)
17. What type of words did Paul not use? (2:5)
18. Who was witness of that fact? (2:5)
19. Over what did Paul not put a "cloke"? (2:5)
20. Who was witness of that fact? (2:5)
21. What two meanings are given for the word "glory"? (2:6)
22. As apostles of Christ, what could Paul have demanded? (2:6)
23. Paul was gentle among the Thessalonians, like a what? (2:7)
24. What two things was Paul willing to have imparted to the Thessalonians? (2:8)
25. When did Paul labor while he was among them? (2:9)

CHAPTER TWO

26. In what three ways had Paul behaved himself toward them that believe? (2:10)
27. Paul had exhorted them as a _____ would do. (2:11)
28. How did Paul exhort them to walk? (2:12)
29. Into what does God call us? (2:12)
30. What is the second main point in the outline of chapter two? (Point B)
31. What are its Scripture limitations?
32. As what did the Thessalonians receive the message which Paul preached? (2:13)
33. What did the way the Thessalonians received his words make Paul do? (2:13)
34. What did the word of God do in the Thessalonians? (2:13)
35. Of whom had the Thessalonians become followers because of their sufferings? (2:14)
36. Of whom had the Thessalonians suffered? (2:14)
37. What had the Jews done to Jesus? (2:15)
38. What had the Jews done to their prophets? (2:15)
39. What had the Jews done to Paul? (2:15)
40. What proof is given in the notes that Paul was correct when he said, "The Jews please not God"?
41. What attitude did the Jews have toward all men? (2:15)
42. What did the Jews try to keep Paul from doing? (2:16)
43. Whom did the Jews resemble in that they "filled up their sins always"? (2:16)
44. How far was God's wrath come upon the Jews? (2:16)
45. At what event was God's wrath upon the Jews especially demonstrated? (2:16)
46. Write out from memory (or recite) I Thess. 2:13. It begins, "For this cause also thank we ... "

Chapter Topic:

Paul's Current Dealings
with The Thessalonians

"When I could no longer forbear, I sent Timothy unto you." 1
Thess. 3:1-2

CHAPTER THREE BEGINS AT 2:17

Perhaps it looks as if we have a lot of nerve to say that chapter three should begin at 2:17. But if we regard the chapters as being rather complete and unified discussions of one particular topic, then we should by all means include 2:17-20 along with the material in chapter three. 2:17-20 is plainly a part of the same subject matter that Paul writes more about in chapter three.

Notice in the outline of chapter three how that the material in 2:17-3:10 all flows together into one discussion of "Paul's Current Dealings With The Thessalonians":

III. Paul's current dealings with the Thessalonians; 2:17-3:10
   1. Paul's desire for personal visit hindered; 2:17-3:10
   2. Timothy sent; 3:1-5
   3. Joy upon Timothy's return; 3:6-10.

THINKING THROUGH THESSALONIANS
I Thessalonians, chapter three (2:17—3:13)

Chapter Topic—"Paul's Current Dealings With the Thessalonians"

1. Paul had been taken from the Thessalonians for a short time in _____ but not in _____. 2:17

2. What had Paul endeavored to do? 2:17
_____.

3. Who prevented Paul from coming unto them? 2:18.
_____.

4. The Thessalonians were Paul's _____, and _____, and _____ of rejoicing. 2:19

5. The Thessalonians were Paul's hope, etc., "in the _____ of our Lord Jesus at his _____." 2:19

6. The Thessalonians were Paul's _____ and _____. 2:20.

7. Where was Paul when he decided it would be good to be left alone? 3:1. _____.

8. Whom did Paul send back to Thessalonica to establish them? 3:2. _____.

9. Paul desired that they would not be moved from their faith by these _____. 3:3

10. Unto what are we appointed? 3:3
_____.

11. When Paul was with them, what had he told them would happen? 3:4.

_____

CHAPTER THREE

12. When Paul could no longer forbear his fears for the Thessalonians, he _____ to know (about) their _____. 3:5
13. By whom did Paul fear that they might have been tempted? 3:5. _____.
14. If they had yielded to temptations, Paul's labors could have been _____ _____. 3:5
15. Were the tidings from the Thessalonians good or bad? (Circle which.) 3:6
16. Timothy brought back tidings of their _____ and _____. 3:6
17. True or false (circle which)—The Thessalonians wanted to see Paul again, just as he wanted to see them. 3:6
18. True or false (circle which)—Timothy's report from Thessalonica distressed Paul. 3:7
19. True or false (circle which)—When Paul wrote this letter, he was in pleasant circumstances. 3:7
20. In 3:8, Paul said, "Now we _____ if ye _____ in the Lord."
21. Was Paul able to express his thankfulness for the Thessalonians? 3:9. Yes or no. (Circle which)
22. What was Paul praying that he might get to do? 3:10. (2 answers)

_____;

_____

23. True or false (circle which)—Paul considered the faith of the Thessalonians to be complete. 3:10
24. To whom did Paul address his prayer? 3:11. (Two answers)

_____;

_____.

25. Paul prayed that the Lord would "direct _____ _____ unto you." 3:11
26. Paul prayed that God would make to increase and abound in what? 3:12. _____.
27. The end (or object) of Paul's prayer was that the Lord "may _____ your _____unblameable in _____ before God." 3:13
28. At what time are we to be before God, even our Father? 3:13.

_____

_____.

29. Who will be with Jesus when He comes? 3:13

_____.

30. Memorize I Thess. 3:12-13.

I THESSALONIANS, CHAPTER THREE (2:17—3:13)
Chapter Topic, *"Paul's Current Dealings With the Thessalonians"*
Outline

I. Paul's current dealings with the Thessalonians; 2:17-3:10
  A. Paul's desire for personal visit hindered; 2:17-20
    1. Paul's desire to see them; 2:17
    2. His efforts hindered; 2:18
    3. How much the Thessalonians meant to Paul; 2:19-20
  B. Timothy sent; 3:1-5
    1. Paul remained at Athens alone; 3-1
    2. Timothy sent to establish and comfort them; 3:2-5
      a. So that no man would be moved by afflictions; 3:2-4
        (1) We are appointted unto afflictions; 3:3
        (2) Paul had warned them of afflictions; 3:4
        (3) They knew afflictions had occurred.
      b. So that Paul could know of their faith; 3:5
        (1) Lest the tempter had tempted them.
        (2) Lest his labor had been in vain.
  C. Joy upon Timothy's return; 3:6-10
    1. What Timothy reported; 3:6
      a. Their faith and charity.
      b. They had good remembrance of Paul always.
      c. They desired greatly to see Paul again.
    2. Paul's reaction to Timothy's report; 3:7-10
      a. Comforted; 3:7
      b. Caused to live; 3:8
      c. Too thankful to express his joy; 3:9
      d. Praying to see them again; 3:10

Conclusion; The apostle's prayer for the Thessalonians; 3:11-13
    1. That God would direct his way unto them; 3:11
    2. That their love would increase and abound; 3:12-13
      a. Toward one another and all men; 3:12
      b. Abound as Paul's love abounded toward them; 3:12
      c. Purpose of this petition—that their hearts would be established unblameable; 3:13

You should NOW memorize the topic of this chapter, and the three main points (A, B, and C) under it, and their Scripture limitations.

THOUGHTS FROM THE OUTLINE
Of I Thessalonians, chapter three

Paul's dealings with the Thessalonians AFTER he left Thessalonica show the feelings of a true man of God toward his converts after he has departed from them. They never cease to be upon his heart. He will do anything possible to help them remain true to the Lord, and he has no greater joy than to hear news of their continued faithfulness and spiritual growth.

Christians should realize that it is a great grief to a minister whom they may love, if they do not remain true to Christ when he has gone away from them.

Text (2:17)

17 But we, brethren, being bereaved of you for a short season, in presence not in heart, endeavored the more exceedingly to see your face with great desire:

Translation and Paraphrase

17. But we, brethren, being bereaved (by our separation) from you, (like a father is grieved when he has lost his children, even though it has been but) for a (short) time (such as the passing) of an hour, (and we have been separated from you only) in presence, not in heart, we, (because of our grief) have hurried (about, seeking) more abundantly (than you can imagine) to see your face with great desire.

Notes (2:17)

1. Can you imagine how a father in a Communistic country would feel to see his children taken out of his house by the police, and sent away to state schools, while he himself was sent off to a slave labor camp? Paul's feelings when he was driven away from the Thessalonians were equally intense.

   Paul uses the word *aporphanidzo* (the root of which gives us our word "orphan") to describe his feelings. The word means "to bereave, as one separated from parent or child."

   We love the churches where we have served. But probably most preachers do not have the intensity of love and yearning for them that Paul had.

2. Paul had not been separated from the Thessalonians very long when he wrote this letter. He says it was "a short time, such as the time of an hour." McGarvey says that "this short time" was about six months. But though the time had not been long, the pain of being separated was not any less keen.

3. Christian people have many farewells to say in this life. Thank God, we shall not have these in the world to come. But even in this life, Christians are not separated in heart nor affection, merely in presence. Thus Paul was separated from the Thessalonians only in presence, not in heart. Paul wrote a similar thought to the Colossians. Col. 2:5.

4. We do not know just what all Paul had done to try to get back to Thessalonica. But he had earnestly endeavoured (literally, "hastened" or "hurried" about) to get back to see them.

5. Not only did Paul desire to get back to see the Thessalonians, but he also desired to see his brethren in other places. He wrote to the Romans, "I long to see you." Rom. 1:11, 13. Paul's heart was big enough to love all of his brethren with all of him. Like a parent with a dozen children, he did not love any of them the less, just because there were so many to love.

Text (2:18)

18 because we would fain have come unto you, I Paul once and again; and Satan hindered us.

Translation and Paraphrase

18. Wherefore, we were resolved to come to you, even I Paul (myself), once and twice (once and again), and (then) Satan cut us off (so we could not come).

Notes (2:18)

1. Paul could not get back to Thessalonica because Satan hindered him. Satan has always tried to interfere with the work of Christian teachers. It was Satan who tried to break up the church in Jerusalem by forbidding the apostles to preach, and persecuting its members so that they were scattered.

2. The word "hindered" (Gr., *egkopto*) is a military term, and indicates the obstruction of an enemy's progress by breaking up the road, destroying bridges, etc. Did you ever think of Satan as a "road-breaker"? This surely explains why missionaries sometimes have so much trouble getting to various places. Paul used the same term, "hindered," in writing to the Romans. Rom. 15:22.

80

3. We do not know exactly what means Satan used to block Paul so he could not get back to Thessalonica. But Satan has many means—sickness, poverty, persecution, etc. Perhaps Satan hindered Paul by the "distress and affliction," mentioned in I Thess. 3:5.

4. Paul had an unhesitating belief in the reality and personal activity of Satan. See Ephesians 2:2; 4:27; II Cor. 4:4; 12:17; Acts 26:18; I Timothy 5:15. We must believe that the devil is real, if we claim to have an apostolic faith.

Text (2:19-20)

19 For what is our hope, or joy, or crown of glorying? Are not even ye, before our Lord Jesus at his coming? 20 For ye are our glory and our joy.

Translation and Paraphrase

19. (We have desired so greatly to see you,) for what is our hope, or joy, or crown in which we rejoice (like an athlete rejoices in his laurel of victory)? Are not even you (Thessalonians our hope, joy, and crown)? (Indeed you are those very things to us, and you will be our crown when we stand) before our Lord Jesus at his coming.

20. For ye are our glory and joy.

Notes (2:19-20)

1. To a gospel preacher like Paul, his converts are his . . .
    (1) Hope
    (2) Joy
    (3) Crown of rejoicing
    (4) Glory; 2:20

2. When we stand before Christ at His coming, the souls that we have won, and the work that we have done for Christ, will be our hope, and joy, and glory, and crown. Let us therefore win souls while we have opportunity.

3. Numerous references in the New Testament teach us that Christians shall be rewarded according to their works. We did not say *saved* by their works, but rewarded according to their works. I Cor. 3:14: "If any man's work shall abide . . . he shall receive a reward."

   This fact partly explains why Paul was so uneasy when he thought that the Thessalonians might have forsaken the faith. If they stood fast for Christ, he would have a reward. If they shrunk back from the Lord, he would suffer loss. I Cor. 3:15. (Of course Paul's concern for them was prompted more by love for them than by self-interest.)

4. Victorious athletes in Paul's time often received garland crowns as symbols of their victories. They could point to the crowns as objects of pride and proof of victory. Likewise Paul could point to the churches he had established as emblems of victory and tokens of his joy. Philippians 4:1: "Therefore, my brethren dearly beloved and longed for, my joy and crown, so stand fast in the Lord."

In the absence of his king, Paul had won a crown, the Thessalonians. When he met the king, he would lay his crown before the king's feet.

5. The fact that the Thessalonians would be Paul's joy and crown in heaven should make it plain once for all that we shall know one another in the future life. Otherwise how could Paul glory in them before Christ at His coming?

6. To explain how the souls we win will be our *glory*, we can do no better than to quote Daniel 12:3: "They that be wise shall shine as the brightness of the firmament; and they that turn many to righteousness as the stars forever and ever."

7. This verse mentions the "coming" of our Lord Jesus. The Greek word translated *coming* is *parousia*. It is used here for the first time in the Thessalonian epistles. You should get to know this word as you will often find it in books, even those all written in English.

Parousia literally means "a being alongside," and is usually translated "coming" or "presence." It is frequently used in Greek literature to refer to the visit (or coming) of some official or prominent personage. It refers in the New Testament to the "coming" or arrival of men, such as Stephanas (I Cor. 16:17) and Titus (2 Cor. 7:6-7). It is applied seventeen times to the second coming of Jesus.

Parousia is used twenty-four times in the New Testament. In the King James version it is translated "coming" twenty-two times and "presence" twice. It is found in Matt. 24:3; 24:27, 37, 39; I Cor. 15:23; 16:17; II Cor. 7:6, 7; 10:10; Phil. 1:26; 2:12; I Thess. 2:19; 3:13; 4:15; 5:23; II Thess. 2:1, 8, 9; James 5:7, 8; II Peter 1:16; 3:4, 12; I John 2:28.

We have given all these detailed facts, so that when we come to this word, *parousia*, in future verses, you will already know its meaning and uses.

STUDY SUGGESTION

Turn to the "Did You Learn?" questions following chapter 3, and see if you can answer questions 1 through 9. These deal with the section, 2:17-20.

(We started the study of chapter three at 2:17. For our reasons for doing this, the outline of chapter three, and the "Thinking Through Thessalonians" questions over chapter three, turn back to the pages following notes on 2:16.)

Text (3:1)

1 Wherefore when we could no longer forbear, we thought it good to be left behind at Athens alone;

Translation and Paraphrase

1. Wherefore (on account of your being so dear to us, and the fact that I could not personally return to you), when we could no longer conceal (and endure the pain of being separated from you), we thought it (would be) good to be left behind at Athens alone (rather than to continue suffering anxiety over you).

Notes (3:1)

1. Christians frequently discover that things do not work out as they sincerely believe they should. God often leads us in paths not of our own choosing, and not according to the way we understand things. Of course, God knows best and can foresee the future, and always works things out for the best. Romans 8:28.

   Paul probably thought very sincerely that it was the will of God that he return to Thessalonica. But God did not open up the way (and when Satan blocks us, only God can open the way). Meanwhile his fears about the young Thessalonian Christians were heaping up day after day.

2. Finally Paul could stand the anxiety no more, and decided that it would be better for him to remain at Athens alone, than to enjoy the assistance of Timothy and continue worrying about the Thessalonians. So Paul sent Timothy back to Thessalonica from Athens. For further details about the moves of Paul, Timothy, and Silas at this time, see Introductory Section VI, paragraphs 16 to 20.

3. When Paul says that *we* could no longer forbear, it is certain that he was speaking only of himself. He could not have been left *alone* if Silas or other helpers had been with him. Writers

often refer to themselves as "we" (an editorial "we"). It does not sound as boastful to say, "We did something," as to say, "I did it."

4. The word translated "forbear" (Gr., *stego*) means "cover, cover up with silence, bear up against, endure, bear, forbear." (Thayer) Paul finally reached the point where he could not cover up his fears about the Thessalonians. He had to do something.

5. Although Paul sent Timothy to Thessalonica from Athens, he wrote this epistle from Corinth later.

Text (3:2)

2 and sent Timothy, our brother, and God's minister in the gospel of Christ, to establish you, and comfort *you* concerning your faith;

Translation and Paraphrase

2. And (so) we sent Timothy, our brother (in the Lord, and minister of God), and fellow-worker with God in the (work of spreading the) good news of Christ, so that he might establish you (in the right beliefs and practices) and exhort you concerning your faith.

Notes (3:2)

1. While the anger of the Jews was directed at the whole church and the gospel itself, their anger was focused on Paul. So Paul sent Timothy to Thessalonica. Timothy apparently encountered no trouble in making the trip. Paul would certainly have had trouble.

2. Paul calls Timothy:
   (1) Our brother.
   (2) Minister of God.
   (3) Fellowlabourer in the gospel. Compare I Cor. 3:9.
       (The title "minister" is omitted in the American Standard Version, Nestle's Greek text, etc. It has only limited support in the oldest manuscripts of the New Testament.)

3. Preachers of the gospel should revel in the way Paul speaks of his fellow-workers. Compare Phil. 4:2. Paul calls them "brothers," "fellow-workers," etc. Paul had no jealousy. Whenever anyone did anything for Christ, Paul was glad.

4. Timothy had two things to do for the Thessalonians:
   (1) *Establish* them. This means to make them stable, and set them fast in the faith.

(2) *Comfort* them. This is the term also translated "exhort." For the meaning of "exhort" and "exhortation," see notes on I Thess. 2:3, par. 2.

Establishing and comforting are two things necessary for every young Christian, and many older ones also.

Text (3:3-4)

3 that no man be moved by these afflictions; for yourselves know that hereunto we are appointed. 4 For verily, when we were with you, we told you beforehand that we are to suffer affliction; even as it came to pass, and ye know.

Translation and Paraphrase

3. (I sent Timothy unto you) so that none (of you) would be shaken about (and distressed) by these troubles (which you are having). For you yourselves know that (in God's arrangement of things) we are appointed unto this (very) thing (affliction).
4. For (you surely remember that) even while we were (still) with you, (that) we kept telling you before (anything had yet happened), that we (as Christians) were certain to be pressed (with afflictions), just as it (soon) came to pass, and (as) you know (very well how) it has happened. (Therefore, do not be disturbed by this turn of events.)

Notes (3:3-4)

1. Often when people become Christians and discover that they experience trouble and sorrow afterwards, they wonder if they have made a mistake. They wonder if they are actually saved, thinking that their sufferings are an indication of God's judgment upon them.
2. But notice that Paul says in these verses that we are actually appointed in God's arrangement of things to suffer tribulation. The "we" refers to all Christians. Let them all hear it.

   The words "tribulation" and "affliction" come from the Greek *thlipsis* and mean "a pressing, pressing together, pressure, oppression, affliction, distress, etc." (Thayer) Tribulation is our lot as Christians.

   John 16:33—"In the world we shall have tribulation."

   Acts 14:22—We enter into the kingdom of God through much tribulation. See also John 15:18-19; Mark 10:30.
3. But let us remember that God is not the instigator of all our troubles. God did not bring the sufferings of Job upon him. The

devil did it. (See Job, chapters 1 and 2.) If Job had accused God of hurting him, Job would have accused God foolishly. Job 1:22. Christians are appointed to suffer, probably because the evil world cannot stand the contrast of sanctified lives to its wickedness. God permits this evil to exist, but the time is coming when God will punish those who afflict us, and give rest to those who are afflicted. II Thess. 1:6-7.

4. We are happy to report that Paul's hope that the Thessalonians had not been moved by affliction was found to be a fact. II Thess. 1:4. They did continue to bear their tribulations without giving up the faith. It *is* possible for suffering people to be victorious over persecutions, so that "no man should be moved (or shaken) by these afflictions."

5. Paul seems to have had to jog the memory of the Thessalonians several times. In this verse he asks, "Don't you remember how that while I was with you I told you that we would have suffering?" Compare II Thess. 2:5; 3:10. Such verses as Acts 14:22 indicate that Paul did indeed warn his converts of tribulation to come.

Text (3:5)

5 For this cause I also, when I could no longer forbear, sent that I might know your faith, lest by any means the tempter had tempted you, and our labor should be in vain.

Translation and Paraphrase

5. Because of this (tribulation which I knew would befall you), I also, when I could no longer conceal (and endure) (my fears about what might have happened to you) sent (Timothy unto you), so that I could know (how) your faith (had held out), lest by any means the tempter (Satan) had (successfully) tempted you, and our toil (among you) had become in vain (because you had fallen away from the faith).

Notes (3:5)

1. The fears of a true minister that Satan may have destroyed the faith of his converts can be an overpowering burden to him. Paul's fears about the Thessalonians were so intense that he could not even preach in Corinth, until Timothy and Silas arrived with the reassuring news from Thessalonica. Acts 18:5; I Thess. 3:6-7.

2. This verse is so closely joined to the preceding verses that it cannot be understood without reading them, but when those verses are read along with this one, this one becomes very plain.

The "cause" which made Paul send Timothy to learn about their faith, is the "tribulation" (mentioned in 3:3-4) which he knew would befall them and indeed had.

3. Paul was mainly concerned about the *faith* of the Thessalonians. He sent Timothy to learn about their *faith*. I Thess. 3:7. Their faith was his main concern rather than their physical welfare or even their survival. There is a rather obvious point in this for us.

4. Of course, "the tempter" is Satan. I Thess. 2:18. Satan's temptations could have turned the Thessalonians away from the faith.

5. Satan tempts us "by any means." Some of his methods are smooth and slick. Some of them are iron-fisted and cruel. Satan can tempt people by incontinency. I Cor. 7:5. Satan beguiles and corrupts us from the simplicity that is in Christ. II Cor. 11:3.

6. When Satan's temptations are successful, the preacher's *labor* is in vain. (The word *labor* used here is *kopos*. For its meaning, see notes on I Th. 1:3, par. 2.) Paul often expressed the fear that his work might be *in vain*.

Gal. 2:2—"Let by any means I should run, or had run *in vain*."

I Cor. 3:15—"If any man's work shall be burned, he shall suffer loss: but he himself shall be saved; yet so as by fire."

Phil. 2:16—"That I may rejoice in the day of Christ, that I have not run *in vain*, neither laboured *in vain*."

7. The fact that Paul's work among the Thessalonians would have been *in vain* if Satan had successfully tempted them, shows that people CAN be lost, even after they are once saved.

No one can deny that the Thessalonians were saved. They were elect. I Th. 1:4. They had the joy of the Holy Spirit. I Th. 1:6.

As long as they remained saved, Paul's work among them could not have been in vain. The fact that Paul feared that his work among them might be in vain proves that they could become lost again. They were elect, but not unconditionally elect.

STUDY SUGGESTION

Turn now to the "Did You Learn?" questions at the end of chapter 3, and see if you can answer questions 10 to 18.

Text (3:6)

6 But when Timothy came even now unto us from you, and brought us glad tidings of your faith and love, and that ye have good remembrance of us always, longing to see us, even as we also to *see* you;

Translation and Paraphrase

6. But now since Timothy has come (back) to us from you, and told us the good news about (your steadfast) faith and your love, and (how) that you have (such affectionate and) good recollection of us at all times, desiring to see us, just as we also (desire to see) you (again),

Notes (3:6)

1. "As cold water to a thirsty soul, so is good news from a far country." Proverbs 25:25. The news which Timothy brought back to Paul from Thessalonica was fully that refreshing to him.

2. This verse (3:6) starts a new section in the outline, entitled "Joy upon Timothy's return." (3:6-10).

3. Timothy and Silas came to Paul in Corinth. Acts 18:1,5. It was there that he wrote I & II Thessalonians.

4. The fact that Paul writes, *"Now when Timothy came,"* seems to indicate that he sat down and wrote this letter almost immediately upon Timothy's return.

5. Here is what Timothy's report about the Thessalonians contained:
   (1) Good news about their faith (inward religion).
   (2) Good news about their love (outward religion).
       (The word translated "charity" actually means "love.")
   (3) The report that they had good remembrance of Paul always.
   (4) Also the news that they desired to see Paul again.
       This was an encouraging report in every way.

6. You have no doubt often heard it said that the phrase "preach the gospel" means "bring good news." That is true, and this meaning is clearly pointed out in this verse. Paul uses the same word *(euaggelidzo)* to describe Timothy's bringing a good report to him, that is used in many other places to describe preaching the gospel of Christ. Timothy's report was good news of one kind. The gospel is also good news, but of a greater kind.

Text (3:7-8)

7 for this cause, brethren, we were comforted over you in all our distress and affliction through your faith: 8 for now we live, if ye stand fast in the Lord.

Translation and Paraphrase

7. Because of this (good news about you), we are (greatly) comforted, brethren, about you (even) in all our distress and tribulation on account of your faith.

8. (This comfort means more to us than you can imagine), because now we live if you stand fast in the Lord.

Notes (3:7-8)

1. The depth of Paul's longing for the Thessalonians can be seen in his statement, "We live if ye stand fast in the Lord." This statement implies an opposite one: "We die if you don't stand fast."

2. Paul had certainly been in affliction and distress before Timothy returned from Thessalonica with good news. Before Timothy's arrival he had not even been stirred to preach. Acts 18:5. In Corinth the Jews blasphemed against him. Acts 18:6. The Lord even saw fit to appear to Paul in Corinth to encourage him. Acts 18:8-9.

3. Paul urged the Thessalonians to "stand fast" in the Lord. It may not be enough in itself to "stand still," but we certainly ought to "stand" against the onslaughts of Satan and not to yield. Ephesians 6:11, 13, 14. "Put on the whole armor of God, that ye may be able to *stand*." I Cor. 15:1: "The gospel ... wherein ye *stand*."

4. The people of a church are so close to a minister that they have power to make his life happy or supremely miserable. The ministerial life and energy of even an apostle seemed dependent on the sympathy, faith, and steadfastness of the brethren. Elijah wanted to die when he thought that all the people had forsaken Jehovah. I Kings 19:4. John the apostle had no greater joy than to hear that his children walked in truth. III John 4.

Text (3:9)

9 For what thanksgiving can we render again unto God for you, for all the joy wherewith we joy for your sakes before our God;

Translation and Paraphrase

9. For what kind of thanks can we (possibly) repay to God (that would truly show our feelings) about you? For (such thanks would have to be great enough to include all the joy in which we rejoice on account of you (as we pray) before our God;

Notes (3:9)

1. This verse all boils down to a simple question: "How can we ever be thankful enough for you?"
2. The question begun here in 3:9 extends on through the tenth verse, where it is extended into a description of how Paul prayed long and hard for them. To make the question more apparent in our paraphrase, we have inserted the question mark into the ninth verse, and made a separate sentence out of the last half of verse nine and all of verse ten.
3. Paul felt like he should "repay" or "recompense" back to God sufficient thanks to show how grateful he was for the Thessalonians. Paul found this to be impossible, for he was too thankful for the Thessalonians to express it.
4. The expression, "joy wherewith we joy," is rather a Hebrew way of expressing tremendous, superlative joy.

Text (3:10)

10 night and day praying exceedingly that we may see your face, and may perfect that which is lacking in your faith?

Translation and Paraphrase

10. (For we do pray) night and day, more than can be measured, asking (God to make it possible for us) to see your face (once again), and to perfect the things which are lacking in your faith.

Notes (3:10)

1. Paul candidly states in this verse that the faith of the Thessalonians was imperfect. He indicates in chapters four and five what some of the things were which were lacking in their faith.
2. Perhaps it seems rather blunt to tell someone, as Paul told the Thessalonians, "I want to come and see you, so I can perfect your understanding and development." This is especially so in matters of religion, where usually every man's way is clean in his own eyes. Prov. 16:2. But undoubtedly the Thessalonians had the right attitude, and knew very well that they were im-

perfect in faith and knowledge. They doubtless would have been extremely glad to have had Paul instruct them further.

3. Paul prayed "exceedingly." The word means "superabundantly," "beyond measure."

4. The way Paul prayed day and night concerning the Thessalonians reminds us of the way King David often prayed in the night. Psalm 119:55. Have you ever awakened in the night, and found yourself thinking about God's law and desiring to pray to God?

5. New converts are only spiritual babes. I Peter 2:2; Hebrews 5:13; I Corinthians 3:1. New converts need to be taught to observe all the things which Jesus commanded us. Matt. 28:20. They need to recognize their limited knowledge and development in spiritual things. They should not be appointed to positions of leadership in churches. I Tim. 3:6, 10. However, they can grow rapidly. And when they have been taught, they should not hold back from serving Christ just because they feel inadequate for the work of witnessing for Christ.

6. Paul prayed for two things concerning the Thessalonians:
   (1) That he might see their face.
   (2) That he might perfect that which was lacking in their faith.

7. The prayer of Paul that he might get to visit the Thessalonians was answered in due time, for Paul visited Thessalonica on his third missionary trip, and again afterwards. See Introductory Section VI, paragraphs 27 and 28.

Text (3:11)

11 Now may our God and Father himself, and our Lord Jesus, direct our way unto you:

Translation and Paraphrase

11. But (now) may our God and Father himself, and our Lord Jesus, direct our path (once again) unto you.

Notes (3:11)

1. There are numerous brief prayers, such as this one, in the Thessalonian epistles. I Thess. 3:11-13; 5:23; II Thess. 1:11; 2:16; 3:5, 16. These written prayers show the character of Paul's mind. He could break into prayer in speaking or writing at any time. He prayed without ceasing. We should develop a similar habit of praying to God at every moment of joy or need. It should be just as easy as talking to any dear loved one.

2. The prayer which is started in this verse (and goes to the end of the chapter) forms the conclusion of Part One of I Thessalonians. There is also a prayer near the end of Part Two (at 5:23).

3. This prayer that God would direct Paul's path back to the Thessalonians was answered in due time. See the notes on I Thess. 3:10, par. 7.

4. There is a very notable, even if incidental, testimony to the glory of the Lord Jesus in this verse. Note that Paul addresses his prayer BOTH to God and to Jesus. Evidently Jesus answers prayers as well as God.

   But while the subject in this verse is PLURAL (God and the Lord Jesus), the verb is SINGULAR. (This is not apparent in English, but the Greek text shows it plainly.) This should go far to prove that God and Christ Jesus are ONE in the godhead, even though they are separate personalities. (This very Scripture was used by Athanasius against Arius back in the fourth century, to prove the deity of Jesus.)

5. The American Standard Version and the Greek text omit the word "Christ" after Jesus. The word "Christ" is not found in most of the ancient texts. Its omission does not affect the thought one bit.

Text (3:12)

12 and the Lord make you to increase and abound in love one toward another, and toward all men, even as we also *do* toward you;

Translation and Paraphrase

12. And may the Lord (Jesus) make you to increase and (even) abound in love for one another, and (also) toward all (men), just as we (do) unto you.

Notes (3:12)

1. It humbles us to read this prayer of Paul. For we notice that Paul asks the LORD to make them increase in love. We dare not forget at any time, that though we may teach and labor and set an example with all our power, it is the *Lord* who transforms men. We may plant and water, but it is the LORD that gives the increase. I Cor. 3:6. We cannot do God's work for Him.

2. There are two requests in this prayer: (3:11-13)
   (1) That God may direct our way unto you. 3:11

(2) That God will make you to increase and abound in love. 3:12
    (a) In love toward one another.
    (b) In love toward all men.

3. Paul addressed the second petition of his prayer to the *Lord.* The Lord is Jesus. Acts 2:36; 10:36.

4. The petition in 3:12 is for the *increase of their love.* Love is the greatest thing in the world. Faith, abilities, knowledge, and even good works, without love are of no avail. I Corinthians 13:1-3. "This is the message which ye have heard from the beginning, that we should love one another." I John 3:11.

5. For the Thessalonians to have loved all men, in the face of the abuse they were receiving, was indeed a development of character that only God could produce. Christians must love all men, even their enemies and persecutors. True followers of Jesus do not persecute even the worst of men. They may rebuke them and withdraw from them, but they do it out of a desire to lead them to a change of mind, and not as a punishment.

6. Paul's prayer that the Lord might make their love to increase, seems to have been answered rather definitely. For in II Thess. 1:3, we find Paul expressing thanks that "the charity (love) of each one of you all toward each other aboundeth." God does answer prayer.

7. After reading Paul's expressions of unlimited love for the Thessalonians in 2:17, 3:8-9, etc., it almost staggers us to read here in 3:21 that Paul says his love for them was increasing. How could it do so? But surely Paul was telling the truth.

Text (3:13)

13 to the end he may establish your hearts unblamable in holiness before our God and Father, at the coming of our Lord Jesus with all his saints.

Translation and Paraphrase

13. (We long to see such love abound among you) so that (by means of love) he may establish your hearts (to be) unblameable in holiness before our God and Father, at the coming of our Lord Jesus with all of his holy ones. (Amen)

Notes (3:13)

1. The goal of Paul's fervent prayer for the Thessalonians is something that the world does not want in any degree. Paul agonized

that they would be "unblameable in holiness before God." People in the world are proud of, and distinguished by, how wicked they can be. Whoever can curse the most violently, drink the most liquor, have the most wives and women, and make the most cutting remarks against "blue-nose," "Victorian," "Puritan" Christians is the most esteemed among the world's elite.

2. Paul prayed that we might be *stablished* unblameable in holiness. "Stablish" (or "establish") means to "set fast, place firmly, fix, make firm, render constant." Holiness is not to be a Sunday style, but is to be the well-established pattern of our whole lives.

3. The Thessalonians would become "unblameable in holiness" as the result of the increase of their love. (I Thess. 3:12) You cannot build a holy life without a sincere foundation of love.

4. This holiness within us is to be fully exhibited at the "coming of the Lord Jesus Christ." We shall never reach the "unblameable" perfectly attained stage in this life, but we shall reach it at the coming of the Lord Jesus. "When he shall appear, we shall be like him; for we shall see him as he is." I John 3:2. Do you have the hope of being like Jesus (and God) when He appears? "Every one that hath this hope in him, purifieth himself, even as he (Jesus or God) is pure." I John 3:3.

(The word "coming" in this verse is *parousia*. See notes on 2:19, par. 7, concerning this word.)

5. The Lord Jesus will come *with all his saints*. The word here translated *saints* simply means "holy ones." It is applied to angels as well as people. It probably refers to angels in this verse. Jesus will come back with His holy ones, the angels. (See Special Study on page 247, "The Coming of the Lord With All His Saints.") Will you be unblameable in holiness when you see Jesus, the holy one, with all His holy angels? God grant us determination and His help that we shall so be.

6. Many ancient manuscripts of the Bible have "Amen" at the close of this verse. We include it in our paraphrase. The "Amen" here fittingly closes not only this prayer, but the whole Part One of the epistle.

STUDY SUGGESTIONS

1. We urge you now to go back and review the outline of chapter 3 (which is found at 2:17).

2. Also we urge you now to answer (preferably by writing out) questions 19 to 38 from the section that follows immediately.

CHAPTER THREE

DID YOU LEARN?

(Questions over I Thessalonians, chapter three)

1. What is the chapter topic of chapter three (2:17—3:10)?
2. Why have we included 2:17-20 with the chapter topic of chapter three?
3. What is the title of the section, 2:17-20?
4. What had Paul endeavoured to do after being driven from Thessalonica? (2:17)
5. Paul was separated from the Thessalonians in presence, but not in what? (2:17)
6. Who had hindered Paul from doing what he desired to do? (2:18)
7. What four things were the Thessalonians unto Paul? (2:19-20)
8. When would the Thessalonians be Paul's crown of rejoicing? (2:19)
9. What is the Greek word which is translated "coming"? (2:19)
10. What is the section (or paragraph) 3:1-5 called in the outline?
11. Whom did Paul send to Thessalonica for him? (3:2)
12. Where was Paul when he sent him? (3:1)
13. What two things was this man to do for the Thessalonians? (3:2)
14. Unto what are we appointed as Christians? (3:3)
15. What had Paul told the Thessalonians while he was still with them would happen? (3:4)
16. Paul was mainly concerned about the _____ of the Thessalonians. (3:5)
17. Who did Paul fear had tempted them? (3:5)
18. What effect would there have been on Paul's labor if the Thessalonians had yielded to temptation? (3:5)
19. What is the section 3:6-10 called in the outline?
20. With what does Part One of I Thessalonians close? (See outline)
21. Give the Scripture limitations of this conclusion.
22. Where did Timothy and Silas come to Paul? (3:6)
23. What four things did Timothy report about the Thessalonians to Paul? (3:6)
24. How long after Timothy brought his report from Thessalonica was it before Paul wrote I Thessalonians? (3:6)
25. What effect did Timothy's report have on Paul? (3:7)
26. Paul declared, "Now _____ _____ if you stand fast in the Lord." (3:7)
27. Was Paul fully able to express his thanks for the Thessalonians? (3:9)

28. For what two things relating to the Thessalonians did Paul pray that he might be permitted to do? (3:10)
29. Was the faith of the Thessalonians perfect? (3:10)
30. When was Paul's prayer request to visit the Thessalonians granted? (3:10)
31. To whom does Paul address his prayer in 3:11?
32. Paul prayed that the Thessalonians might increase in what? (3:12)
33. Toward whom was this increase to be shown? (3:12)
34. What did Paul pray would be established unblameable in holiness? (3:13)
35. When would these be established unblameable? (3:13)
36. What other expression means the same as "saints"? (3:13)
37. Who are the "saints" who will come with Jesus? (3:13)
38. Write out, or recite, from memory I Thess. 3:12-13. It begins, "And the Lord make you to . . . "

Chapter topics

1. The Walk of the Christian.

2. The Dead in Christ and the Lord's Coming.

"The dead in Christ shall rise first——." I Thess. 4:16

THINKING THROUGH THESSALONIANS
I Thessalonians, chapter four

Chapter Topics—1. The Walk of the Christian. 4:1-12
   2. The dead in Christ, and the Lord's coming. 4:13-18

1. The Thessalonians had "received _____ _____ how they ought to walk and to please God." 4:1
2. In instructions on how to "walk," Paul urged that they "would _____ _____ and _____." 4:1
3. The commandments of Paul were given "by the _____ _____." 4:2.
4. "Your _____" was the will of God for the Thessalonians. 4:2
5. From what were the Thessalonians to abstain? 4:3.

   _____.
6. What should we know how to possess in sanctification and honor? 4:4. _____.
7. What people live in the "lust of concupiscence?" 4:5.

   _____. (The notes will explain these words.)
8. No man should "go beyond (or go too far) and _____ his brother in the matter." 4:6
9. Who is the avenger of sins? 4:6. _____.
10. God has not called us "unto _____ but unto _____. 4:7
11. Whom do we despise when we despise Paul's commands? 4:8.

   _____.
12. Concerning what did Paul not need to write to the Thessalonians? 4:9. _____.
13. Who taught the Thessalonians to love one another? 4:9.

   _____.
14. What three things did Paul tell them to do in 4:11?

   _____;

   _____;

   _____.
15. For what two reasons were they told to work? 4:12.

   _____

   _____;

   _____

   _____.

16. Concerning what did Paul not want them to be ignorant? 4:13. _____.

17. Paul gave them information so "that ye _____ not, even as others which have no _____. 4:13

18. What event gives us assurance that the dead will rise again? 4:14. _____

19. The dead Christians are described as "them which _____ in _____." 4:14

20. Whose word did Paul speak? 4:15. _____.

21. "We which are _____ and remain unto the _____ of the Lord shall not prevent (or go ahead of) them which are _____. 4:15

22. With what three things will the Lord descend from heaven? 4:16. _____; _____; _____.

23. Before we are all caught up, "the _____ in Christ shall rise _____." 4:16

24. After the Christian dead are raised, "we which are _____ and remain shall be _____ up _____ with them in the _____, to meet the _____ in the _____." 4:17

25. How long shall we remain with the Lord? 4:17. _____.

26. What are we to do with these words of Paul? 4:18. _____.

27. Memorize I Thess. 4:13-17.

I THESSALONIANS, CHAPTER FOUR

Chapter Topics—1. *The Walk of the Christian.* 4:1-12
2. *The Dead in Christ and the Lord's Coming.* 4:13-18

Outline

I. The walk of the Christian; 4:1-12
   A. Abound according to the apostles' teaching; 4:1-2
   B. Abstain from fornication; 4:3-8
      1. This is the will of God; 4:3
      2. Know how to possess your vessel; 4:4-5
         a. In sanctification and honor;
         b. Not in lust like the Gentiles; 4:5

99

     3. No one should defraud his brother; 4:6-7
       a. The Lord is the avenger of all such.
       b. God has not called us to uncleanness; 4:7
     4. We despise God when we disobey; 4:8
  C. Practice brotherly love; 4:9-10
     1. Paul did not need to write about this; 4:9a
     2. They were taught by God to do this; 4:9b
     3. The Thessalonians did this; 4:10a
     4. They needed to increase more and more; 4:10b
  D. Study to be quiet; 4:11a
  E. Do your own business; 4:11b
  F. Work with your own hands; 4:11c-12
     1. As Paul had commanded them; 4:11c
     2. That they might walk honestly toward outsiders; 4:12
     3. That they might have need of nothing.

II. The Lord's Coming; 4:13-5:11
  A. The dead in Christ and the Lord's coming; 4:13-18
     1. We should not be ignorant about this; 4:13
     2. Jesus's resurrection gives us assurance; 4:14
       a. We believe that Jesus died and arose.
       b. Even so will God bring the dead in Christ with Him.
     3. The living shall not precede the dead; 4:15
     4. Events at the Lord's coming; 4:16-17
       a. The Lord descends;
         (1) With a shout;
         (2) With the voice of the archangel;
         (3) With the trump of God.
       b. The dead in Christ rise first; 4:16
       c. Those which are alive are caught up with them; 4:17
       d. We meet the Lord in the air; 4:17
       e. We shall ever be with the Lord.
     5. Comfort one another with these words. 4:18

THOUGHTS FROM THE OUTLINE
Of I Thessalonians, chapter four

Chapter four includes two distinct topics.

The first of these concerns the *walk* of the Christian, that is, the way he lives. In this world the gospel depends very heavily upon the lives of those who believe it for its success. Also the salvation of those who believe the gospel depends on how they continue to walk. For these reasons the teaching about the walk of the Christian is very urgent.

The second section about the dead in Christ and the Lord's coming is always of much interest. The discussion about the Lord's coming extends on into the next chapter (to 5:11), where the matter of the times and seasons of the Lord's coming is brought up and discussed.

Text (4:1-2)

1 Finally then, brethren, we beseech and exhort you in the Lord Jesus, that, as ye received of us how ye ought to walk and to please God, even as ye do walk,—that ye abound more and more. 2 For ye know what charge we gave you through the Lord Jesus.

Translation and Paraphrase

1. (Now) therefore, brethren, (changing the subject to some remaining matters.) we ask you and urge (you) by the (authority and goodness of the) Lord Jesus, that, just as you have received from us (teachings concerning) how you ought to walk (that is, how to live your lives each day) and (how) to please God,—as indeed you are walking—(we urge you not merely to continue doing as you are, but) that you will increase (and even exceed) more (and more in doing so.)

2. For you know what (the) commandments (were, which) we gave to you through the (authority and commission of the) Lord Jesus.

Notes (4:1-2)

1. In all of Paul's letters to Gentile churches, there is a closing exhortation to purity of life, a warning against such sins as the Gentiles commonly practiced. These exhortations to the Thessalonians begin with the fourth chapter, and continue through the fifth.

2. It is hard for us to visualize the degeneration of pagan society and morals. In one of the rooms uncovered in Pompeii, the city that was buried by the volcano Veseuvius in 79 A.D., there is a frieze picturing immoral scenes. This was the atmosphere in which many of the Gentiles of Paul's time wanted to live.

3. Paul's prayer that they might be "unblameable in holiness" is carried right over into this new chapter with very specific instructions as to what they should do to be holy. Paul was always careful in his instructions to his converts to dwell on the practical side of Christianity, for—

> Vice is a monster of such frightful mien,
> That to be hated needs but to be seen;
> Yet seen too oft, familiar with her face,
> We first endure, then pity, then embrace.

4. Chapters four and five of I Thessalonians make up Part Two of the epistle, which is entitled in the outline "Exhortations and Teachings."

5. The first part of chapter four (4:1-12) deals with the "Walk of the Christian." The word *walk* refers to the way we live, as if life were a journey through which we are walking. Paul uses the word *walk* in this manner nearly thirty times in his epistles.

6. No one could ever say that Paul was shy about asserting his authority, and claiming divine approval. Paul declares that the Thessalonians had received "of *us* how ye ought to walk," and that his commandments were "by the Lord Jesus."

   Although Paul may appear to have been rather forward, we are thankful that he was not shy about these things, because Paul told us the truth, and we must know the truth to be saved. Throughout this chapter Paul asserts his inspiration.

   This leads us to repeat a necessary teaching: We must follow what the *apostles* said if we are going to be saved. The apostles spoke the words which Jesus gave to them. The Holy Spirit led *them* into all truth. John 16:13-14. No church council, pope, or modern day prophet has any thing new from God to add to what the apostles said. Therefore we must do what the apostles said, and abound more and more in the way they taught us to walk and to please God.

7. The American Standard version inserts a phrase, "even as ye do walk," after the words "please God" in 4:1. This addition has much support in the oldest New Testament manuscripts. It indicates that the Thessalonians had made a great change in their way of living since they had received the gospel.

Text (4:3)

3 For this is the will of God, *even* your santification, that ye abstain from fornication;

Translation and Paraphrase

3. For (among other things) this is the will of God (for you—yes, it is even) your sanctification, (the process of your becoming free from sin and consecrated to God—and it is this:) that you should abstain from (every form of) sexual vice.

Notes (4:3)

1. Christianity never delivers us, as by the stroke of a magician, from the lusts and wickedness which have become habitual in the heathen world. Rather a long and constant fight is necessary for vanquishing them.

2. For example, fornication was considered no sin among the Gentiles. Therefore, Paul often had to warn about it in his letters. "Fornication" refers to unlawful sexual intercourse in general. "Adultery" is generally used to describe the sin of married people who are unfaithful. "Fornication" is a broader term. It includes adultery and all related vices. Notice some of Paul's words about fornication:

    I Cor. 6:13—"The body is not for fornication."

    I Cor. 6:18—"Flee fornication. Every sin that a man doeth is without (outside) the body; but he that committeth fornication sinneth against his own body."

    Hebrews 13:4—"Fornicators and adulters God will judge." (See also Rev. 21:8)

3. If our sanctification is the will of God, we ought to give more attention to the subject than we usually hear given. "Sanctification" is the action of making us free from sin and consecrated to God. It is the opposite of "pollution." It means "holiness" in its general sense, and the same word which is translated "holiness" is the one translated "sanctification." Sanctification (or holiness) is commanded in I Peter 1:12. In Hebrews 2:11 Christ is described as "he that sanctifieth" us.

4. In this verse Paul makes it very plain that the "sanctification" that he is referring to is "abstaining from fornication." There are other things necessary in sanctification, of course, but that is the only matter that Paul is dealing with in this verse.

5. It would be wrong to quote just part of this verse—"This is the will of God, even your sanctification"—and then by using that part of the verse to urge people to seek a "second work of grace." Some denominations hold to a doctrine that after a person has been saved, he may have a second work of grace, a sanctification by baptism of the Holy Spirit, in which all desire for and practice of sin is taken out of his nature.

    John the apostle says, "If we say we have no sin (present tense), we deceive ourselves." I John 1:8. Surely this verse cancels out any doctrine that we can be so totally sanctified that we utterly cannot sin.

6. The two stages in sanctification:
    (1) Sanctification at conversion.

Paul wrote to the Corinthians, "But ye are washed, but ye are sanctified." The spirit of every believer is sanctified, cleansed, and set apart for the Master's use at conversion. I Cor. 6:11; Heb. 10:14; I Peter 1:2; II Thess. 2:13; Eph. 5:26.

    (2) Sanctification after conversion.

Hebrews 12:14: "Follow ... the holiness (or sanctification) without which no man shall see the Lord." Sanctification is something we must follow or pursue (Gr., *dioko*) constantly. We cannot get a one-shot inoculation of sanctification that will permanently guarantee our immunity against sin.

"Now being servants of God, we have fruit unto holiness (or sanctification)." Romans 6:22.

Text (4:4)

4 that each one of you know how to possess himself of his own vessel in sanctification and honor,

Translation and Paraphrase

4. (And) that each (one) of you should know (and act like you knew) how to (get hold of yourself and) get possession of your own vessel (your body, so as to live) in sanctification and honor.

Notes (4:4)

1. It is no honor to commit fornication. It is an honor to be modest, pure, and (for the unmarried) virgin.

2. What do you think Paul means by telling us to possess our *vessel* in sanctification and honor? What is the *vessel* he refers to? The natural thought that comes to our minds is that the vessel is our *body,* and that we are to keep control of it, and not permit ourselves to look upon a woman to lust after her, nor to commit fornication. We believe that this is the correct meaning of the verse.

3. However, many scholarly interpreters say that the *vessel* is a wife, and that Paul in this verse is telling the men to procure for themselves wives as vessels for the satisfaction of their passions, rather than for them to commit fornication. Now it is a fact that the word *vessel* is used in I Peter 3:7 to describe a woman. And it is interesting to note that the Revised Standard Version of the Bible and the versions of Moffatt and Goodspeed

all boldly insert the word "wife" into their versions. This is
more of an interpretation than it is a translation.

4. Here are our reasons for thinking that the *vessel* to which Paul
refers is our body and not a wife:

    (1) There is nothing particularly spiritual in knowing how to
take a wife. In fact the wicked are often the most pro-
ficient in doing it.

    (2) In I Cor. 7:8, 27, 32-33, 38, Paul rather discourages
marriage for many people. It therefore seems unlikely
that he would here recommend marriage as a universal
panacea for fornication.

    (3) The verses both immediately before and after this one
caution us about fornication and lust. This leads us to
think that this verse must refer to controlling our bodies
and not to marrying a wife.

5. It is beyond question that in the Scriptures our bodies are often
called *vessels*. Note I Sam. 21:5: "Of a truth women have been
kept from us about these three days, since I came out, and the
vessels of the young men are holy." Also II Cor. 4:7: "We have
this treasure (the gospel) in earthen vessels (referring to the
fact that our bodies are made of dust)." See also II Tim. 2:21;
Acts 9:15; Romans 9:21-23.

6. We mentioned that some versions of the Bible boldly interpret
the word "vessel" as "wife." But others just as openly interpret
it as "body." So Phillips, New English Bible, and Amplified
New Testament.

7. This verse is similar to Romans 6:19: "As ye have yielded your
members servants to uncleanness and to iniquity unto iniquity,
even so now yield your members to righteousness unto holiness
(or sanctification)."

Text (4:5)

5 not in the passion of lust, even as the Gentiles who know not God;

Translation and Paraphrase

5. (By possessing our vessel in sanctification, we shall) not (live)
in the passion (which) lust (arouses) as (do) the Gentiles who
do not know God.

Notes (4:5)

1. The big word "concupiscence" in this verse (pronounced—kon-
KUE-pi-s'ns) will derail the thought of most readers from what
this verse says, as it is a stranger in modern English.

Actually, the word simply means "ardent desire, hence, sexual lusts." (Webster's Collegiate Dict.)

The American Standard Version translates "lust of concupiscence" as "passion of lust."

2. There is little difference in meaning between the words "lust," "concupiscence," and "passion." Thayer says that the phrase "passion of lust" is a genitive of apposition. The word translated "concupiscence" *(epithumia)* may be a slightly more comprehensive term, describing desire and lust as a way of life; whereas the word translated "lust" *(pathos)* can refer to a more momentary passion, the ungovernable desire. Hence in our paraphrase we have rendered the phrase, "the passion (which) lust (arouses)."

3. Some men think that nothing can be done about sexual passions except to gratify them. This verse teaches us that this is not so. We can pray to God for deliverance. We can deliberately turn our minds toward other matters. We can do physical work which will absorb the energy that is showing itself in the form of lust.

4. Once again here Paul emphasizes the moral degeneration of the Gentiles. "The heathen moralists condemned unchastity only in the case of a child-bearing wife, as it would wrong her husband not to know the paternity of her children." (B. W. Johnson) See also paragraph 2 of the notes on 4:1-2.

5. The statement that the Gentiles do not know God is more than just a casual bit of information. It is a judgment upon them. The reason that they do not know God is that they refused to have God in their knowledge. Romans 1:28. God will take vengeance on them that know not God. II Thess. 1:8. "Pour out thy fury upon the heathen that know thee not." Jer. 10:25. See also Ps. 79:6; Gal. 4:8; I Cor. 15:34.

Text (4:6)

6 that no man transgress, and wrong his brother in the matter; because the Lord is an avenger in all these things, as also we forewarned you and testified.

Translation and Paraphrase

6. (And) that none (of you) should go too far and (covetously) take advantage of his brother in the matter (of sexual vice). Because the Lord is (an) avenger (who will punish severely when He deals with all) of these things, just as we told you previously and most solemnly charged (you)."

106

Notes (4:6)

1. The phrase "in any matter" is interpreted by some scholars to refer to business dealings. Therefore they say that the teaching of this verse is that we should not cheat one another in business. (Indeed we should not do that.)

2. However, the fact that the matter of sexual vice is discussed in the verses immediately before and after this verse leads us to think that this verse also deals with that subject.

3. Also the phrase "in any manner" is rendered "in *the* matter" in the Greek text and the American Stan. version. While this reading is a bit uncertain, it is probably the correct one. *The* matter to which it refers would, therefore, seem to be the matter under discussion in the verses just preceding, the matter of sexual vice.

4. For us to covet and take another man's wife would be to "go beyond" (and overreach) what we have a right to do. It is "going too far." (The same word is used in 2 Cor. 7:2; 12:17-18.)

5. No one can commit fornication without defrauding and wronging someone. It is a sin that always wrongs and hurts others, and not just ourselves. By it men can wrong someone's wife, or future wife, someone's sister, someone's marriage or future marriage, someone's home or family life. Besides that, it is a sin against GOD. Psalm 51:4. And it is a sin against our own body. I Cor. 6:18.

6. Many Scriptures teach that God is an avenger, one who punishes and takes vengeance. Psalm 94:1-2; II Peter 2:3; Rom. 2:9-11, 16. The successful thief may conclude that crime has no penalty. But God's justice will not be thwarted.

   Heathen gods were often pictured as indulging in human vices. But the true God is the avenger of vices.

7. Paul reminds the Thessalonians that he had already forewarned them about this matter of sexual vice. Compare Gal. 1:9. Evidently when the apostles of Christ once spoke, their teaching was not to be modified later to suit someone's pleasure and convenience.

Text (4:7-8)

7 For God called us not for uncleanness, but in sanctification. 8 Therefore he that rejecteth, rejecteth not man, but God, who giveth his Holy Spirit unto you.

Translation and Paraphrase

7. For God has NOT called us (into his kingdom) upon (the basis of liberty to practice moral) uncleanness, but (he has called us) in sanctification (or holiness).

8. Consequently, he who disregards (this command) is not disregarding (any mere) man (like myself) but the (very) God who also gives to you His Holy Spirit.

Notes (4:7-8)

1. God told the Israelites in olden times: "I am the LORD your God: ye shall therefore sanctify yourselves, and ye shall be holy; for I am holy." Leviticus 11:44.

2. The same instructions are given to Christians: "Be ye holy; for I am holy." I Peter 1:16. Therefore we beseech you, as strangers and pilgrims in this world, abstain from fleshly lusts, which war against the soul. I Peter 2:11. Avoid entertainments, reading material, and thoughts which are immoral and lustful. These things are fighting against your soul.

3. "For God did not call us with a permission of impurity, but in sanctification." (Rotherham's translation of 4:7.)

4. It is a serious thing to despise the preacher's message, for you are actually despising and rejecting God in so doing. Jesus said to His disciples, "He that heareth you heareth me; and he that despiseth you despiseth me; and he that despiseth me despiseth him that sent me." Luke 10:16.

5. Note that it is in the voluntary power of a man to resist or accept truth. But it is not in man's power to escape the consequences of that choice.

6. The Holy Spirit is given to every one who repents and is baptized. Acts 2:38; 5:32; Gal. 4:6. "What, know ye not that your body is the temple of the Holy Spirit which is in you, which ye have of God, and ye are not your own?" I Cor. 6:19.

   The Holy Spirit had brought joy to the Thessalonians. I Thess. 1:6. God had given them the Holy Spirit. They therefore could not honorably disobey God when He had given them such a blessing.

Text (4:9-10)

9 But concerning love of the brethren ye have no need that one write unto you: for ye yourselves are taught of God to love one another; 10 for indeed ye do it toward all the brethren that are in all Macedonia. But we exhort you, brethren, that ye abound more and more;

Translation and Paraphrase

9. But concerning brotherly love, you have no need that (anyone) should be writing unto you. For (verily) you yourselves are God-taught to love one another.

10. For indeed you do that (very thing) to all the brethren which are in all of Macedonia. But we (must) urge you, brethren, to exceed (your past good works and abound yet) more (and more).

Notes (4:9-10)

1. In the second century, the scoffing writer, Lucian, in speaking about Christians, declared, "It is incredible to see the ardor with which the people of that religion help each other in their wants. They spare nothing. Their first legislator has put it into their heads that they are all brethren."

2. Lucian was right. We are brothers. We have brotherly love, because we are taught of God to love one another. Brotherly love is not a natural thing in man. Hatred is the natural instinct in sinful mankind. Titus 3:3. Love is "God-taught." (Rotherham.) Compare John 6:45; Isa. 54:13. God taught the Thessalonians to love one another. Love is a fruit of the Holy Spirit. Gal. 5:22. The love of God is shed abroad in our hearts by the Holy Spirit which is given unto us. Romans 5:5.

3. INTERPRETER'S BIBLE observes that the word "brotherly-love" (*philadelphia*) is almost absent from the Greek of the pre-Christian period, and where found, refers to love for a natural brother. In the New Testament it is always love for a Christian brother.

4. Brotherly love as a Christian duty is laid upon us in other verses also. See Rom. 12:10; Heb. 13:1; I Peter 1:22; II Pet. 1:7. Brotherly love is combined with hospitality in Heb. 13:1-2.

5. Jesus said, "A new commandment I give unto you, That ye love one another, as I have loved you." John 13:34. The whole gospel taught us to love one another, and love is the essence of the gospel.

6. Love of the brethren is quite the opposite of the passion of lust, concerning which Paul spoke in preceding verses. Uncleanness is an offense against brotherly love.

7. We may love one another and do many other good things, but it is always needful for us to increase and abound more and more in doing good. I Thess. 4:1, 10; 3:12; Phil. 1:9; II Th. 1:3.

Text (4:11-12)

11 and that ye study to be quiet, and to do your own business, and to work with your hands, even as we charged you; 12 that ye may walk becomingly toward them that are without, and may have need of nothing.

Translation and Paraphrase

11. And (we beseech you) to make it your goal (because of your love of honor) to lead a quiet (settled) life, and to keep busy with your own affairs, and to work with your own hands, just as we commanded you;

12. So that (by thus working) you may walk (or live) in a manner that will present a good appearance to those (who are) outside (of the kingdom of Christ), and (so that) you may have a lack of none (of the necessities of life).

Notes (4:11-12)

1. There is nothing that some people dread as much as being quiet. They delight in a row, and if one is not in progress, they stir one up.

2. "The Greeks were naturally mercurial and restless." (McGarvey.) Note how the Athenians sought only to hear some new thing. Acts 17:21.

3. We must *study* to be quiet. This means to make it our ambition to live a quiet settled life. A peaceful spirit cannot be attained without studied effort. The word "study" (Gr., *philotimeomai*) means "to be fond of honor ... to be ambitious, to strive earnestly, to make it one's aim." (Thayer)

4. Being "quiet" (Gr., *esuchadzo*) means "to lead a quiet life, rest, keep quiet." It describes those who are not running hither and thither, but staying at home and minding their business.

   It is very hard to live quietly in our age with its blare, honking horns, hurry, clatter, rush, activities, TV, etc. How can we "be quiet"? We grant that it is not easy, but its rewards are great.

5. The exhortation to "Study to be quiet," is repeated as a *command* with greater force in II Thess. 3:12. Obviously they did not heed Paul's *exhortation* to work in this letter. So a stronger approach was used.

6. We should be ambitious to work at our own business and not meddle in other people's business. The Greeks were a restless

110

people, often given to intermeddling in the business of other people.

7. "Every fool will be meddling." Prov. 20:3. Christians do their own business and leave other people's business alone. "Be not eavesdroppers, or news droppers. Wide ears and wide tongues dwell together." (Jewell)

8. Supporting ourselves by working with our own hands is definitely commanded in God's word. See Eph. 4:28. Paul's own hands often supported him. Acts 20:34. He left us an example, and Paul's example of a gentleman is not one whose hands are too dainty for work.

Many people make it their life's pattern to do just as little work as they can get by with, and then to depend upon unemployment compensation, or state, county, or federal welfare to care for them. Such people need the nobly independent attitude of Paul.

9. Many Bible interpreters have speculated that the Thessalonians were loafing and living off their Christian brethren, because they expected Christ to come at any moment. There is utterly no hint in the Scriptures that this was the case. Nothing in the Scriptures connects any false ideas about Christ's return with the people not minding their own business.

10. Paul gives two reasons why they should be quiet, and mind their own business, and work:
    (1) To present an honorable appearance to outsiders.
    (2) To lack none of the necessities of life.

11. I Thess. 4:12 brings out the stern reality that people on the outside of the church view our manner of living as being more important than what we teach, and that idleness and parasitic behavior are especially reprehensible to them. Human nature is more impressed by appearances than by doctrines.

12. A spirit of quietness, combined with honest labor, brings to us a satisfying independence, causing us to "have need of nothing." (The Revised Standard Version renders "nothing" as "nobody." This is a permissible rendering, as the word may be either neuter or masculine. We should have need of nothing, and have to depend on nobody.)

13. With the close of verse 12, we end, the section 4:1-12, which is entitled "The Walk of the Christian." Notice again, and memorize the six points in this section:
    (1) Abound according to the apostles' teaching; 4:1-2
    (2) Abstain from fornication; 4:3-8

    (3) Practice brotherly love; 4:9-10
    (4) Study to be quiet; 4:11
    (5) Do your own business; 4:11
    (6) Work with your own hands; 4:11-12

STUDY SUGGESTION

Turn now to the "Did You Learn?" questions at the close of chapter four, and see if you can answer questions 1 to 26.

Text (4:13)

13 But we would not have you ignorant, brethren, concerning them that fall asleep; that ye sorrow not, even as the rest, who have no hope.

Translation and Paraphrase

13. But we do not want you to be ignorant, brethren, concering those (of our Christian brethren) who are sleeping (in death), so that you may not be burdened with sorrow as indeed the rest (of mankind) who have no hope (so often are).

Notes (4:13)

1. A Christian missionary to American Indians wrote in Dec. 1962: "Tonight there is heard the sorrowing of our poor Indian people as they chant their sacred funeral songs, beat the seven sacred tom-toms, mingled with the weeping and wailing of those who have no hope. Oh, how the FEAR of DEATH seems to GRIP those who do not know the Lord Jesus Christ." (John Runyan, McKinley Indian Mission)

2. The sorrow of the brethren at the time of death is aggravated by their ignorance of the future destiny. Upon the walls of the catacombs beneath Rome are found epitaphs for the dead who were buried there long ago. Some of the pagan epitaphs say things like these:

    "Live for the present hour, since we are sure of nothing else."

    "I lift my hands against the gods who took me away at the age of twenty though I had done no harm."

    "Traveller, curse me not as you pass, for I am in darkness and cannot answer.

But on the tombs of the early Christians in the catacombs are found epitaphs that sing with the bright cheer of immortality:

    "Here lies Marcia, put to rest in a dream of peace."

    Lawrence, to his sweetest son, borne away of angels." (From *Fox's Book of Martyrs*)

3. This verse (4:13) opens a new section, having the topic "The Dead in Christ, and the Lord's Coming." The section covers 4:13-18. Paul opens this section by saying, "We would not have you to be ignorant." Paul used similar expressions in numerous places in his writings to introduce new topics. See Rom. 1:13; 11:25; I Cor. 10:1; 11:3; 12:1; II Cor. 1:8; Phil. 1:12; Col. 2:1.

   Christians have no excuse for being ignorant about their faith, and there certainly is no honor in being ignorant.

4. "Sleep" is a common metaphor for death in the Scriptures, being used fifteen times in the N.T. See I Cor. 15:6, 20. "Sleep" implies the possibility of an awakening. The grave become the couch in which the body rests until the awakening at the resurrection.

   But those who say that the spirits of the dead also sleep, greatly pervert the meaning of "sleeping" in death. For the Scriptural descriptions of souls after death, see Rev. 6:9-11 and Luke 16:22-24. See also Special Study VI page 253, "Questions About Spirit and Soul."

5. Does this verse teach that it is wrong to weep at the death of our loved ones? Of course not. Jesus himself wept at the tomb of Lazarus. John 11:35. Devout men carried Stephen to his burial weeping. Acts 8:2. See also Acts 9:39.

   The thing which we are not to do is to weep *as those who have no hope* weep. They often wail and carry on in uncontrollable sorrow. We who have a hope of reunion at the coming of the Lord Jesus Christ should not weep as if death ended everything eternally.

6. Aeschylus, the Greek tragic dramatist (525-456 B.C.), said, "Once dead, there is no resurrection more." The apostle Paul said, "The trumpet shall sound, and the dead shall be raised incorruptible." The pagans had no hope in death. Eph. 2:12. Christians have great hope in death.

7. This paragraph about sorrowing over the Christians who had died, indicates that the Thessalonians had a misunderstanding about the subject. What we know about the difficulty is only what we can infer from this paragraph (4:13-18). But it appears that the Thessalonians, expecting a speedy return of the Lord, feared that in some way the Christians who had died would not share the glories and benefits of the Lord's return.

8. It has been well suggested that Christians should mourn for those who are living in sin, and not for the dead who are in the Lord.

Text (4:14)

14 For if we believe that Jesus died and rose again, even so them also that are fallen asleep in Jesus will God bring with him.

Translation and Paraphrase

14. For since we believe that Jesus died and rose (again from the dead, we have the assurance that) in the same manner (as God raised up Jesus) God will also through Jesus (and the salvation Jesus provides) bring those who have fallen asleep (into eternal life and glory) with him (that is, with Jesus).

Notes (4:14)

1. Although Paul begins this verse by saying, *"If* we believe that Jesus died and rose again," we must not think for a moment that Paul doubted that Jesus died and rose again. While our version uses the word, "If," to begin the sentence, the Greek construction (*ei.* w. indic.) is one which is used when one wished to assume that what he said was true.

2. The evidence that Jesus did rise from the dead is overpowering. He was seen alive after his death and resurrection on at least ten occasions, over a period of fifty days, by as many as five hundred people at once. We must believe that Jesus arose, if we expect to be saved. Romans 10:9. See also Rom. 4:25.

3. The phrase, "sleep in Jesus," is literally translated "those who have fallen asleep *through* Jesus."

   This phrase, "through Jesus," should probably not be connected with "asleep" but with God "bringing" them.

   We say this because the Devil has the power of death. Heb. 2:14. And it is therefore not likely that Paul meant to say that Christians fall asleep through the work of Jesus. Rather, Paul surely meant that through Jesus (and the salvation He provides) God will bring those who have fallen asleep back from the dead with Jesus.

   The Revised Standard Version renders this clearly: "For since we believe that Jesus died and rose again, even so, through Jesus, God will bring with him those who have fallen asleep."

4. I Corinthians 15:12—"If Christ be preached that he rose from the dead, how say some of you that there is no resurrection of the dead?" The fact that Jesus arose never to die again is a proof that we also can rise from the dead. The fact that Jesus promised that He would resurrect the dead, combined with the power He exhibited when He arose Himself, makes us absolutely con-

fident that "there will be a resurrection of the dead, both of the just and unjust." Acts 24:15; John 5:28-29.

5. The word "sleep" in this verse is an aorist (a kind of past tense) passive participle, and is probably best rendered "those who have fallen asleep," rather than as "them which sleep." Concerning the use of the word "sleep" to describe death, see notes on I Thess. 4:13, par. 4.

Text (4:15)

15 For this we say unto you by the word of the Lord, that we that are alive, that are left unto the coming of the Lord, shall in no wise precede them that are fallen asleep.

Translation and Paraphrase

15. For this we tell you (not by our own guesses or hopes, but) by the (very) word of the Lord, that we which are living (and) remaining (alive on earth) until the coming of the Lord, (that) we shall most certainly not go ahead of those who have fallen asleep.

Notes (4:15)

1. If we had only Paul's hopes or opinions as support for our hope that the dead will be raised, it would not be very solid assurance. But Paul informs us that what he speaks is the very "word of the Lord." Since the Lord Himself informed Paul about this matter, we place our total reliance upon it.

2. The expression, "word of the Lord," is often used to describe the prophetic messages which God gave to various men. See Micah 1:1; Hosea 1:1; Jer. 1:2; Luke 3:2, and many other such references.

3. Paul uses the phrase, *"We* which are alive and remain unto the coming of the Lord." But the *we* in this verse does not indicate that Paul expected to be living when Christ returned. In II Cor. 4:14, Paul used the word *us* in such a manner that indicates that he expected to be resurrected: "Knowing that he which raised up the Lord Jesus, shall raise up *us* also by Jesus."

   Neither here, nor elsewhere in the New Testament is the coming (parousia) of the Lord stated to be very soon (by human standards of time). Some people in New Testament times assumed that it would be that way, but Paul never said so.

4. Concerning the word "coming" (parousia), see notes on I Thess. 2:19, par. 7.

5. What did Paul mean when he said that we which are alive when the Lord comes back shall not *prevent* them which are asleep? The word *prevent* now means to hinder or restrain. But in 1611, when the King James version was translated, it meant to "go before" or "come before." It is from the Latin word *praevenio*, meaning "to come before, to get the start of."

David said in Psalm 119:147: "I prevented the dawning of the morning and cried." David did not keep the morning from dawning. What he meant was that he got up before the dawning of the morning to pray.

Paul meant, then, that those who are alive when Christ returns will not go ahead of, or have a head start on, those who will have died before that time.

6. Paul uses a very strong negative *(ou me)* to affirm that we who are living will most certainly NOT go ahead of those who have died before the Lord's coming.

8. For the significance of the word "sleep" as applied to the dead, see notes on I Thess. 4:13, par. 4.

Text (4:16)

16 For the Lord himself shall descend from heaven, with a shout, with the voice of the archangel, and with the trump of God: and the dead in Christ shall rise first;

Translation and Paraphrase

16. Because the Lord himself shall come down from heaven with the awakening cry, (and) with the voice of (Michael) the archangel, and with the trumpet of God (sounding forth), and (then) the dead (which are) in Christ (the Christians) will rise first.

Notes (4:16)

1. Jesus is not going to send any substitute or assistants back to the earth for Him. "The Lord HIMSELF shall descend from heaven."

Rev. 1:7: "Behold, he cometh with clouds, and every eye shall see him, and they *also* which pierced him: and all kindreds of the earth shall wail because of him. Even so, Amen."

(The fact that those who pierced, or crucified, him will see him, indicates that they too will be resurrected.)

2. Three sounds are to accompany the Lord's coming:

(1) *A shout.* We think that this shout will be the Lord's own cry. For John 5:28 says that all that are in the graves shall

116

hear *his voice.* This word *shout* (Gr., *keleusma*) means an order, or command, specifically a stimulating cry such as is given to rouse animals or horses by charioteers, or as a signal to men.

When our Lord was on earth, he did not cry nor lift up, nor cause his voice to be heard in the stret. Isa. 42:2. But when He returns, "Our God shall come, and shall not keep silence." Psalm 50:3,4

(2) *The voice of the Archangel.* Michael (not Gabriel) is the archangel. Jude 9; Rev. 12:7. (Where did people ever get the idea that Gabriel will blow the trumpet?) Rotherham translates the word "archangel" as "chief-messenger," and that is literally correct.

(3) *The trump of God.* The trumpet of God was heard at Mt. Sinai, when God gave the law to Moses. It blew "exceeding loud," so that all the people that was in the camp trembled. See Ex. 19:16; Heb. 12:19. This trumpet will be equally frightening when it is heard again.

I Cor. 15:52: "At the last *trump,* for the trumpet shall sound, and the dead shall be raised incorruptible."

Matt. 24:31: "And he shall send his angels with a great sound of a trumpet."

3. When the Lord comes and the dead are raised, "the dead shall be raised INCORRUPTIBLE, and we shall be CHANGED." I Cor. 15:52. Christ is going to change our vile body, that it may be fashioned like unto his glorious body. Phil. 3:21.

4. Personally, we believe this verse about the Lord's coming, and the trumpet, etc., literally. However, one author says in reference to this verse: "We must not look for literal exactness where things are depicted beyond the reach of sense." Such an attitude as this is often only a pious way of explaining away what the Scriptures say.

5. Sometimes people connect this verse with Rev. 20:5:

"The dead in Christ shall rise *first.*" I Thess. 4:16.

"But the rest of the dead lived not again until the thousand years were finished." Rev. 20:5.

This is a good example of "grasshopper exegesis," that is, the practice of jumping around in the Scriptures, combining pieces of verses here and pieces of verses there, and producing conclusions not actually taught by any of the Scriptures.

We cannot connect I Thess. 4:16 with Rev. 20:5, because the word *first* in I Thess. 4:16 has no reference at all to what is to happen to the rest of the dead, such as are mentioned in Rev. 20:5.

6. With what, then, is the word "first" in I Thess. 4:16 contrasted? It is contrasted with the catching up of the living Christians. "The dead in Christ shall rise *first*."

"Then we which are alive and remain shall be caught up together with them." (I Thess. 4:17)

To place any other significance upon the expression that the "dead in Christ shall rise *first*" can only be speculation.

Actually the Scriptures indicate rather plainly that there is only going to be ONE resurrection of all the dead. John 5:28-29: "The hour (singular) is coming in the which ALL that are in the graves shall hear his voice, and shall come forth; they that have done good——and they that have done evil." Acts 24:15: "There shall be a resurrection (singular, not plural), both of the just and unjust."

"The first resurrection" mentioned in Rev. 20:4-5 is a resurrection of "the souls of them that were beheaded for the witness of Jesus." Nothing is said about any bodily resurrection there. It is a resurrection of souls, whatever that may signify. The bodily resurrection is mentioned later in Rev. 20:13.

7. To gain a true picture of the events connected with the coming of the Lord and the resurrection of the dead, we should by all means notice Matthew 24:29-31:

"Immediately AFTER the tribulation of those days shall the sun be darkened, and the moon shall not give her light, and the stars shall fall from heaven, and the powers of the heavens shall be shaken: And then shall appear the sign of the Son of man in heaven: and then shall all the tribes of the earth mourn, and they shall see the Son of man coming in the clouds of heaven with power and great glory. And he shall send his angels with a great sound of a trumpet, and they shall send his angels with a great sound of a trumpet, and they shall gather together his elect from the four winds, from one end of heaven to the other."

Notice that this Scripture destroys the idea that Christ will come secretly and take the church out of the earth leaving sinners behind. (See Special Study II page 242, "A Secret Rapture Considered.") For Christ's elect are to be gathered at the same time that all the tribes of the earth shall mourn.

It also rules out the idea that there will be a tribulation period AFTER Christ returns. For notice that the elect will still be here after the tribulation, and that then Christ will come and send his angels to gather them. (See Special Study IV page 247, "The Coming of the Lord With All His Saints.")

8. Besides this Scripture in Matt. 24:29-31, we ought also to consider Matthew 13:40-42. It tells what is going to happen to the wicked when Christ comes:

> "As therefore the tares are gathered and burned in the fire: so shall it be in the end of this world. The Son of man shall send forth his angels, and they shall gather out of his kingdom all things that offend, and them which do iniquity, And shall cast them into a furnace of fire: there shall be wailing and gnashing of teeth."

Text (4:17-18)

17 then we that are alive, that are left, shall together with them be caught up in the clouds, to meet the Lord in the air; and so shall we ever be with the Lord.

18 Wherefore comfort one another with these words.

Translation and Paraphrase

17. Then (after that,) we who are living (and) remaining shall at the same time be caught up with them (the resurrected saints) in (the) clouds, unto (the) meeting with the Lord in the air. And in this manner we shall be (united) with the Lord (to be with him) always.

18. Wherefore (seeing that we have such a glorious hope), comfort (and exhort) one another by these words.

Notes (4:17-18)

1. There is a gospel song entitled, "The Meeting In the Air." That is a fine title. I Thess 4:17 talks about *meeting* the Lord in the air, and the word *meeting* is actually a noun (Gr., *apantesis*, meaning "meeting"). Will you join in that "meeting in the air" with the Lord?

2. I am sure that no Christian will have acrophobia (fear of heights) when our bodies have been transformed, and we have been caught up in the air. "Caught up" means "to seize, carry off, snatch out or away." It is the same word used in Acts 8:39 to describe how the Spirit of the Lord caught away Philip after he baptized the Ethiopian.

3. Many Scriptures teach that the Lord is coming with clouds. Rev. 1:7; Matt. 24:30. The Lord's presence is often associated with clouds and smoke. Exodus 19:18; Isa. 6:4; Psalm 18:11-12; Matt. 17:5

4. Note that we are to meet the Lord in the *air,* the atmospheric region.

5. The glorious meeting with the Lord shall never end.

6. This Scripture brings to our minds other blessed passages:

John 14:3—"I will come again, and receive you unto myself, that where I am, there ye may be also."

John 17:24—"Father, I will that they also, whom thou hast given me, be with me where I am." (Jesus wants us to be with him. Death can be a fulfillment of the desire of Jesus for us to be with him personally.)

Rev. 21:3 and 22:3 speak of eternally dwelling with God.

7. Because of all the glorious hope we have in Christ's second coming, we are commanded to tell Christians who mourn, that they will meet their dead in Christ on that day when Christ appears, and that in sweet union and communion they will ever be with their Lord and their loved ones.

8. The word "comfort" is the same word also translated "exhort." The coming of Christ and the resurrection of the dead is both a comfort and a stimulus to us to serve Christ more fully. On the meaning of "comfort" or "exhort," see notes on I Thess. 2:3, par. 2.

STUDY SUGGESTION

We urge you now to turn to the "Did You Learn?" questions which follow immediately, and try to answer (preferably by writing out the answers) questions 27 to 46

DID YOU LEARN?

(Questions over I Thessalonians, chapter four)

1. What is the title and Scripture limitation of Part Two of I Thessalonians?

2. What is the first topic of chapter four, and what are the Scripture limitations of it?

3. What did Paul include in all of his letters to Gentile churches? Why? (4:1-2)

4. What does Paul mean by the word "walk"? (4:1-2)

5. List the six points (A to F) in the outline of the first topic of chapter four.

6. By whom did Paul give the commandments which he gave? (4:2)

7. What is fornication? (4:3)

8. What is sanctification? (4:3)

9. What are the two stages in sanctification? (4:3)
10. What is the "vessel" which we should know how to possess? (4:4)
11. What other interpretation is sometimes given to the word "vessel"? (4:4)
12. Did the Gentiles regard immorality as sin? (4:5)
13. What is concupiscence? (4:5)
14. How had it come about that the Gentiles did not know God? (4:5)
15. What does the phrase "go beyond" in 4:6 mean?
16. By doing what sin will we "go beyond and defraud" our brother? (4:6)
17. Who is the avenger of sins? (4:6). What is an avenger?
18. God has not called us unto uncleanness, but unto what? (4:7)
19. If we despise (or disregard) Paul's teaching on holiness, whom are we actually despising? (4:8)
20. Concerning what subject did Paul not need to write them? (4:9)
21. Who taught them to love one another? (4:9)
22. Explain the sentence, "Study to be quiet." (4:11)
23. Whose business should we do? (4:11)
24. Were the Thessalonians loafing because they expected the Lord's coming very soon? (4:11-12)
25. Was Paul's exhoration about working carried out by the Thessalonians? (4:11-12). How do you know?
26. For what two reasons should we be quiet and work? (4:12)
27. What is the second chapter topic of I Thessalonians, chapter four, and what are its Scripture limitations?
28. Concerning what did Paul not want them to be ignorant? (4:13)
29. For what is "sleep" a common metaphor? (4:13)
30. Are we forbidden to sorrow for our dead? (4:13)
31. In what way are we to "sorrow not"? (4:13)
32. What misunderstanding did the Thessalonians apparently have about the dead Christians? (4:13)
33. What fact gives us assurance that the dead shall rise? (4:14)
34. Did Paul teach that Christ was coming within his lifetime? (4:15)
35. What does the word "prevent" in 4:15 mean?
36. With what three sounds will the Lord descend? (4:16)
37. Who is the archangel? (4:16)
38. At what occasion on earth has the trumpet of God been previously heard? (4:16)

39. Who shall rise first when Christ returns? (4:16)
40. With what does the word "first" make a contrast? (4:16)
41. Why cannot we connect the statement that the "dead in Christ shall rise *first*," with Revelation 20:5? (4:16)
42. What will happen after the dead in Christ are raised? (4:17)
43. Where shall we be caught up to meet the Lord (4:17)
44. How long shall we be with the Lord? (4:17)
45. What should we do with the words about Christ's coming and the resurrection? (4:18)
46. Write out (or recite) from memory I Thess. 4:13-17. It begins, "But I would not have you——."

I THESSALONIANS, CHAPTER FIVE

Chapter Topics

1. Times and Seasons of the Lord's Coming. 5:-11
2. Practical Exhortations. 5:12-22

"Let us not sleep (and be drunken) as do others; but let us watch
and be sober." I Thess. 5:6, 7

I THESSALONIANS CHAPTER FIVE

Chapter Topics:—1. Time and Seasons of the Lord's
Coming. 5:1-11
2. Practical Exhortations. 5:12-22

1. Concerning what did Paul have no need to write to them? 5:1.
_____ and _____.
2. "The day of the Lord so cometh as a _____ in the
_____." 5:2.
3. What will people be saying when the Lord returns? 5:3.
"_____ and _____."
4. True or false (circle which)—Those who are saying, "Peace
and safety," will escape on the day of the Lord. 5:3.
5. Christians are not in _____. 5:4.
6. True or false (circle which). The day of the Lord will overtake
Christians as a thief. 5:4.
7. Christians are "children of _____ and children of the
_____." 5:5.
8. As children of the day, what should we not do? 5:6 _____
_____.
9. As children of the day, what should we do? 5:6. (two answers)
_____; _____.
10. What two things are done in the night? 5:7 _____;
_____.
11. Rather than being drunken, we are to "be _____."
5:8
12. What spiritual armor are we to put on? 5:8
(1) _____
_____;
(2) _____
_____.
13. God has "not appointed us to _____, but to _____
_____ _____ by our Lord Jesus
Christ." 5:9
14. Christ "_____ for us," that whether we are alive or dead,
"we should _____ _____ with him."
5:10
15. Paul begged the Thessalonians "to _____ them which
_____ among you, and are _____ you in the
Lord and _____ you." 5:12.

16. The Thessalonians were to "_____ them very _____ in love for their work's sake." 5:13
17. "Be at _____ among yourselves." 5:13
18. "_____ them that are unruly." 5:14
19. "_____ the feebleminded (or faint-hearted)." 5:14
20. "_____ the weak." 5:14
21. "Be _____ toward all men." 5:14
22. "See that none render _____ for _____ unto any man." 5:15
23. "_____ evermore." 5:16
24. "_____ without ceasing." 5:17
25. "In every thing _____ _____." 5:18
26. "_____ not the Spirit." 5:19
27. "_____ not prophesyings." 5:20
28. "_____ all things; _____ _____ that which is good." 5:21.
29. "_____ from all _____ of evil." 5:22
30. "The very God of peace _____ you wholly." 5:23.
31. Paul prayed God that their "whole _____, and _____, and _____ be preserved blameless unto the _____ of our Lord Jesus Christ." 5:23
32. We shall be preserved blameless, because God, who calls us, is _____. 5:24
33. What did Paul ask the Thessalonians to do for him? 5:25. _____.
34. With what were the Thessalonians to greet their brethren? 5:26. _____.
35. Unto whom was this epistle to be read? 5:27 _____ _____.
36. What did Paul wish would be with the Thessalonians? 5:28.
_____
_____
_____
37. Memorize I Thess. 5:1-2, 23

CHAPTER FIVE

I THESSALONIANS, CHAPTER FIVE

Chapter Topics—1. *Times and Seasons of the Lord's Coming.* 5:1-11
2. *Practical Exhortations.* 5:12-22

Outline

II. The Lord's Coming; 4:13-5:11
  A. The dead in Christ and the Lord's coming; 4:13-18
  B. Times and seasons of the Lord's coming; 5:1-11
    1. Comes as a thief; 5:1-3
      a. No need of Paul to try to write to them; 5:1-2
      b. When men are saying, "Peace and Safety;" 5:3
      c. As travail upon a woman
    2. Will not come to Christians as a thief; 5:4-11
      a. Why it won't overtake us thus; 5:4-5
      (We are not in darkness.)
      b. What we should be doing; 5:6-8
        (1) Let us not sleep; 5:6
        (2) Let us watch;
        (3) Let us be sober; 5:6-8a
        (4) Put on the armor of God
          (a) Breastplate of faith and love;
          (b) Helmet of the hope of salvation; 5:8-10.
        (5) Comfort and edify one another; 5:11
III. Practical exhortations; 5:12-22
  1. Know them which labor among you. 5:12-13
  2. Warn the unruly; 5:14
  3. Comfort the faint-hearted; 5:14
  4. Support the weak; 5:14
  5. Be patient toward all men; 5:14
  6. Render to no man evil for evil; 5:15
  7. Rejoice evermore; 5:16
  8. Pray without ceasing; 5:17
  9. In everything give thanks; 5:18
  10. Quench not the Spirit; 5:19
  11. Despise not prophesyings; 5:20
  12. Prove all things; 5:21
  13. Abstain from all appearance of evil; 5:22
CONCLUSION
  1. Prayer for their entire sanctification; 5:23-24
  2. Request for prayer; 5:25

127

3. Command to greet the brethren; 5:26
4. Command to read the epistle; 5:27
5. Benediction of grace; 5:28

(You should now memorize the two chapter topics of chapter five, and the two divisions (1 and 2) in section 5:1-11.)

THOUGHTS FROM THE OUTLINE
Of I Thessalonians, chapter five

The first eleven verses of this chapter are actually a continuation of the discussion of the Lord's coming, which was started at 4:13.

In 4:13-18 Paul discussed the relation of the *dead in Christ* to the Lord's coming. In 5:1-11, Paul discusses the relation of the *living* to the Lord's coming.

The Lord's coming will affect the living in two completely opposite ways. Neither the Christians nor the unsaved can know the times and seasons of the Lord's coming. But to sinners that day will come as a thief, bringing destruction. To Christians it will *not* come as a thief, because they are always watching, and spiritually awake, and sober.

What a sermon it makes to compare the way the Lord's coming will come like a thief to sinners, but to the ch ldren of God, since they are always looking for His coming, it will *not* come as a thief.

Paul closes his epistle with some brief pointed exhortations. The exhortations may be brief, but their application is very broad.

Text (5:1)

1 But concerning the times and the seasons, brethren, ye have no need that aught be written unto you.

Translation and Paraphrase

1. But concerning the (general) times (when the Lord may return) and the (particular) seasons (when that would be most likely to occur), brethren, you have no need that (aught) should be written to you (giving you further information on the subject).

Notes (5:1)

1. When we think about the Lord's second coming, we all long to know WHEN it may be. We are like the disciples who asked Jesus, "Master, *when* shall these things be?" Luke 21:7. We have an expectancy of the Lord's coming. "Even so, come, Lord Jesus." Rev. 22:20. This expectancy naturally raises the question, "When?"

2. In the outlines we have entitled the section 5:1-12 as "Times and Seasons of the Lord's Coming." The section is closely connected with the preceding section, 4:13-18. Both are listed under

the heading, "The Lord's Coming," in the outline.

3. There are three points of resemblance between sections 4:13-18 and 5:1-11:

(1) Both sections tell how people will fare on the day of the Lord. 4:13-18 tells how the dead in Christ will fare on that day. 5:1-11 tells how the living will fare on that day.

(2) Both sections raise a problem, and both give an answer to the problem.

(a) 4:13-18 raises the problem, "What will happen to the dead in Christ when the Lord comes?" Answer: They will be resurrected before the living are caught up.

(b) 5:1-11 raises the problem, "Exactly when is the Lord coming?" Answer: No one can know, but since Christians are always watching, his coming will not take us by surprise.

(3) Both sections close with an exhortation to comfort one another. 4:18; 5:11

4. The expression, "times and seasons," is also found in Acts 1:7 and Daniel 2:21. "Times" refer to time in general. "Seasons" refer to limited portions of time, with the added notion of suitableness. Note the paraphrase for this distinction.

5. Many people have set the date for the end of the world and the Lord's coming, and all have been wrong. Any such efforts are bound to be in vain.

Jesus said, "It is not for you to know the time or the seasons, which the Father hath put in his own power." Acts 1:7. While Jesus was on earth he said, "But of that day and hour knoweth no *man*, nor the angels of heaven, but my Father only." Matthew 24:36. We think that Christ NOW has been given authority over and knowledge of the future (for this is suggested by Revelation chapter 5), but it still remains true that NO MAN on earth knows when Christ is coming. "In such an hour as ye think not, the Son of man cometh." Matthew 24:44.

6. God changes the times and seasons. Daniel 2:21. God had a time set to destroy Nineveh, but He changed His mind when Nineveh repented. Jonah 3:4, 10. Perhaps God has changed His time schedule on the return of Christ, not wishing that any should perish, but that all should come to repentance. II Peter 3:9.

7. The Thessalonians knew that the coming of the Lord would be unpredictable and unexpected. Paul had told them that. There-

fore it was unnecessary for him to go into a discussion of the times and seasons. Probably God had not revealed anything on this subject to Paul anyway.

8. Some interpreters make a distinction between the "day of the Lord," discussed in 5:1-11, and the taking up of the saints (the "rapture") discussed in 4:13-17. They maintain that the "Day of the Lord" discussed here is several years after the taking up of the saints, and follows a great tribulation.

This interpretation always reminds us of the bed of Procrustes. Procrustes (in mythology) placed his guests on a bed, and stretched short men and chopped off tall men to fit it. There is not the slightest suggestion in the text that this paragraph (5:1-11) is talking about a different event from that discussed in 4:13-18. If one did not have a certain theory about what will happen when Christ returns, he would never from this Scripture itself (4:13-5:11) get the idea that two different events were being described. We should not force the Scriptures to fit our theories, but make our theories to fit the Scriptures.

(For our reasons for questioning the idea of two returns of Christ, a secret rapture, followed by a tribulation, see notes on I Thess 4:16, and the Special Studies on pages 238-260, particularly studies II and IV.)

Text (5:2)

2 For yourselves know perfectly that the day of the Lord so cometh as a thief in the night.

Translation and Paraphrase

2. For you yourselves know very clearly (how) that (the) day of the Lord is coming (unexpectedly just) as a thief (comes) in the night.

Notes (5:2)

1. The coming of the Lord will be like the coming of a thief in that it will be unannounced and unexpected. It will NOT be like the coming a thief in being quiet, sneaky, and concealed. His appearance will be like lightning that comes out of the east and shines even unto the west. Matt. 24:27.

2. The Thessalonians may have sent an inquiry to Paul when Timothy returned from Thessalonica: "Tell us precisely (Gr., *akribos*) when the Lord will return." Paul here writes that they already know "precisely" (or perfectly) that nothing can be known on the subject.

3. Numerous Scripture passages compare the Lord's coming to a thief:

Matt. 24:43—"If the goodman of the house had known in what watch the *thief* would come, he would have watched."

II Pet. 3:10—"But the day of the Lord will come as a *thief* in the night."

Rev. 3:3—"If thou dost not watch, I will come as a *thief*, and thou shalt not know what hour I come unto thee."

Rev. 16:15—"Behold, I come as a *thief*; Blessed is he that watcheth and keepeth his garments.

4. It is difficult to imagine how the day of the Lord could come as a *thief* if only seven years before that day every eye had seen the Lord, and all the saints had been taken out of the earth, and a great shout and the trumpet of God had been heard, and a period of great tribulation had followed.

5. The expression, "day of the Lord," is used frequently in the Old Testament. It is applied to numerous occasions when God's judgment has been poured out upon sinners. Amos 5:18-20 uses it to refer to Israel's destruction by Assyria. Zephaniah 1:14-18 uses it to refer to the destruction of Judah and Jerusalem by Babylon. Joel 2:1-3 uses it to refer to a locust plague that was near at hand. It is applied to the end of the world in II Peter 3:10.

We mention these uses of the expression, "day of the Lord," because some interpreters seem to apply automatically any Scripture that uses the expression, "day of the Lord," to Christ's second coming, regardless of what the context is referring to.

Text (5:3)

3 When they are saying, Peace and safety, then sudden destruction cometh upon them, as travail upon a woman with child; and they shall in no wise escape.

Translation and Paraphrase

3. (For) when they are saying, (It is a time of) peace and security, then unexpected destruction shall come upon them, just as labor pains (come upon the woman that is with child. And they shall (most certainly) not escape (from the terrors of that day).

Notes (5:3)

1. They shall not escape: They will not be able to conceal themselves in the dens or the rocks and mountains. Rev. 6:16. The drunkard will have his cup at his lips, the swearer his oath in his mouth, the murderer his gun in his hand, and some in the act of adultery.

131

2. How little men know about the true danger to their souls: When they are saying, "Peace and safety," then sudden destruction: As it was in the days of Jeremiah, men will be saying, "Peace peace, when there is no peace." Jer. 6:14. And as it was in the days of Noah, "they knew not till the flood came and took them all away; thus shall it be in the coming of the son of man." Matt. 24:39.

3. Luke 21:34: "And take heed to yourselves, lest at any time your hearts be overcharged with dissipation and drunkenness, and cares of this life, and so that day come upon you unawares." (The word translated "unawares" in Lk. 21:34 is the same word *(aphnidios)* translated as "sudden" here in I Thess. 5:3.)

4. The statement, "They shall not escape," is emphatic in form (using *ou me,* as in I Thess 4:15). Our translation and paraphrase renders it, "They shall (most certainly) not escape."

5. Note that the fate of sinners is said to be "destruction." "Destruction" (Gr. *olethros*) does not indicate annihilation of body and soul. But it describes the total ruin of everything the sinner is and hoped for. The word is used in this sense by Greek writers. For a full discussion of its meaning and uses, see notes on II Thess. 1:9.

Text (5:4)

4 But ye, brethren, are not in darkness, that that day should overtake you as a thief:

Translation and Paraphrase

4. But you, brothers, are not in (the) darkness (like the unsaved people in the world who do not watch for the Lord's return. For if you were, it would happen) that the day (of the Lord) would come upon you as a thief (just as it is coming upon them).

Notes (5:4)

1. Here is a happy reversal: The day of the Lord is coming like a thief. But that day will NOT overtake Christians like a thief, because they are always watching for it. The Lord comes as a thief in the night, but we Christians are not in the dark.

2. What a joy it is not to be in spiritual darkness. "For God who commanded the light to shine out of darkness, hath sh ned in our hearts, to *give* the light of the knowledge of the glory of God in the face of Jesus Christ." II Cor. 4:6. "Arise, shine; for thy light is come, and the glory of the LORD is risen upon thee. For behold, the darkness shall cover the earth, and gross darkness the people; but the Lord shall arise upon thee, and his glory shall be seen upon thee." Isaiah 60:1-2.

3. A few ancient manuscripts render this verse, "that that day should overtake you as *thieves*." (Moffatt, Goodspeed, Rotherham, and American Standard Vers. margin give this rendering.) This rendering gives the meaning that if we are living in the spiritual darkness of sin, the day of the Lord will surprise us as thieves are surprised when the police appear unexpectedly. Actually this reading has little support in the ancient texts, and we mention it only in case you see it in some version, and wonder about it.

Text (5:5)

5 for ye are all sons of light, and sons of the day: we are not of the night, nor of darkness;

Translation and Paraphrase

5. (But you cannot be in such darkness,) for you are all sons of (the) light (seeing how the Lord has shined upon us), and sons of (the) day. We (Christians) are not (sons) of (the) night nor of darkness.

Notes (5:5)

1. Thieves and evil doers work at night, because they are evil. They hope that the darkness will cover their activities. "For everyone that doeth evil hateth the light, neither cometh to the light, lest his deeds should be reproved. But he that doeth truth cometh to the light, that his deeds may be made manifest, that they are wrought in God." John 3:20-21.
2. Christians are children of the light and of the day. The light of Christ has shined upon them. They have come to the light, and put away sinful things, for these are the works of darkness. Therefore God has shined in our hearts, to give the light of the knowledge of God in the face of Jesus Christ." II Cor. 4:6.
3. When we are out of the darkness and in the light, we have such comforting assurance. We know our sins are forgiven. We know there is a life to come. We know that we have eternal life. I John 5:13.
4. Jesus said, "I am the light of the world; he that followeth me shall not walk in darkness." John 8:12. Compare I John 1:5-6.
5. Ephesians 5:8: "For ye were sometimes darkness, but now are ye light in the Lord: walk as children of light."
6. Romans 13:12: "The night is far spent, the day is at hand: let us therefore cast off the works of darkness, and let us put on the armour of light."

7. Paul makes a shift in this verse, so as to include himself with the children of light: First, *"Ye* are;" Then, *"We* are."

Text (5:6-7)

6 so then let us not sleep, as do the rest, but let us watch and be sober. 7 For they that sleep sleep in the night; and they that are drunken are drunken in the night.

Translation and Paraphrase

6. Wherefore then, let us not fall asleep, as the rest (of mankind who are in spiritual darkness have done), but let us be watching and be sober (alert and wary).

7. For those who are sleeping sleep in the night (of spiritual ignorance and darkness), and those who get drunk are drunken at night.

Notes (5:6-7)

1. If you were told that a certain child came from a wealthy home, you might say, "I suppose he has lots of nice clothes." This would seem like an inevitable conclusion, since wealthy people do usually have nice clothing.

    Likewise there are certain things that are inevitable for us as children of light. (The Gr. conj. *ara oun* indicates the logicalness or inevitability of the conclusion.)

2. As children of light, we should NOT——
    (1) sleep; (2) Be drunken.
    As children of light, we should——
    (1) Watch; (2) Be sober; (3) Put on the armor of righteousness. 5:8.

3. Obviously "sleep" in this verse refers to being asleep about spiritual things. Many people are just as unaware of sin, salvation, the Lord's return, and everlasting life as sleeping people are unaware of the time of day.

    "And, that knowing the time, that now it is high time to *awake out of sleep;* for now is our salvation nearer than when we first believed." Rom. 13:11.

4. Watching is a most necessary thing for the children of light. We need to watch for our Savior, watch the devil, watch ourselves, and watch what is going on around us. We "watch," not to be meddlesome, but to protect our own souls, and to help others to walk in the right way. "Be sober, be *watchful;* your adversary the devil, as a roaring lion, walketh about." I Peter 5:8 (American Stan. vers.). See also Heb. 13:17; Acts 20:31; Matt. 26:41; 24:42; Luke 21:36.

5. Furthermore it is necessary for us to *be sober*. This means to be calm, collected, and alert in our thinking. Compare I Tim. 3:2. A person cannot be sober when he is drunken, for alcohol destroys the ability to think clearly.

6. Our Lord personally warned about being drunken, and fighting, and eating with the drunken, while we are waiting for the Lord to return. See Matt. 24:48-50; Luke 12:45-46. Such a person will be cut in sunder, and have his portion with unbelievers. (As you think of these matters, note how well the picture at the start of this chapter illustrates the thought.)

7. It is an obvious fact that "they that be drunken are drunken in the night." The apostle Peter defended himself against a charge of drunkenness, by declaring that men would not be drunken at nine o'clock in the morning, the time it happened to be. Acts 2:15.

   Not only is the drunkard most likely to be drunken in the hours of darkness, but he lives that way because he is in spiritual darkness to begin with.

Text (5:8)

8 But let us, since we are of the day, be sober, putting on the breast-plate of faith and love; and for a helmet, the hope of salvation.

Translation and Paraphrase

8. But (rather than sleeping and being drunken) let us who are (children) of the day be sober, (and this we can do by) putting on a breastplate of faith and love, and (as) a helmet (the) hope of salvation.

Notes (5:8)

1. When the captain of our salvation returns, will we be alert, disciplined, armed soldiers, or will be be drunken, sleeping, sprawling slackers lying about in the barracks?

2. Paul urges upon us the necessity of being *sober*. This is the opposite of both sleeping and being drunken. The Greek word *(nepho)* means to be calm and collected in spirit. It is the same word as is used in 5:6.

3. Paul's thoughts in this verse are echoed in Romans 13:12-13: "The night is far gone (and) the day is almost here. Let us then drop (fling away) the works *and* deeds of darkness and put on the full armor of light. Let us live *and* conduct ourselves honorably *and* becomingly as in the (open light of) day; not in

135

revelling (carousing) and drunkenness, not in immorality and debauchery (sensuality and licentiousness), not in quarreling and jealousy." *(Amplified New Testament)*

4. The Scripture often compares righteousness, faith, and such things to armor such as soldiers wear. See Isa. 59:17 and Ephesians 6:13-17.

5. The breastplate of *faith* and love will protect the heart from evil thoughts, and keep us watching for the Lord's coming.

   Since *faith* cometh by hearing, and hearing by the word of God (Rom. 10:17), we ought to devote time to reading or hearing the word of God every day. But very few Christians even spend fifteen minutes a day with God's word. And few churches are truly grounded in the word of God. We need to take more seriously this command to put on the breastplate of *faith* and love.

6. Love must be combined with faith. "Though I have all faith so that I could remove mountains, and have not love, I am nothing." I Cor. 13:2.

7. In this verse Paul urges us to put on the hope of salvation as a helmet. In Ephesians 6:17, salvation itself is called the helmet. A helmet serves both as a protection in battle, and as an adornment when the battle is won. Our salvation is a protection to us. God will not let Satan tempt us more than we can endure. I Cor. 10:13. Our salvation is an adornment, shining from our faces in friendliness, happiness, seriousness, kindness, and assurance.

8. The Christian life is——
   (1) A battle requiring armor. I Thess. 5:8.
   (2) A prize-fight, requiring self-discipline. I Cor. 9:26-27.
   (3) A race requiring training and patience. I Cor. 9:24; Heb. 12:1.

Text (5:9-10)

9 For God appointed us not unto wrath, but unto the obtaining of salvation through our Lord Jesus Christ, 10 who died for us, that, whether we wake or sleep, we should live together with him.

Translation and Paraphrase

9. (We have this hope of salvation) because God (in His work of setting us into his kingdom for his own use) has not appointed us to (suffer the terrors of his everlasting) wrath (against sin),

136

but (he has appointed us) unto the obtaining of salvation through the Lord Jesus, the anointed one.

10. (The Lord Jesus Christ is he) who died for us (bearing our sins in his own body) so that whether we (live and) are watching (when the Lord returns) or (die and) are sleeping (at that time), we might live together with him.

Notes (5:9-10)

1. Christ's death is so perfect a guarantee of salvation that even death cannot rob us of it. Whether we are alive or dead when Christ comes, we shall live together with Him. Our fellowship with the Lord will be uninterrupted by either life or death.

2. Christians have not accepted God's offer of pardon without God responding to their acceptance. For God has *appointed us* unto salvation.

   (The word here translated "appoint" (*tithemi*) is in the Greek middle voice. In this voice it means "to place for one's self." (Thayer.) We have emphasized this meaning in our paraphrase by the rendering, "In his work of setting us into his kingdom for his own use.")

3. The *wrath* of God awaits the disobedient and drunken. See Luke 12:45-46; I Thess. 5:7. See notes on I Thess. 1:10, paragraph 8.

4. The "wrath" (to which we are NOT appointed) is wrath (Gr., *orge*) or indignation which has arisen gradually and become more settled. It is not a fit of anger (Gr., *thumos*) which rises and then subsides.

   God has been infinitely patient with sinners. But His just wrath has been building up for a long time, and will finally bring upon them their just destruction.

5. Some interpreters think that the "wrath" mentioned here refers to a tribulation period to occur on earth after Christ has taken the church out of the world at the "rapture."

   However, "wrath" here is not opposite to "rapture," but is opposite to "salvation." The wrath probably refers to hell, and such judgments upon sinners. (See the notes on I Thess. 4:16, and Special Studies II and IV.)

6. There is considerable meaning in the word "obtain" in the phrase "obtain salvation." This word (Gr., *peripoiesis*) means an "obtaining, or a preserving, or preservation." (Thayer) The same word is used in II Thess. 2:14: "to the obtaining of the glory of our Lord Jesus." Also in Heb. 10:39: "We are of them who have faith unto the *saving* of the soul."

The idea is that salvation (safety and deliverance) is something that can be obtained and held onto, or it can be lost unto us. (How terrible to lose such a valuable thing:)

It is a blessed consolation, that God has not appointed us unto wrath, but to the obtaining of salvation. Christians do not fear the judgment day. Their sins have been taken away, and will be remembered against them no more. Their sins, having once been laid on Jesus, will never be laid on them.

7. The fact that Christ died for us is an essential part of the gospel. I Cor. 15:3; Rom. 5:8.

8. The result of Christ's death is that, for those who accept him, whether they live, they live unto the Lord, or whether they die, they die unto the Lord. Rom. 14:8.

9. It will make no difference in our fellowship with the Lord, whether we have died and are asleep when He returns, or whether we are living and watching. In either event we shall live with Him.

Text (5:11)

11 Wherefore exhort one another, and build each other up, even as also ye do.

Translation and Paraphrase

11. Wherefore comfort (and exhort) one another, and each one of you build up the other (in the most holy faith), even as (I know) you are doing.

Notes (5:11)

1. This passage is very comforting, but there is no comfort in it for those who are not saved. Only those who are watching for the day of the Lord Jesus, so that that day will not overtake them as a thief, will find any comfort in this verse (and the preceding ones).

2. The word "comfort" used here is the same one translated "exhort" in other places. Note Heb. 3:13. For its meaning, see notes on I Thess. 2:3, par. 2.

3. This command to comfort one another is similar to that in I Thess. 4:18.

4. The word *edify* means to "build up." So often people tear one another down, and discourage one another. What we say to one another is tremendously important. Often a word of encouragement can change a person's entire outlook and attitude, and actions.

138

This word translated "edify" is also used in Jude 20: "*Building up* yourselves in your most holy faith." Also it is in Rom. 15:2: "Let each one of you please his neighbor for his good to edification."

STUDY SUGGESTIONS—

(1) Review the outline of 5:1-11.

(2) Turn ahead to the "Did You Learn?" questions at the end of chapter five, and see if you can answer questions 1 to 18.

Text (5:12-13)

12 But we beseech you, brethren, to know them that labor among you, and are over you in the Lord, and admonish you; 13 and to esteem them exceedingly highly in love for their work's sake. Be at peace among yourselves.

Translation and Paraphrase

12. But we do request of you, brothers, that you give heed to those who toil among you, and are (appointed to be) over you in the Lord, and who admonish you.

13. And (that you) regard them highly, (yes even) beyond measure in (your) love (that you show,) because of their work (which they do for your sake. And) keep peace among yourselves.

Notes (5:12-13)

1. These verses begin a section of *Practical Exhortations*. (5:12-22.) There are thirteen of these exhortations. See outline. We sum up the first exhortation to say, "Know them which labor among you."

2. An excessive modesty prevents many ministers, evangelists, and elders from calling attention to the sacred work which they do, and to the respect with which it is to be regarded. Such a modesty is most harmful to the church. Let not the minister hesitate, even at the risk of being thought egotistical, to speak on this subject and enforce the New Testament teaching.

3. Roman Catholics are forced to knuckle down to the authority of their priesthood. Protestants have rightly rebelled against such unauthorized tyranny. But generally they have gone too far the other way. They not only disregard human authority in religion, but God's authority too. Without fear of God they neglect to worship, never pray nor pay, and feel no obligation to work. They do not hesitate to find fault with minister, even when he speaks the word of God. My brethren, let us take the yoke of Christ upon us. We are slaves of a divine Lord.

4. It is possible that Paul inserted the command here concerning the respect due to elders and evangelists, because some of the Thessalonians were insubordinate, and despised those with gifts such as prophesying. I Thess. 5:20.

5. Three duties of those who are "over you in the Lord" are indicated:
   (1) Labor; (The word means *toil.*)
   (2) Rule
   (3) Admonish

6. Two duties toward those that are over us in the Lord are laid down for us:
   (1) Know them.
   (2) Esteem them highly.
       (The adverb, "very highly," used here is the same word used by Paul to describe his longing to return to Thessalonica in I Thess. 3:10. Appreciation for the ministry and eldership should be most warm.)

7. The expression, *"Know* them which labour among you," of course means more than just to get acquainted. It is a Hebrew way of expressing "to have regard for, cherish, pay attention to."

8. The duty of Christians to be obedient to their church elders and evangelists is also taught in other Scriptures:
   (1) Heb. 13:17: "Obey them that have the rule over you, and submit yourselves: for they watch for your souls, as they that must give account, that they may do it with joy, and not with grief."
   (2) I Cor. 16:16: "That ye submit yourselves unto such, and to every one that helpeth and laboreth."

9. Nothing is indicated in these verses that would warrant our assigning to different church officers the various responsibilities of laboring, ruling, and admonishing. All of these jobs are to be done by the elders of churches. I Tim. 5:17; Titus 1:5, 9; Acts 20:28. Also preachers (or evangelists) must labor and admonish people. Titus 3:10; II Tim. 4:2.

10. It is easy for some men to abuse their authority, and take too much power unto themselves because they love the preeminence. III John 9.
    Those who are leaders among the churches of Christ are not to rule over their brethren like the kings of the Gentiles rule. Luke 22:24-26. Whosoever would be greatest shall be the serv-

ant of all. Jesus forbade us to assume titles of honor, like "Father" or "Rabbi." Also the title, "Reverend," belongs to God alone, and should not be worn by the Lord's servants. See Psalm 111:9.

We notice that in I Thess. 5:13, that those who are "over you in the Lord," are to be esteemed very highly *for their work's sake,* rather than because they hold some office with a high-sounding title.

The Lord's church does not have any "district ministers," "state secretaries," "district superintendents," cardinals, patriarch, or popes.

11. As true as all this is, we feel that among many churches people need to be MORE subject to authority, and not less. Of course, the authority must be God's authority, and rest upon Scriptural teachings.
12. "Admonish" means to "warn, exhort, place in one's mind."
13. Paul concludes his exhortation about the church's attitude toward its minister by saying, "Be at peace among yourselves."

Let there be peace between the minister and his flock, between the members themselves, and between ministers in different places.
14. If we have a factious spirit and cannot get along with our brethren in the church, or with the elders or preacher, we should take the matter to the Lord in prayer immediately, with humiliation and self-judgment.
15. Some of the Thessalonians were not working to support themselves. II Thess. 3:11-12. It is easy to imagine that this caused tension in the church, and may have partly been the reason Paul said, "Be at peace among yourselves."

Text (5:14)

14 And we exhort you, brethren, admonish the disorderly, encourage the fainthearted, support the weak, be longsuffering toward all.

Translation and Paraphrase

14. But we exhort you, brothers, warn those who are (idle and) not obeying orders; encourage the faint-hearted; support the weak; be longsuffering toward all (men).

Notes (5:14)

1. No one enjoys being told he is wrong or being warned about something he is doing. Warning many people merely makes them stubborn. But Christians should both expect and appre-

ciate warnings and exhortations that are given from God's word by sincere people who are more advanced in the faith than they are.

2. Paul urged the Thessalonians (in 5:12) to obey those who admonished them. Now in this verse, they themselves are instructed to admonish (or warn) others.

3. The word "unruly" (Gr., *ataktos*) means "disorderly, out of the ranks (often so of soldiers), irregular." The INTERPRETER'S BIBLE says that the Greek papyri sometimes uses the word to refer to idleness and loafing, and that is probably its application here.

   We say this because II Thess. 3:11 says, "We hear that there are some which walk among you *disorderly,* working not at all, but are busybodies." The word "disorderly" in II Thess. 3:11 is the same one as is translated "unruly" here in I Thess. 5:14.

4. In I Thess. 5:8 Paul compared Christians to armored soldiers. Now he says, "Don't be disorderly, or out of the ranks." Paul himself was not "disorderly" among them. II Thess. 3:7. Too many Christians are like soldiers out of line. Their actions interfere with the forward march of the whole church.

5. "Admonish (warn and seriously advise) those who are out of line—the loafers, the disorderly." (*Amplified New Testament*)

6. This verse is "an admonition against a too strictly disciplinarian spirit. The disorderly are not too hastily to be considered apostates, nor are the fainthearted to be regarded as cowards, nor the weak called blacksliders, nor are any to be hastily cast out." (McGarvey)

7. Paul's second Thessalonian letter indicates that these people who were unruly and disorderly and not working did not obey his exhortation and warning here in I Thessalonians. Therefore, in the second letter, Paul dealt with them roughly, saying, "If any will not work, neither let him eat." II Thess. 3:10.

8. The feeble-minded are not those who are mentally weak, but those who are faint-hearted and easily discouraged. They are the timid ones, those easily discouraged by persecutions, or cast down by trouble.

   We do not condone their faulty understanding or weak will, but we must make concessions to their weakness and support them. We comfort, exhort, and encourage them. I Cor. 8:12.

   Paul himself set an example of encouraging the fainthearted.

For in I Thess. 2:11, he tells how he exhorted and comforted, and charged every one of you as a father does his children.

Furthermore, God Himself comfort the fainthearted. Isa. 57:15: "I dwell in the high and holy place with him also that is of a contrite and humble spirit, to revive the spirit of the humble, and to revive the heart of the contrite ones."

9. The idea in the phrase, "Support the weak," is to "stick with them." Hold the weak firmly to you.

The law of the jungle says that the weak shall perish and only the fittest survive. The law of Christ is that the strong shall support the weak. Romans 15:1: "We that are strong ought to bear the infirmities of the weak, and not to please ourselves."

Every church has people in it who are weak in knowledge, trust, courage, and strength. Let us stick to these people and support them until they become strong and can uphold others.

10. To be "patient" (Gr., *makrothumeo*) means to "persevere patiently and bravely in enduring misfortunes and troubles; to be patient in bearing the offences and injuries of others; to be mild and slow in avenging." (Thayer.) It is the very opposite of being exasperated, short tempered, and despairing.

It takes a lot of long-suffering and patience before some of the children of God develop into the kind of people they should be. See I Cor. 13.4.

Text (5:15)

15 See that none render unto any one evil for evil; but always follow after that which is good, one toward another, and toward all.

Translation and Paraphrase

15. See that none (of you) return to anyone (an) evil (deed) for (an) evil (deed), but (rather) always seek (to do) the good (thing, both) to each other (as Christians), and (also) to all (men).

Notes (5:15)

1. This teaching about not returning evil for evil is contrary to everything the world does and believes. But it is repeatedly commanded in the Scriptures.

Prov. 20:22: "Say not thou, I will recompense evil; but wait on the Lord, and he shall save thee."

Matt. 5:39: "But I say unto you that ye resist not evil." See also Romans 12:17-21; I Peter 3:9; Matt. 5:39-41.

2. The caution to "see" is a warning that this practice of returning evil for evil can creep into our actions without our being aware that it is happening.
3. Note that the practice of not returning evil for evil, but rather returning good, is to be done by Christians to two groups:
    (1) Among themselves;
    (2) To all men.
4. Savonarola said years ago, "A Christian's life consists in doing good and suffering evil."
5. Four ways to react—
    1. The cruel (or Communist) way . . . Return evil for good.
    2. The common way . . . . Return evil for evil.
    3. The courteous (or civil) way . . . . . Return good for good.
    4. The Christian way . . . . Return good for evil.

Text (5:16-17)

16 Rejoice always; 17 pray without ceasing;

Translation and Paraphrase

16. Rejoice always (in tribulation as well as in comfort).
17. Pray without ceasing. (Always be in an attitude of communion with God.)

Notes (5:16-17)

1. Christianity is not sullen and sour, but full of joy, so full of joy that saints can be joyous even when the world frowns. Christianity is not recommended by sepulchral tones and suppressing every outward manifestation of gladness.
2. "Rejoice evermore" means "rejoice always." The word "rejoice" is found in Paul's letters more than two dozen times. See Phil. 3:1; 4:4. Paul even rejoiced in his sufferings. Col. 1:24; Acts 16:25; See also I Peter 4:13.
3. The secret of true joy is to avoid trying to be happy, and just go on quietly doing our work and service. Then happiness will come to us without our looking for it. But chasing happiness itself is like chasing rainbows. It is always just beyond reach.
4. I Thess. 5:16 is actually the shortest verse in the Bible. Perhaps you have thought that "Jesus wept" was the shortest verse. (John 11:35.) In the English Bible it is the shortest. But in the Greek text John 11:35 actually has three words and sixteen letters, while I Thess. 5:16 has only two words and fourteen letters. The shortest verse in the Old Testament is I Chronicles 1:25.

5. How can we "pray without ceasing"? We cannot always be saying words in prayer. However, we can always be in an attitude of prayer, and break out spontaneously in prayer at opportune times. Review the notes on I Thess. 3:11, paragraph 1.

6. The command to pray always was also given by Christ. See Luke 18:1. Paul also stated it in other Scriptures. See Romans 12:12; Colossians 4:2; Ephesians 6:18.

Text (5:18)

18 in everything give thanks: for this is the will of God in Christ Jesus to you-ward.

Translation and Paraphrase

18. Give thanks in every thing (that happens to you), for (doing) this is the will of God for you in (your service to) the anointed one, Jesus.

Notes (5:18)

1. We should not only feel thankful for God's benefits, but also always *express* our thanks. No doubt exists but that all ten of the lepers whom Jesus healed were thankful for their healing, but only one of them came back and expressed the thanks that were due. Luke 17:15-18.

2. It has been well observed that it is backwards to have only one day a year for Thanksgiving, and three hundred sixty-four for grumbling. We ought to have one day a year for expressing our grumbles, groans, grunts, and grouching, and three hundred sixty-four days a year for blessing the Lord who satisfies our mouth with good things.

3. Ephesians 5:20: "Giving thinks always for all things unto God and the Father in the name of our Lord Jesus Christ."

Text (5:19)

19 Quench not the Spirit;

Translation and Paraphrase

19. Do not quench (and put out the fire of) the (Holy) Spirit, (for he both brings conviction to you, and endows you with gifts and miracles).

Notes (5:19)

1. On the day of Pentecost, when the Holy Spirit was first poured out upon all flesh, the Spirit came with the appearance and likeness of *fire*. Acts 2:1-3, 16-17. The Holy Spirit caused men to

145

prophesy, see visions, work miracles, and do many other wondrous things. Acts 2:17. These miraculous works of the Spirit continued throughout the early generations of the church.

2. In this verse Paul compares the Spirit to a *fire* which can be quenched.

3. The statement about not quenching the Spirit refers primarily to not quenching the miraculous gift and powers that the Spirit empowered men to do. The Thessalonians were to give free expression to the prophesying, speaking in tongues, etc., that the Holy Spirit might perform in them. For a list of the gifts and workings of the Spirit, see I Cor. 12:7-10.

4. The fact that the Thessalonians could *quench* the Spirit harmonizes with what Paul said in I Cor. 14:32: "The spirits of the prophets are subject to the prophets." Unlike what happens in most modern cases of speaking in tongues (so-called), when people exercise these gifts in a state of uncontrollable ecstasy, the people in New Testament times who had these gifts were in perfect control of what they said, and could even suppress the revelations entirely.

5. Numerous other Scripture references contain similar exhortations about not quenching or suppressing the workings of the Spirit. See Numbers 11:28-29; I Cor. 14:39; Luke 9:50.

6. Should we in our time permit and encourage a free exercise of speaking in tongues and such gifts? We will not say "No" to anything that God's Spirit does. But in view of the plain Scriptural predictions that miraculous works of the spirit, such as tongues, prophesying, etc., were to cease (I Cor. 13:8; Zechariah 13:1-3), and in view of the fact that these gifts were given by the laying on of the apostles' hands (See Rom. 1:11; Acts 8:17-19), we do not expect to see such things as speaking in tongues and prophesying in our own time. (For further discussion of this matter, see the notes on I Thess. 5:20, and the notes on Ephesians 4:13 in THE GLORIOUS CHURCH, by the author of this book.)

7. Even if we do not have miraculous workings by the Spirit, the Holy Spirit is still very definitely at work within us. See Philippians 2:3. The Spirit stirs us to do things for the Lord, brings conviction of sin to us, and many other things. When you may think of a job you ought to do for the Lord because His word commands it, go do it; don't quench the Spirit. If we suppress

the Holy Spirit's message to our conscience, we shall soon lose our fire, become lukewarm, and then cold and formal.

8. But remember, in all matters, the Spirit leads us by the word of God, and if any spirit leads us otherwise, it is not the Spirit of truth, but the spirit of error. I John 4:6.

9. The Scripture speaks of "resisting the Spirit" (Acts 7:51) and "grieving the spirit" (Eph. 4:30) and "doing despite unto the Spirit of grace" (Heb. 10:29). Sinners may "resist the spirit" by rejecting the message which is preached. See Genesis 6:3. But only believers can "quench" or "grieve" the Spirit.

Christians can quench the Spirit by disobeying the word of God, by living sensual lives, by ignoring their consciences, and by disregarding the counsel of those who are led by the Spirit.

Text (5:20)

20 despise not prophesyings;

Translation and Paraphrase

20. Do not treat with contempt (the) prophesyings (which your) teachings may give through divine inspiration).

Notes (5:20)

1. This negative command, "Despise not prophesyings," is equivalent to an emphatic positive: "Don't despise prophesyings; rather delight in them."

2. This verse is closely related to the verse preceding it, "Quench not the Spirit." Both refer to restraining the work of the Spirit as He sought to do miraculous things.

3. The office of the *prophet* and prophesying was very important in the early church. God's revelation was made known unto the apostles and *prophets* by the Spirit. Eph. 3:5. The church was built upon the foundation of the apostles and *prophets*. Eph. 2:20. The prophets were second in the church only to the apostles. I Cor. 12:28. Prophesying was greater than speaking in tongues or any other spiritual gift. I Cor. 14:1-5. Paul told the Corinthians to, "Covet to prophesy." I Cor. 14:39.

4. Therefore, to despise and treat with contempt the utterances of their inspired teachers was a serious wrong.

5. Silvanus himself, who joined with Paul in sending this letter, was a prophet. Acts 15:32; I Thess. 1:1.

6. How does this verse apply to twentieth century Christians?

If we interpret the word "prophesyings" to refer merely to the preaching of the gospel and to teaching believers to observe whatsoever Christ has commanded us, then certainly people need to be warned to "Despise not prophesyings." For there is a general disregard for God's word and the instruction of the Scriptures in our time.

7. However, we cannot honestly nor accurately say that the word "prophesyings" (Gr., *propheteia*) means simply preaching. This word is found nineteen times in the New Testament, and in *every* reference it indicates speaking by supernatural revelation or help. See II Pet. 1:20-21 and Rev. 1:3 for examples.

The same thing is true of the related verb, *propheteuo,* which means "to prophesy." It is found twenty-eight times in the New Testament, and in every reference where it occurs, it has a plain or implied reference to supernatural assistance in speaking. Notice Luke 1:67; Acts 2:17; Acts 19:6; etc.

8. The question then arises, "Are such supernaturally inspired 'prophesyings' still to be found in the churches?"

We think not. Paul plainly predicted that "when that which is perfect is come," such partial things as prophecies would fail. I Cor. 13:8-10. Zechariah the prophet prophesied that in the day that a fountain for sin and uncleanness was opened that the prophet would pass out of the land. Zech. 13:1-3.

9. Both the predictions of Paul and of Zechariah appear to us to have been fulfilled.

We now have a perfect salvation and a perfect revelation of the will of God given to us in the New Testament. Therefore, surely "that which is perfect" (not "*he* who is perfect") has already come, and prophecies should have failed and tongues ceased in the churches long ago.

Concerning Zechariah's prophecy we notice that—

(1) The blood of Jesus has long ago been shed, and a fountain thereby opened to the inhabitants of Jerusalem for sin and for uncleanness.

(2) The prophets and the unclean spirit were to pass out of the land in that day (or time).

In view of these two Scriptures, we feel that the office of the *prophet* as it existed in the times of the apostles has ceased in the churches of God.

10. Therefore, the only way that we in our times could "despise not prophesyings" would be to despise the messages of God's prophets and apostles that have been preserved for us in the Holy Scriptures. This we should NOT do. John the apostle cautions us in Rev. 22:18-19:

> "I testify unto every man that heareth the words of the *prophecy* of this book, If any man shall add unto these things, God shall add unto him the plagues that are written in this book: And if any man shall take away from the words of the book of this *prophecy,* God shall take away his part out of the book of life, and out of the holy city, and from the things which are written in this book."

With this warning reverberating in our minds, we should take heed to "despise not prophesyings."

Text (5:21-22)

21 prove all things; hold fast that which is good; 22 abstain from every form of evil.

Translation and Paraphrase

21. Test all things (whatever you may hear or see. Then) hold fast (only that which is) the good (in the mixture of good and evil that constantly confronts us).
22. Depart from every(thing that has the) appearance of evil.

Notes (5:21-22)

1. Many people accept any teaching, simply because "Our preacher said so," or because they have always thought it was that way. The command to "Prove all things" forbids such a gullible attitude. We should not accept anything we hear or see until we know it is in harmony with God's word.
2. In our life we are always confronted with a mixture of evil and good in everything. Therefore we must prove (or test) all things, and hold fast only to that which is good.

   Paul urged the Philippians to "approve the things that are excellent." Phil. 1:10. (The same Gr. verb, *dokimadzo,* is used both in Phil. 1:10 and I Thess. 5:21.)

   Error is never so dangerous as when it is mixed with some truth.
3. The command to "Prove all things," may have had reference to the "prophesyings" mentioned in 5:20. While they were not to despise prophesyings, yet they were to test all things. The apostles commanded us to "Try the spirits whether they are of

God." I John 4:1. (The word "try" in I John 4:1 is the same Gr. word that is translated "prove" in I Thess. 5:21.)

Some of the early Christians had the gift of "discerning of spirits" which would enable them to spot false teaching without the aid of written Scriptures. We who have the Scriptures have a perfect yardstick to measure all things against.

4. Not only were the Thessalonians to hold fast to that which was good, but to avoid all appearance of evil. This would be very difficult for them to do in their pagan surroundings. They would have to be careful about where they went, whom they were seen with, under what conditions, etc. This would be difficult, but with God's help not impossible. II Thess. 3:3.

5. Most English versions of the Bible seem to prefer to translate 5:22 in some way similar to that in the American Standard version: "Abstain from every form of evil."

The translation hinges on the meaning given to the word *eidos* (translated "appearance" in the King James version). Basically the word means "external appearance, form, figure, shape." (Thayer.) It can mean "kind" or "form," as in the American Standard version. But it seems to us that the King James translation, "Abstain from all *appearance* of evil," is to be preferred.

6. There is a play on words in 5:21-22 which is not apparent in the English versions. We will try to bring it out by the following contrast:

   (1) In 5:21, we are told to "hold fast" (Gr., *katecho*) that which is good.

   (2) In 5:22, we are told to "hold off" (Gr., *apecho*) from all appearance of evil.

7. Keeping away from evil is essential for the child of God. God is holy and we too must be holy. Note Exodus 23:7; Job 1:8; 2:3. We must not use the members of our body as servants of unrighteousness. Romans 6:13, 19.

8. Avoiding all *appearance* of evil means that Christians should avoid going to places where people might think they were doing evil. To go into a night club, pool hall, tavern, etc., even for a legitimate reason, might cause some one to think we were indulging in evil. We should not only avoid the evil itself, but we must avoid even the appearance of evil.

Text (5:23)

**23 And the God of peace himself sanctify you wholly; and may your
spirit and soul and body be preserved entire, without blame at the
coming of our Lord Jesus Christ.**

Translation and Paraphrase

23. But (now) may the God (who is the creator and giver) of peace
(may he) his own self consecrate you in every respect (even
unto the end of the age). And may your entire spirit, and soul,
and body be (kept from sin and found) blameless at the coming of our Lord Jesus, the anointed one.

Notes (5:23)

1. Just as Part One of I Thessalonians closed with a prayer (3:11-
13), so also Part Two closes with this prayer in 5:23.

  Paul's prayer in this verse is that the God of peace may do
two things for the Thessalonians:

  (1) Sanctify them wholly.

  (2) Preserve their entire nature blameless unto the coming
of Christ.

2. This closing prayer of Part Two reflects both the greatness of
the heart of Paul and the greatness of the power of God. Medi-
tate a minute about how great the requests in this prayer are.

3. The title, "God of peace," means "the peaceful God." Also it
carries the idea that God is the creator and author of peace.

  This title, "God of peace," is also found in Romans 15:33;
16:20; Phil. 4:9; II Cor. 13:11; Heb. 13:20; II Thess. 3:16.

  How thankful we should be that the true God is the God of
peace, and not of hate and war.

4. To "sanctify" means to "render sacred, declare holy, consecrate, separate from things profane, dedicate to God, purify."
To "sanctify" is to separate something from God, and consecrate it to holy uses.

  The entire nature of Christians is being sanctified. For a discussion of "sanctification," see the notes on I Thess. 4:3.

5. We are to be sanctified "wholly." The word "wholly" (Gr., *holoteles*) means perfect, complete in all respects, and through all
time. It is a combination of two words, one meaning "whole"
and the other meaning "end." We have tried to bring out this
double significance in our translation and paraphrase by rendering it "in every respect (even unto the end of the age)."
(The word *holoteles* is used as a predicate adjective, almost as
an adverb.)

151

It is comforting to think that we shall be wholly sanctified. We shall no longer be in danger of temptation. We shall not lose anything that is dear to us on earth. If we have lost a mother whose saintly disposition has made her memory dear, we can be comforted to know that God is not permitting any of her precious nature to escape His preservation and sanctification. The best that is on earth will become better and none of it will be lost.

6. The words, "I pray God," in this verse are written in italics because they are added to the text. They should not be included, because all *three* men—Paul, Silvanus, and Timothy—joined in sending this letter. The Amer. Stan. Vers. correctly omits the "I" here, as also in I Thess. 4:9.

7. This verse indicates that man has a three-fold nature:
   (1) He has a spirit.
   (2) He has (and is) a soul.
   (3) He has a body.
   (For a full study and analysis of the Scriptural uses of the words, "spirit" and "soul," see Special Study VI, "Questions About 'Spirit' and 'Soul'.")

8. Concerning the difference between "spirit," "soul," and "body," we shall only make the following observations here:
   (1) "Spirit" (Gr., *pneuma*) is the life-principle in man. It is the divine breath that gives him life. It is the "inward man" (II Cor. 4:16) that feels, things, wills, decides, and lives.
   (2) "Soul" (*psuche*) refers to our personal identity. It includes all those things that make us a particular person —our life, our mind, our affections, our emotions, our whole self.
   (3) "Body" *(soma)* is almost a self-explanatory term. It is the "outward man" (II Cor. 4:16), the fleshly, material part of our being, to which life is given by the *spirit*, and which with the spirit becomes a living *soul*, YOU!

9. All three parts of man's nature—spirit, soul, and body—have presently been corrupted by sin. But they will all be sanctified wholly at the coming of Christ.
   Our bodies will be sanctified when they are transformed at the resurrection of the dead. Until that time we must keep cleansing ourselves from all defilement of flesh and spirit. II Cor. 7:1; I Cor. 15:51-53.

10. While we ourselves need to do all we can to make ourselves ready for the coming of the Lord, it is GOD who actually preserves us and delivers us from sin.

Jude 24: "Unto him who is able to keep you from faling, and to present you faultless before the presence of his glory with exceeding joy." Compare I Cor. 10:13; 1:8; Phil. 1:10.

11. As Paul draws this first epistle to the Thessalonians to a close, he points once again to the pole-star of our home, the coming (*parousia*) of our Lord Jesus Christ. (Concerning the meaning of *parousia*, see notes on I Thess. 2:19, par. 7.)

It would be profitable for you at this time to go back to Introductory Section III and review what Paul said about the Lord's coming in the Thessalonian epistles.

Text (5:24)

24 Faithful is he that calleth you, who will also do it.

Translation and Paraphrase

24. He who calls you (into his kingdom and glory) is faithful, who will also do (this thing, that is, preserve our spirit, soul, and body blameless).

Notes (5:24)

1. In I Thess. 5:23, Paul prayed that God would sanctify us wholly, and preserve our spirit, soul, and body at the coming of Christ. If God were not faithful and did not help us to be sanctified, it would never be accomplished.

2. Christians both can and must trust God. We cannot let fear rule our lives. Fear will make us timid and hesitant. Faith in a faithful God will drive out fear.

3. Many Scriptures tell of the faithfulness of God. He never fails to do what He says He will do. See I Cor. 1:9; 10:13; II Thess. 3:3; I John 1:9; II Tim. 2:13; Deut. 7:9.

4. God calls us into His kingdom and glory. I Thess. 2:12. He calls us by the gospel. II Thess. 2:14.

5. We can be confident in what God can and will do. He is able to do exceeding abundantly above all we ask or think. Eph. 3:20. He will perfect our good work until the day of Christ. Phil. 1:6.

Text (5:25-26)

25 Brethren, pray for us. 26 Salute all the brethren with a holy kiss.

Translation and Paraphrase

25. Brethren, (please) pray (also) for us (continuously).

153

26. Greet all the brothers (your fellow-Christians) with an holy kiss.

Notes (5:25-26)

1. How very often Paul requested the prayers of his Christian brethren: See Eph. 6:19; Romans 15:30; Col. 4:3, 18; II Thess. 3:1-2; II Cor. 1:8-11; Hebrews 13:18. If an inspired apostle such as Paul needed the prayers of his brethren, how much more your preacher needs your prayers.

2. In 5:26 Paul lays upon us the duty of knowing and greeting all of our Christian brethren. They should be very dear to us. The people we associate with on Sunday ought to mean much more to us than the people with whom we mingle during the week. It is good to see churches where the members greet and talk freely to one another.

3. The kiss was a common greeting in the East in Bible times, and still is in places. Jesus criticized his host on one occasion by saying, "Thou gavest me no kiss." Luke 7:45. This was assumed to be part of a sincere welcome into a home.

   This kiss was given on the cheek, the forehead, the beard, the hands, the feet, but not (in Palestine) the lips. There is reason to believe that, as a rule, men only thus greeted men, and women women. It was so enjoined in the Apostolic Constitutions (third century).

4. The "holy kiss" is also mentioned in I Cor. 16:20; II Cor. 13:12; I Peter 5:14.

5. After checking all the references to kissing in the Bible (and they are numerous), it appears to us that people in Bible times just did NOT go around kissing everyone they met. It was something rather special. There were kisses of greeting, farewell, worship, respect, and kisses of affection between people very close (such as Ruth and Naomi), and kisses of pretended affection (Judas kissing Jesus, for example).

6. That unrestrained kissing was not the universal custom in Bible times is indicated by the fact that King David's son, Absalom, attracted a lot of attention to himself by kissing any man who came near to him (along with giving out flattery). If kissing had been extremely common, Absalom's actions would not have attracted the notice they did. II Samuel 15:5-6.

7. We read of the father kissing the prodigal son (Luke 15:20), Paul and the Ephesian elders weeping and kissing in farewell (Acts 20:37), Aaron greeting Moses with a kiss (Ex. 4:27), etc.

By far the majority of cases of kissing involved those of the same sex. (This was not always the case, however, as Jacob kissed Rachel before he even introduced himself. However, she was a relative, and he knew it even before she did! Gen. 29:11.)

8. Erotic kissing is never referred to in the Bible, except possibly in Song of Sol. 1:2, and in that place the couple were unquestionably married.

9. In this verse Paul did not say that we had to kiss every time we met or said "Good-bye." Neither was he instituting a new church custom or ordinance. Since kissing was a form of greeting common in the world of that time, he could not have meant to institute a new practice, but he is here purifying an old one, insisting that the greeting be *holy*. This instruction applies to all our greetings, whether they be by handshake, embrace, or occasionally a holy kiss. We see people here in America sometimes greet those who are very dear to them with an embrace or kiss. If such is the custom, let it be a *holy* kiss, and do not try to interpret Paul's words to mean that we ought to kiss all our brethren every time we meet them.

Text (5:27)

27 I adjure you by the Lord that this epistle be read unto all the brethren.

Translation and Paraphrase

27. I adjure you by the Lord (and His authority, as a judge might demand of people under oath), that this letter be read to all the (holy) brothers (to your whole congregation).

Notes (5:27)

1. Paul evidently thought that his letter could be understood by the common people in the church, as he gave strict orders that it be read to all of them.

   The Roman Catholic clergy has often held back the Bible from their people, saying that the laity cannot interpret correctly the Bible without an infallible guide. However, Lois, Eunice, the Bereans, the Ephesians, and many others all read and understood the Scriptures without any official interpreter to explain them. II Tim. 1:5; 3:15; Acts 17:11; Eph. 3:4.

2. Public reading of the Scriptures does more good than we ever dream of. People will make many applications of the word of God as the Holy Spirit lays it on their hearts.

3. When we read the Scriptures publicly, we might well remember the example of Ezra who read *distinctly* and gave the sense. Nehemiah 8:8.

4. Paul's command to the Thessalonians to read his epistle publicly is put in the form of a judicial oath. He placed them under oath to do this. This certainly emphasized the importance that Paul attached to his writings. (The force of this command as an oath is brought out in our paraphrase.) For a similar oath, see Acts 19:13.

5. Paul also commanded the Colossians to read their epistle to the Laodiceans, and that they likewise read the one from Laodicea. Colossians 4:16.

Text (5:28)

28 The grace of our Lord Jesus Christ be with you.

Translation and Paraphrase

28. (Now) may the favor of our Lord Jesus, the anointed one, be with you. (Amen)

Notes (5:28)

1. The benediction of "grace" is found at the end of every one of Paul's letters (including Hebrews). See Romans 16:24; I Cor. 16:23; etc.

2. It is not found at the close of the letters by Peter, Jude, James, or John. The book of Revelation, however, closes with a benediction of grace. Rev. 22:21.

3. "Grace" means "favor," as explained in the notes on I Thess. 1:1, paragraph 12.

4. The word "Amen" is not given at the close of Nestle's Greek text (it is in the margin), nor in the American Standard version. But it is included in many ancient manuscripts, and we include it in our paraphrase. It seems such an appropriate closing, both here and at the end of Part One of the epistle. See notes on I Thess. 3:13, paragraph 6.

5. The postscript at the close of I Thessalonians in the King James version, "The first *epistle* unto the Thessalonians was written from Athens," is NOT part of the inspired text by Paul, and also it is not true. See Introductory Section IV, paragraph 4.

STUDY SUGGESTION—

Turn now to the "Did You Learn?" questions on the following pages, and answer questions 19 to 51.

CHAPTER FIVE

DID YOU LEARN?

(Questions over I Thessalonians, chapter five)

1. What are the two topics of chapter five, and what are the Scripture limitations of each? (See outline)
2. What are the two divisions in the first topic of chapter five? (See outline)
3. What are three points of resemblance between sections 4:13-18 and 5:1-11? (5:1)
4. Concerning what subject did Paul say (in 5:1) that he had no need to write to them?
5. As what will the day of the Lord come? (5:1)
6. What will men be saying before the day of the Lord? (5:3)
7. What will come upon people as travail upon a woman with child? (5:3)
8. Why will not the day of the Lord overtake Christians as a thief? (5:4)
9. Of what are Christians children? (5:5)
10. Of what are Christians NOT children? (5:5)
11. What two things should the children of light NOT do? (5:6-7)
12. What three things should the children of light do? (5:6-8)
13. What armor are the children of light to put on? (5:8)
14. Unto what has God NOT appointed us? (5:9)
15. Unto what has God appointed us? (5:9)
16. Christ died for us, so that whether we wake or sleep we should do what? (5:10)
17. In I Thess. 5:11, what two things are the Thessalonians told to do for one another?
18. What word the word "edify" mean? (5:11)
19. How many practical exhortations are listed in the outline of section 5:12-22?
20. What two duties do we have toward them which are "over us in the Lord"? (5:12-13)
21. At what are we to be among ourselves? (5:13)
22. What does "unruly" in 5:14 mean?
23. What were some of the Thessalonians doing (or not doing) that caused Paul to call them "unruly"? (5:14)
24. What does "feebleminded" in 5:14 mean?
25. What are we to do for the weak? (5:14)
26. Toward whom are we to be patient? (5:14)
27. What are we to return for evil? (5:15)

THINKING THROUGH THESSALONIANS

28. When are we to rejoice? (5:16)
29. How can we pray without ceasing? (5:17)
30. What are we to give in every thing (or every experience)? (5:18)
31. To what is the Spirit compared in the verse, "Quench not the spirit"? (5:19)
32. To what does the statement about not quenching the Spirit primarily refer? (5:19)
33. How important were prophets and prophesying in the early church? (5:20)
34. To what activity does the word "prophesying" refer in the New Testament? (5:20)
35. What two Scriptures are given in the notes to support the view that "prophesyings" are not now to be found in the churches? (5:20)
36. What are we to do with all things? (5:21)
37. From what are we told to abstain in 5:22?
38. With what does Part Two of I Thessalonians close? (5:23)
39. What two things did Paul request that the God of peace might do for the Thessalonians? (5:23)
40. What are the three parts in man's nature? Explain what each is. (5:23)
41. Paul prayed that our entire nature might be preserved blameless at what event? (5:23)
42. Who is going to sanctify and preserve us? (5:24)
43. According to 5:24, the one who call us is _____
____.
44. In 5:25, what did Paul ask his brethren to do for him?
45. What is the purpose of the holy kiss? (5:26)
46. Is the holy kiss a church ordinance? (5:26)
47. What did Paul command the Thessalonians to do with his letter? (5:27)
48. Under what form did Paul issue his charge to read his letter publicly? (5:27)
49. What is the benediction in every epistle of Paul? (5:28)
50. Recite or write out from memory I Thess. 5:1-2, 23.
    5:1-2 begins, "But of the times ... "
    5:23 begins, "And the very ... "
51. As a final question over I Thessalonians, see if you can say all the chapter topics of the epistle.

II Thessalonians

Introductory Section I

THE RELATIONSHIP OF II THESSALONIANS TO I THESSALONIANS

1. *II Thessalonians was sent only a few months after I Thessalonians.*

2. *The same three men* (Paul, Silvanus, and Timothy) *sent both of the Thessalonian epistles.* And in both epistles, Paul was the main author.

3. *II Thessalonians was sent from the same place as I Thessalonians, Corinth.*

4. *In both of the letters Paul expresses thanks for their faithfulness.* I Thess. 1:2-3; II Thess. 1:3-4.

5. *Both of the letters have the theme of Christ's second coming.*
   (I Thessalonians discussed Christ's coming as it related to the dead and living saints. II Thessalonians discusses the coming as it relates to the everlasting perdition of the wicked, and to the *man of sin* who shall come before the Lord comes. See Introductory Section III of I Thessalonians.)

6. *Both epistles deal with the same problems:*
   (1) *Persecutions and trials;* I Thess. 3:3-4; II Thess. 1:4
   (2) *Misunderstanding about the Lord's coming.*
      (a) In I Thessalonians there were questions about what would happen to the dead in Christ at the Lord's coming, and exactly when the coming would be.
      (b) In II Thessalonians there was the problem that some believed that the day of Christ had already come. II Thess. 2:1-2
   (3) *People who would not work.* I Thess. 4:11; 5:14; II Thess. 3:10-11

159

Introductory Section II
CHAPTER TOPICS AND OUTLINE
OF II THESSALONIANS

A. *Chapter Topics of II Thessalonians*

Chapter 1—"God's Righteous Retribution"
Chapter 2—"The Man of Sin"
Chapter 3—"Withdraw From Idlers"
(Memorize these chapter topics NOW. While these topics do not cover everything that is in each chapter, if you will only remember these, you will have a general idea of what is in each chapter of the whole epistle.)

B. *Outline of II Thessalonians*

(More complete outlines are given at the beginning of the notes on each chapter. Note that each chapter closes with a prayer. Aside from the chapter topics, you will not need to memorize more of this outline now. The outlines will be studied more carefully as each chapter is considered.)

CHAPTER 1—"GOD'S RIGHTEOUS RETRIBUTION"
    I. Address and greeting; 1:1-2
   II. Thanks for their faith and love; 1:3-4
  III. God's righteous retribution; 1:5-10
  IV. Prayer for God's blessings; 1:11-12
CHAPTER 2—"THE MAN OF SIN"
    I. Paul's entreaty about the Lord's coming; 2:1-3a
   II. The man of sin; 2:3b-12
  III. Thanksgiving for God's choosing the Thessalonians; 2:13-15
  IV. Prayer that they be comforted and stablished; 2:16-17
CHAPTER 3—"WITHDRAW FROM IDLERS"
    I. Request for prayer; 3:1-2
   II. Expressions of confidence; 3:3-5
  III. Withdraw from idlers; 3:6-15
  IV. Prayer for peace; 3:16
Conclusion; 3:17-18

Introductory Section III
FACTS ABOUT II THESSALONIANS

(Memorize all facts in *italics*.)
  1. *It was written by Paul the apostle.* Silvanus and Timothy joined with Paul in sending the letter.

2. *It was written from* the city of *Corinth,* during Paul's second missionary trip.

(That the letter was written at Corinth during the second missionary trip is evident from the fact that Silvanus, or Silas, was with Paul up till that time, and apparently never afterwards. Silas became separated from Paul while he was at Corinth, for he is never afterwards mentioned as being associated with Paul.)

3. *It was written* about *A.D. 53,* just a few months after Paul sent I Thessalonians.

(The time between the two was probably only as long as it took I Thessalonians to be delivered, and a report brought back to Paul from Thessalonica.)

4. *The following problems are discussed in II Thessalonians:*
   (1) They were enduring *continued persecutions.* II Thess. 1:4
   (2) *Some had been misled to believe,* either by a supposed revelation, or by misunderstanding Paul's teachings, or perhaps even by a letter which Paul supposedly wrote, *that the day of Christ had already arrived.* II Thess. 2:1-2. This notion had caused them to become shaken, troubled, and excited.
   (3) *Some* had not obeyed Paul's exhortation in I Thessalonians about working, and *were not working at all,* but were meddling and being busybodies. II Thess. 3:10-11
       In II Thessalonians Paul *commands* such people to work, and puts some teeth into his command.

Introductory Section IV

DID PAUL REALLY WRITE II THESSALONIANS?

Yes. It is beyond serious question that Paul wrote this letter.

Many very ancient Christian writers quote or refer to passages in II Thessalonians. Polycarp (70-156 A.D.) alludes to 1:4 and 3:15. Justin Martyr (about 150 A.D.) refers to 2:3. Irenaeus (130-190 A.D.) quotes 2:8. Clement of Alexandria (about 195 A.D.) quotes 3:2. Tertullian (about 200 A.D.) quotes 2:1-2 as part of Paul's epistles.

It would have been impossible for men as ancient as these to have regarded II Thessalonians as an epistle of Paul, if it were not well certified as a true apostolic epistle.

Some modern authors have questioned that Paul wrote II Thessalonians on the supposed ground that *the teachings about the second coming of Christ in II Thessalonians differs from that in I Thessalonians.*

In I Thessalonians Paul supposedly indicated that Christ's coming was very near and would be within their lifetime. Then in II Thessalonians he indicates that there would first have to be a falling away from the faith, and the appearance of the man of sin before the Lord came.

This is a manufactured contradiction, not based on truth. Paul was so far from being mistaken in I Thessalonians about Christ's immediate coming, that he could distinctly remind the Thessalonians (in II Thess. 2:5) that he told them while he was yet with them, before he ever wrote I Thessalonians, that the falling away would precede the Lord's coming.

There have been other even more flimsy objections to the fact that Paul wrote II Thessalonians, such as the extreme similarities of parts of the two epistles, and the difference in Paul's apparent attitude toward the church in the two letters.

DID YOU LEARN?
(Questions over the Introductory Sections of II Thessalonians)

1. What three men sent II Thessalonians? (Section I)
2. From what city was it sent?
3. How long after Paul sent I Thessalonians was it before II Thessalonians was sent?
4. For what was Paul thankful in both epistles?
5. What is the theme of both the Thessalonian epistles?
6. What three problems are dealt with in both epistles?
7. What are the chapter topics of II Thessalonians? (Section II)
8. With what does each chapter of II Thessalonians close?
9. During what missionary trip was II Thessalonians written? (Section III)
10. In what year was II Thessalonians written?
11. What had some of the Thessalonians been misled to believe about the Lord's coming?
12. What had caused them to have this misunderstanding?
13. What was the problem in Thessalonica about working?
14. What is a cause for which some have questioned the fact that Paul wrote II Thessalonians? Explain why this objection is not true. (Section IV)

II THESSALONIANS, CHAPTER ONE

Chapter topic:

God's Righteous Retribution

The Lord Jesus shall be revealed from heaven with His mighty angels, in flaming fire taking vengeance———" II Thess. 1:7, 8

THINKING THROUGH THESSALONIANS

Chapter Topic: "God's Righteous Retribution"

1. True of false (circle which)—The same people that sent II Thessalonians also sent I Thessalonians. II Thess. 1:1; I Thess. 1:1

2. True or false (circle which)—Paul requested the same things to be unto the Thessalonians in the second epistle as he did in the first one. II Thess. 1:2; I Thess. 1:1

3. What did Paul feel bound (or obligated) to do? II Thess. 1:3. _____.

4. What did the faith of the Thessalonians do? II Thess. 1:3. __ _____.

5. What did the charity (love) of every one of the Thessalonians do? II Thess. 1:3. _____.

6. Paul glorified (boasted) in the churches of God for the _____ _____ and _____ of the Thessalonians. II Thess. 1:4

7. True or false (circle which)—Persecutions had ceased from the Thessalonians after Paul wrote I Thessalonians. II Thess. 1:4

8. The patience and faith of the Thessalonians was a manifest token of the _____ _____ of God. II Thess. 1:5

9. God's righteous judgment upon the Thessalonians was working things out so "that ye may be _____ _____ of the kingdom of God." II Thess. 1:5

10. What does God recompense to them that trouble you? II Thess. 1:6. _____.

11. Is this a righteous thing for God to do? II Thess. 1:6. Yes or No (circle which.)

12. What will God recompense to those who are troubled? II Thess. 1:7. _____.

13. With what shall the Lord Jesus be revealed from heaven? II Thess. 1:7. _____ _____.

14. In what will Jesus take vengeance? II Thess. 1:8. _____ _____ _____.

15. Upon what two classes of people will God take vengeance? II Thess. 1:8

    _____
    _____;

    _____
    _____.

16. With what shall the disobedient be punished? II Thess. 1:9. __ _____.

17. This punishment will be in a place "from the _____
_____ of the _____." II Thess. 1:9
18. The disobedient shall be punished "when he _____
_____." II Thess. 1:10
19. Christ will come to be _____ in his
_____, and to be _____ in all
them that _____." II Thess. 1:10
20. Paul prayed always that God would "_____ you
_____ of this calling." II Thess. 1:11
21. Paul prayed that God would _____ all the _____
_____ _____ of his goodness, and
the _____ of _____ with _____."
II Thess. 1:11
22. Note the two that will be glorified: II Thess. 1:12
(1) "the name of our _____ _____
_____ may be glorified in _____.
(2) and _____ (be glorified) in _____."
23. According to what will we be glorified? II Thess. 1:12. _____
_____
_____.

24. Memorize II Thess. 1:6-9.

II THESSALONIANS, CHAPTER ONE

Chapter Topic, *"God's Righteous Retribution"*

Outline

I. Address and Greeting; 1:1-2
  1. Paul, Silvanus, and Timothy; 1:1
  2. To the church of the Thessalonians;
  3. Grace and peace; 1:2
II. Thanks for their faith and love; 1:3-4
  1. Their faith and love increase; 1:3
  2. Paul boasted of them in other churches; 1:4
III. God's righteous retribution; 1:5-10
  1. Their patience a token of God's righteous judgment; 1:5
  2. God will recompense trouble to the troublers; 1:6
  3. God will recompense rest to those troubled; 1:7a
  4. Retribution to be done when Jesus is revealed; 1:7b-10
    a. Vengeance to be taken on the ignorant and disobedient; 1:8-9
    b. Jesus to be glorified and admired in His saints; 1:10

IV. Prayer for God's blessings; 1:11-12
  1. The petitions; 1:11
    a. That God would count them worthy.
    b. That God would fulfill all the good pleasure of goodness.
    c. That God would fulfill all the work of faith with power.
  2. The purposes for the petitions; 1:12
    a. That the name of Jesus may be glorified in you.
    b. That you may be glorified in Him.

Text (1:1-2)

1 Paul, and Silvanus, and Timothy, unto the church of the Thessalonians in God our Father and the Lord Jesus Christ; 2 Grace to you and peace from God the Father and the Lord Jesus Christ.

Translation and Paraphrase

1. Paul, and Silvanus, and Timothy (send greetings) to the congregation of the Thessalonians (who are) in God our father, and (in our) Lord Jesus, the anointed one:
2. (May divine) favor and peace (come to you) from God (the) father and (from the) Lord Jesus Christ.

Notes (1:1-2)

1. These two verses and I Thess. 1:1 are almost identical. Only a few words differ. Both of these verses are combined into one verse (1:1) in I Thessalonians. Please refer to the notes on I Thess. 1:1 for comment on these verses.
2. We are thankful that Paul could still address the Thessalonians in this letter with the same warm greeting that he did in his first letter. At least they were not like the Galatians who quickly departed from the gospel. Gal. 1:6.

Text (1:3)

3 We are bound to give thanks to God always for you, brethren, even as it is meet, for that your faith groweth exceedingly, and the love of each one of you all toward one another aboundeth;

Translation and Paraphrase

3. We are obligated (by our sense of debt to God and our debt to you for your faith, hope, and love) to give thanks to God always for you, brethren, just as it is fitting, because your faith increases (so) greatly, and the love of each one of you all toward one another grows (so much);

Notes (1:3)

1. We rejoice when a church grows in number, budget, and the size of its building. But do we rejoice when a church grows in

faith and love? This was what made Paul thankful for the Thessalonian church.

2. This verse reveals that one of Paul's prayers had been answered. Paul had prayed in I Thess. 3:12 that the Lord would make them abound in love toward one another.

   After sending I Thessalonians, Paul received the report back about the Thessalonians that their faith was growing exceedingly, and their *love* was abounding.

3. The expression, "We are *bound* to give thanks," indicates an obligation, such as a debt to be paid. Paul felt bound to give thanks for the Thessalonians, not merely because that was the nice thing to do, but because it was debt he owed.

   This expression about being *bound* (or obligated) to give thanks is found only here and in II Thess. 2:13 in the whole N.T.

4. "As it is meet" (Gr., *axios*) means "as it is worthy," or "as it is fitting." The faith and love of the Thessalonians had weight and value that demanded an equal measure of thanks upon Paul's part. (The word *axios* means "of equal weight, of like value, worth as much." See notes on I Thess. 2:12, par. 4.)

5. The word translated "groweth exceedingly" (Gr., *huperauxano*) means "to increase beyond measure."

   The Thessalonians had grown much in their faith, as all Christians should. They had not lost their first love. Rather they had increased that love. We should ask ourselves if Paul could say the same thing about us that he said about the Thessalonians. For faith that does not grow usually shrinks.

6. In all of Paul's letters, except Galatians and Hebrews, Paul begins with a thanksgiving. We should likewise always express our thanks first, and then give our criticisms if we have any to offer.

7. We prefer to translate the word "charity" as "love." In modern times we think of *charity* as almsgiving and helping the poor. The Greek word *agape* used here means "love" rather than "almsgiving."

Text (1:4)

4 so that we ourselves glory in you in the churches of God for your patience and faith in all your persecutions and in the afflictions which ye endure;

Translation and Paraphrase

4. So (greatly has your faith and love grown) that we ourselves glory about you (expressing the pride and thanks that are due, when we speak) among the churches of God (telling them) con-

cerning your endurance and faith in all the persecutions and the afflictions which you endure.

Notes (1:4)

1. Paul was not a man to keep quiet about something good. He boasted about the generosity of the Macedonian churches to the Corinthians in II Cor. 8:1-5. Here he tells how he "gloried in" (1) the patience, and (2) the faith of the Thessalonians when he spoke to other churches.

   It is always an encouragement and a stimulus to Christians to hear of the good work of churches elsewhere. Ministers do wrongly if they do not advertise to their people about such things.

2. Note here that Paul speaks of the churches as "churches of God." This is the name most often used in the New Testament to describe local congregations. The name "church of God" is used in I Cor. 1:2; 11:22; 15:9; II Cor. 1:1; Gal. 1:13; I Thess. 2:14; II Thess. 1:1, 4; I Tim. 3:5, 15; I Cor. 10:32.

   The term "churches of Christ" is used in Rom. 16:16. We should be happy to be a part of a group called either a church of God or a church of Christ.

3. The word "patience" (Gr., *hupomone*) has the meaning of *steadfastness*; also of endurance and expectation of help and victory. A man, such as Job, who endures one blow after another without giving up his trust in God has "patience."

4. Paul had sent Timothy to Thessalonica to exhort them concerning their faith. I Thess. 3:2. This verse indicates that their faith was doing very well.

5. Paul mentions here their "persecutions and afflictions." The same expression is used in Mark 4:17 in the parable of the sower, to describe the influences that caused those sown on rocky ground to wither.

6. There is little difference in meaning between the words "persecutions" and "tribulations." "Persecution" refers to "pursuit" or "persecution." Tribulation (Gr., *thlipsis*) means "pressure" or "affliction." (See notes on I Thess. 3:3, par. 2.)

Text (1:5)

5 which is a manifest taken of the righteous judgment of God; to the end that ye may be counted worthy of the kingdom of God, for which ye also suffer;

Translation and Paraphrase

5. (You must never become discouraged in these sufferings, for your steadfastness is) an (obvious) evidence of the (fact that

there is a) righteous judgment of God (coming upon mankind). Your steadfastness in suffering, combined with God's righteous judgment, shall work out unto a happy result, namely) that you (shall) be judged worthy of the kingdom of God, for which (I know that) also you are suffering.

Notes (1:5)

1. We come now to the main point of II Thessalonians, chapter 1, the topic of God's righteous retribution. (See outline.)

   So often we see vice flourish and virtue perish. The Thessalonians probably wondered why they should be suffering persecution when they were trying to do the pure will of God. This problem of the prosperity of the wicked has always been perplexing to the righteous. Psalm 73 considers the problem. See also Job. 21:7-17. Many songs reflect on this matter, such as "We'll Understand It All By and By."

   In this chapter Paul, like the writer of Psalm 73, considers the "end" of those who are prosperous, comfortable, persecuting, and ungodly. There is a day of righteous retribution on God's calendar, and He will equalize all things. Until that day we must trust in God, having faith that He will do what is right.

2. What is the *manifest token* of the "righteous judgment of God"? Is it the "persecutions and tribulations" in 1:4, or is it the "patience and faith" in the same verse? Either view is possible, but we prefer the view that the "patience and faith" is the "manifest token."

3. This would seem to be suggested by the fact that "persecutions and tribulations" are plural nouns, while "patience and faith" and "manifest token" are all singular. Since "manifest token" appears to be in apposition to a previous term, it seems most likely that it would refer to a singular word (or words) like itself.

4. The term "manifest token" (Gr. *endeigma*) means "evidence, token, or proof." (Thayer) Rotherham translates 1:5: "A proof of the righteous judgment of God."

5. The patience and faith of Christians often suggest to sinners and persecutors the possibility of a divine origin of the Christian faith, and divine punishment for those who oppose it. It seemed to suggest this to Gamaliel. Acts 5:38-40.

6. A remarkable case of how the patience and endurance of Christians convinced a man of the righteous judgment of God is the case of Justin Martyr (103-162 A. D.). As a youth he sought to find rest for his troubled soul by studying the philosophers, but

found himself growing none the wiser with regard to God. He saw a good deal of persecution of Christians and admired the endurance they displayed. One night, while walking near the seashore, he met an aged Christian, with whom he conversed freely, and by whom he was convinced of the truth of Christianity. He spent his life seeking to win men to the gospel and writing articles to defend the faith. During the reign of Marcus Aurelius, he refused to obey a command to sacrifice to pagan idols. Hence he was condemned to be scourged, and then beheaded, which was executed with all imaginable severity.

To Justin, the patient endurance and pure faith of the Christians was a proof of the divine nature of their religion. In our times, the world is also looking for the proof in our lives that the gospel of Christ is true.

7. A related verse to I Thess. 1:5 is Phil. 1:28: "And in nothing (be) terrified by your adversaries: which is to them an *evident token* of perdition, but to you of salvation, and that of God." Note here again the thought that the patience and endurance of Christians is a proof to their adversaries that they are on the road to perdition (destruction) while the Christians are following the truth. They sense this, even if they won't face up to it, or do anything about it.

8. Often we hear people say that we can never be *worthy* of God's blessings. We ourselves believe as strongly as anyone that we are not saved by our own works of righteousness. Titus 3:5; Eph. 2:9.

But even so, this verse says that we "may be counted *worthy* of the kingdom of God," and indicates that being counted worthy is the result of our patience and faith as well as God's righteous judgment. So evidently it is wrong to say that a man can NEVER be worthy. (For the meaning of "worthy," Gr., *axios*, see notes on I Thess. 2:12, par. 4.)

This matter of being worthy is also emphasized in other verses. II Thess. 1:11: "that our God would count you *worthy* of this calling." Col. 1:10: "That ye might walk *worthy* of the Lord." I Thess. 2:12: "That ye would walk *worthy* of God." See also Rev. 3:4.

Let us freely admit that we are not saved by any works we do. But let us also realize that when once saved, Christians CAN and must live in a manner worthy of God. These facts do not contradict and exclude one another.

170

9. What is it that causes us to be counted worthy of the kingdom of God? Is it God's righteous judgment? Or is it our patience and faith? It is both. If either of these were lacking, we could not be counted worthy of God's kingdom.

10. The "kingdom of God" in this verse probably refers to the future and everlasting kingdom of God (as in II Peter 1:11) rather than to the church, which is also called the kingdom of God. Col. 1:13. It is a fact that God has already called us into the kingdom and glory. I Thess. 2:12. But it is also true that "through many tribulations we (Christians) must enter into the kingdom of God." Acts 14:22.

11. All Christians will suffer in some degree and manner. If we do not suffer, we shall not be judged worthy of God's kingdom. Compare Hebrews 12:7-8.

Text (1:6-7)

6 if so be that it is a righteous thing with God to recompense affliction to them that afflict you, 7 and to you that are afflicted rest with us, at the revelation of the Lord Jesus from heaven with the angels of his power in flaming fire,

Translation and Paraphrase

6. (We say that your endurance will work out to this happy result,) assuming (as we do) that it is a righteous (and therefore a predictable) thing on the part of God, to repay affliction to those who are afflicting you,

7. And (to repay) rest to you who are being afflicted (along) with us. (And this will be done) at the revelation of the Lord Jesus from heaven (when He comes) with his mighty angels.

Notes (1:6-7)

1. God is going to recompense (or repay) two things:
   (1) Affliction to those who afflict you.
   (2) Rest to you that are afflicted.

2. God has always repaid people according to their works. "Reward her even as she rewarded you, and double unto her double according to her works." Rev. 18:6; 20:12. Those who afflict will receive affliction. Those that take up the sword shall perish by the sword. Matt. 26:52. See Josh. 7:35. Who can doubt that it is a righteous thing with God to recompense affliction to those who afflict his people?

   Some people argue that God is too kind and loving to punish anyone. But the truth is that God could not be righteous and let sin and cruelty go unpunished. Those who cause you to suffer must be repaid for their wrongs if God is just and righteous.

171

3. There is a similarity in some words in 1:6-7 which is not brought out by the King James text, but is very plain in the American Standard Version:

"If so be that it is a righteous thing with God to recompense *affliction* to them that *afflict* you, and to you that are *afflicted* rest . . ."

Thus also the *New English Bible:*

"It is surely just that God should balance the account by sending *trouble* to those who *trouble* you, and relief to you who are *troubled.* (Copyright, Oxford University and Cambridge University, 1961)

4. We must leave to God the work of taking vengeance. Romans 12:19: "Vengeance is mine; I will repay, saith the Lord." This verse gives us encouragement that all sin will be justly punished, and also keeps in check our own poorly informed and poorly controlled instincts for punishing others.

5. Rest shall be given to the children of God when the Lord Jesus is revealed from heaven. Our eternal life is a time of *rest,* as well as service. Rev. 14:3: "Yea, saith the Spirit, that they may rest from their labours." Hebrews 4:9: "There remaineth therefore a *rest* for the people of God." We must work now. The rest will come later.

6. Rest (Gr., *anesis*) means a "loosing, relaxing, relief, rest." (Thayer). "The slackening of strings that have been pulled tight." (Preacher's Homiletic Commentary)

7. The parousia of the Lord is described in this verse as not only a "coming," but a "revelation" of the glory and judgment of the Lord. (For the meaning of *parousia,* see notes on I Thess. 2:19-20, par. 7.)

This word "revelation" (Gr., *apokalupsis*) means "an uncovering, a laying bare, instruction in things before unknown, manifestation, appearance." (Thayer) It is applied to the coming of the Lord in I Cor. 1:7; II Thess. 1:7; I Peter 1:7, 13; 4:13.

7. We notice that BOTH the rest and the tribulation which the Lord Jesus shall recompense will be given "at the revelation of the Lord Jesus from heaven."

This cancels out the idea that the saints will have been taken out of the earth to be with the Lord several years before Christ appears in glory to all mankind. For BOTH the saints and the sinners will receive their due recompense at the revelation of the Lord. The saints are not to receive their rest several years before the sinners get their tribulation, but both will receive what they have coming at the revelation of the Lord. (For more about this, see Special Studies II and IV on pages 242 and 247.

8. The Lord Jesus is to be revealed along with his mighty angels. Angels are indeed mighty; they even "excel in strength." Psalm 103:20. Numerous Scripture passages teach that the Lord will come with his angels, his holy ones (or saints). See Matthew 24:31; 25:31, and article IV in Appendix.

If one angel laid 185,000 Assyrians low in a single night, the coming of the angels should be terrifying to sinners. Isaiah 37:36.

Text (1:8)

8 rendering vengeance to them that know not God, and to them that obey not the gospel of our Lord Jesus:

Translation and Paraphrase

8. (For He shall be revealed) in flaming fire, giving (and rendering) vengeance upon them who (have not known and) do not know God, and upon them who disobey the gospel of our Lord Jesus.

Notes (1:8)

1. Christ will be perfectly just in taking vengeance on them that know not God. For people are not innocently ignorant. The peoples of the world do not know God, because they refused to have God in their knowledge. Romans 1:28. The heathen truly live in ignorance of the gospel. But they also live in definite rebellion against what little they do know of God and morality. By such law as they have written in their own hearts, they are condemned. Rom. 2:14-15; 3:9-10.

2. Jeremiah 10:25: "Pour out thy fury upon the heathen that know thee not, and upon the families that call not on thy name." See also Psalm 79:6.

3. When Christ is revealed from heaven, it will be a time of vengeance. The day of grace will have ended. The opportunity to obey and be saved will be past and gone.

4. The words, "in flaming fire," can refer either to the way that Christ shall be manifested when He comes, or to the manner in which He shall take vengeance.

In our paraphrase we have connected them with the way Christ shall be revealed. We have done this mainly because we know that sinners will not be sent into the eternal fire prepared

173

for the devil and his angels until AFTER the judgment. See Matt. 25:41; Rev. 20:15. This verse (and 1:7) does not so much refer to the events after the judgment as to the events connected with Christ's revelation in the clouds of heaven. This revelation will be with flaming fire. Of course, it will be followed by a fiery condemnation of sinners after the judgment.

5. Isaiah 66:15, 24: "For behold, the Lord will come with fire . . . neither shall their fire be quenched."

6. The presence of the Lord is often associated with fire and smoke. Thus at Mt. Sinai. Ex. 19:18. And at the burning bush. Ex. 3:2; And over the tabernacle. Numbers 9:15. See also Isa. 10:16-17; Nahum 1:5-6.

7. It is a fearful thing to face the fiery vengeance of the Lord. "There remaineth . . . a certain fearful looking for of judgment and *fiery* indignation, which shall devour the adversaries." Hebrews 10:26-27.

8. This verse makes powerfully plain the necessity for OBEYING the gospel. Truly it is needful to *believe* the gospel. But the gospel not only has facts to be believed and promises to be received, but commands to be obeyed. For a list of the commands to be obeyed in order to be saved, see notes on I Thess. 1:4, par. 5.

9. The word "obey" (Gr., *hupakouo*) basically means to listen or hearken. Rotherham brings out this force of the word in his translation: "And them who decline to hearken unto the glad-message of our Lord Jesus."

10. Paul warns that there shall be indignation and wrath to them that "do not *obey* the truth." Rom. 2:8. Compare Rom. 1:8; 16:26. Christ is the author of eternal salvation to all that *obey* him. Heb. 5:9. "Hereby do we know that we know him, if we keep his commandments." I John 2:3

11. The teaching of I Thess 1:7-9 about Jesus coming with his mighty angels, the flaming fire, etc., is frankly rejected by some theologians (or should we call them diabologians?). The *Interpreter's Bible* comments that the mighty angels, or angels of his power, the flaming fire, the glory of his might, all belong to the traditions of Judaism, and thus is a drapery of language. We accept these descriptions as the revelation of God, and not as some fictitious flight of words.

Text (1:9)

9 who shall suffer punishment, *even* eternal destruction from the face of the Lord and from the glory of his might,

Translation and Paraphrase

9. (These) who (are disobedient) shall pay the penalty (which is) everlasting destruction (in a place far) from the presence of the Lord, and from his (majestic and) powerful glory.

Notes (1:9)

1. How terrible to be forever away from the presence of the Lord: Every good and perfect gift comes from the Lord. James 1:17. All men on earth, even those who do not serve God, enjoy His blessings—His rain, sunshine, the gift of life, godly friends and loved ones, etc. How fearful to be forever banished from the Lord, where none of these blessings can ever come!

2. The punishments of sinners is described as "everlasting destruction." Because of this expression (and similar ones in other references), some have thought that the punishment will be an annihilation, a going out of existence, a being burned into nothingness. This is contrary to the meaning of the word "destruction," and to Scriptural teaching in other references. See Rev. 14:9-11; Mark 9:43-48; Matt. 25:41, 46.

3. The word here translated "destruction is *olethros*. It is used elsewhere in the New Testament only in I Thess. 5:3, I Tim. 6:9, and I Cor. 5:5. Lidell and Scott's definition of *olethros* is "Ruin, destruction, undoing." The word indicates total ruin, but not necessarily an end of existence or annihilation.

   In I Cor. 5:3, Paul speaks of delivering the incestuous man to Satan for the *destruction* of the flesh. In this life neither our literal flesh nor our fleshly instincts are ever totally annihilated. They are brought under control and subjugated, but not annihilated.

   I Tim. 6:9 Paul speaks of hurtful lusts drowning (present tense) men in destruction and perdition. (The present tense indicates a continuous action.) Since the destruction of sinners is said to be presently in the process of being accomplished according to this verse, it would seem to be wrong to say that "destruction" is limited to one irrevocable burning up in the lake of fire.

4. To further illustrate the meaning of *olethros* (or destruction), R. C. Foster (in THE FINAL WEEK, page 118) tells how the word was used by the Greek dramatist Sophocles in his play, "Oedipus Rex." Oedipus was a king who became enmeshed in the most hideous moral mess imaginable, and brought untold shame and misery upon himself. He even married his own mother. In the end of the play, Oedipus, instead of committing suicide, put

out his own eyes. Scholars agree that his tragedy was greater because he had to live on in the moral muck he had created than it would have been for him to have committed suicide and ended it all. Now quoting R. C. Foster:

"In the light of our discussion of eternal punishment, it is of startling importance to find that Oedipus in his agony cries out, 'I am the great olethros (ton megan olethron):' In other words, Oedipus is not saying that he is the great annihilation, but that he is the supreme example of endless suffering. Out of the midst of one of the most famous of all Greek dramas comes powerful evidence as to the meaning which this word carried." (Op. cit., p. 118)

5. "Everlasting destruction from the presence of the Lord" indicates that sinners are to be banished from the presence of the Lord forever. Goodspeed translates this verse as "eternal ruin and exclusion from the presence of the Lord." In Matt. 25:41, the doom of the wicked is to "Depart from me." The wicked are driven forever from His presence. On the other hand the saints are to be "ever with the Lord." I Thess. 4:17.

6. The glory of the Lord's power is vividly described in Deut. 33:2 and I Tim. 6:16. God dwells in light unapproachable. But sinners will not share this light. They will be in outer darkness. Matt. 25:30.

Text (1:10)

10 when he shall come to be glorified in his saints, and to be marvelled at in all them that believed (because our testimony unto you was believed) in that day.

Translation and Paraphrase

10. (This penalty to the disobedient shall be carried out) at the time when He (Jesus) shall come in that (great) day to be glorified (before all creatures of the universe for what He has accomplished) in (the perfecting of) his saints, and to be marvelled at (by all creatures because of what He has accomplished) in all (of you) who have believed, because our testimony was believed by you.

Notes (1:10)

1. While sinners should fear the return of Christ as the time when they will face everlasting destruction, Christ and his brethren,

the Christians, (Heb. 2:12) look forward to that day as a time of glorification.

2. The Thessalonian Christians looked forward to the Lord's coming as a day of glory, because they had believed the message of Christ which Paul preached. We cannot pass into the temple of glory without first passing through the temple of faith. In ancient Athens there were two temples, a temple of Virtue, and a temple of Honor. No one could enter the temple of Honor, except by passing through the temple of Virtue. (Preacher's Homiletic Com.) So also we shall not share Christ's glory, unless we have first believed the divine testimony.

3. Two things are to happen to Christ when He comes:
    (1) He is to be glorified in His saints.
    (2) He is to be marvelled at in all that believe.
    ("Marvelled" is a better translation than "admired.")

4. The expression, "to be glorified in his saints," may not seem very clear. It means (as we have given it in our translation and paraphrase) that Christ is to be glorified before all creatures of the universe (and by them) for what He has accomplished in the perfecting of His saints. When all creatures see the wonderful character which Christ has developed in His saints over the years, and see the glorious bodies in which He shall resurrect us, Christ will thus be glorified in His saints.

   Similar statements about people being "glorified in" someone are Gal. 1:24: "They (the churches) glorified God in me (Paul);" also John 14:13: "The Father may be glorified in the Son." See also John 17:10; 13:31.

5. The parenthetical phrase, "because our testimony among you was believed," is added to identify the Thessalonians with the believers who shall share the glorification of Christ. Abstract facts are often not interesting to us, but if we are personally involved in them, they become very interesting and important to us.

6. "That day" mentioned at the end of the verse is the day when He shall come, the day the Lord Jesus is revealed from heaven. In our translation we have placed the phrase, "in that (great) day," right after the words, "He shall come," to show that the day referred to is the day when He shall come.

Text (1:11-12)

11 To which end we also pray always for you, that our God may count you worthy of your calling, and fulfill every desire of goodness and *every* work of faith, with power; 12 that the name of our Lord Jesus may be glorified in you, and ye in him, according to the grace of our God and the Lord Jesus Christ.

Translation and Paraphrase

11. (Desiring greatly that our Lord may truly be glorified in you,) we pray always unto that (end) concerning you, (asking) that our God may count you worthy of the calling (which we have described), and (that He may) fulfill every good pleasure of (his) goodness (in His dealings with you), and (fulfill every) work of faith with power.

12. (We ask for these things) in order that the name of our Lord Jesus may be glorified in (the work and faith) you (show), and (that) you (in return shall be glorified) by (your fellowship with) Him, according to the (program of the) grace of our God and (our) Lord Jesus Christ.

Notes (1:11-12)

1. We call this prayer that closes chapter one a prayer for God's blessings. It has three petitions in it, and two purposes for the petitions:
   - (1) The petitions; 1:11
     - a. That God would count them worthy of the calling.
     - b. That God would fulfill all the good pleasure of His goodness.
     - c. That God would fulfill the work of faith with power.
   - (2) The purposes; 1:12
     - a. That the name of Jesus may be glorified in you.
     - b. That you may be glorified in him.

2. Have you ever prayed as Paul prayed here, that God would count certain people worthy of His calling? Have you ever prayed that God would fulfill the good pleasure of His goodness in the activities of some church.

3. The "wherefore" beginning vs. 11 literally means, "Unto that end," and refers back to Paul's statement in 1:10 about how Jesus will be glorified in His saints. Paul prayed always that Jesus would truly be glorified in the character and labors of the Thessalonians. Have you ever prayed that such holy character might be developed in your brethren that they would bring glory to Jesus?

178

4. Paul prayed that God would count them *worthy* of the glorious calling we have as Christians (or, more particularly, the calling of glorifying Jesus). This verse brings up again the matter of being *worthy*, which we mentioned in the notes on II Thess. 1:5, par. 8. It is wrong to say that we can never be worthy. God will count us worthy if we strive to attain the goal. (For the meaning of "worthy," see notes on I Thess. 2:12, par. 4.)

5. Then Paul prayed that God would fulfill in them all the good pleasure of His goodness. Knowing that God's goodness is unlimited, this is a GREAT request. "May God accomplish in you all that goodness would desire, and that faith can effect." (Preacher's Homiletic Com.)

6. It is not enough that we have good intentions of goodness. We must *fulfill* them with God's help. Good intentions without fulfillment are insufficient.

7. Then Paul prayed that God would fulfill the work of faith with power. Oh, how we long to see the POWER of God displayed! When we read of how God displayed His power on Mt. Carmel as Elijah called down fire on the Lord's altar, we are tempted to pray, "Lord, do it again!" We are not anticipating miracles of the type God showed to Elijah, but we long to see heart-heating, soul-saving, saint-stirring power in our churches. Maybe modern churches lack this power because they have not asked for it as Paul did here.

8. The conjunction "that" at the beginning of verse twelve indicates the purpose or end desired. In our translation, we have rendered it "in order that."

9. The purposes Paul had in mind in his prayer were that the name of our Lord Jesus may be glorified in us, and we be glorified in him. In the Bible a NAME is not merely a tag of identification, but it is descriptive of the person himself. Note Acts 4:12.

10. We cannot glorify the name of Jesus and be glorified ourselves by our own ability, but only according to the grace (or favor) of God. God supplies the ability and the grace.

11. Concerning how Jesus is to be glorified "in you," see notes on II Thess. 1:10, par. 4.

12. We shall be glorified by Jesus, because our association with Him gives us all the glories of holiness, obedience, immortality, and goodness which Jesus has. He is glorious. We shall be like Him. We are glorified by being in fellowship with Him.

13. Note that Jesus and God are on an equality as being the source of grace that will result in our glorification. Compare notes on I Thess 3:11, par. 4.

STUDY SUGGESTION—See if you can now answer the "Did You Learn?" questions that follow immediately.

DID YOU LEARN?

(Questions over II Thessalonians, chapter 1)

1. What is the topic of chapter one?
2. What men sent the second Thessalonian letter? (1:1)
3. What two things concerning the Thessalonians did Paul feel bound to thank God for? (1:3)
4. What is the meaning of the expression, "*bound* to give thanks"? (1:3)
5. For what two things about the Thessalonians did Paul "glory" in other churches? (1:4)
6. What is patience? (1:4)
7. Had the persecutions which the Thessalonians suffered early in their Christian experience subsided when Paul wrote II Thessalonians? (1:4)
8. According to the notes, what is the "manifest token of the righteous judgment of God"? (1:5)
9. What causes us to be counted worthy of God's kingdom? (1:5)
10. Is it Scriptural to speak of being *worthy*? (1:5)
11. Can God be righteous and yet repay tribulation to people? (1:6)
12. What will be recompensed to those who trouble us? (1:6)
13. What will God recompense to his children who are troubled? (1:7)
14. When shall God recompense these things? (1:7)
15. With whom will the Lord Jesus be revealed? (1:7)
16. To what do the words, "in flaming fire," in 1:8 refer?
17. How can Christ be just, and then take vengeance on them that know not God? (1:8)
18. With what visible thing is the presence of the Lord often associated? (1:8)
19. On what two classes of people will Christ take vengeance? (1:8)
20. What does the word "destruction" mean, and what does it not mean? (1:9)
21. "From" what shall the disobedient be punished? (1:9)
22. When shall Christ be glorified in his saints? (1:10)

23. Explain how Christ shall be "glorified in his saints." (1:10)
24. Why does Paul insert the parenthetical phrase, "because our testimony among you was believed"? (1:10)
25. What is the prayer in 1:11-12 called in the outline?
26. What were Paul's three petitions in the prayer? (1:11)
27. What were the two purposes of the petitions? (1:12)
28. Recite, or write out, from memory II Thess. 1:6-9. Verse 6 begins, "Seeing it is———."

II THESSALONIANS, CHAPTER TWO

Chapter Topic:

The Man of Sin

"There shall come a falling away first, and that man of sin be revealed." II Thess. 2:3

THINKING THROUGH THESSALONIANS

Chapter Topic: "The Man of Sin"

1. By (or concerning) what two things did Paul beseech the Thessalonians in chapter two? 2:1.

   _____

   _____

   _____;

   _____.

2. Paul lists three things by which they were not to be shaken or be troubled. 2:2. What were they?

   _____; _____; "_____ as from us."

3. They were troubled, thinking "that the _____ of _____ _____ was at hand." 2:2.

4. What two things must precede the day of Christ? 2:3. _____

   _____; _____

   _____.

5. The man of sin is called "the son of _____

   _____." 2:3.

6. The man of sin "_____ and _____

   _____ himself above all that is called _____ or that is worshipped." 2:4.

7. The man of sin sitteth in the _____ of God, showing himself that he is _____." 2:4.

8. True or false (circle which)—Paul mentioned the man of sin for the first time in this chapter. 2:5.

9. Concerning the man of sin, Paul says, "Now ye know what _____ that he might revealed in his time." 2:6.

10. What was already working in Paul's time? 2:7.

    _____

11. The man of sin would have appeared sooner, "only he who now letteth (that is, hinders) will let (hinder) until he _____ _____

    _____ _____ of the way." 2:7.

12. By what two means will the Lord destroy that Wicked one? 2:8. _____

    _____; _____

    _____.

13. The wicked one's coming is after the working of whom? 2:9.

    _____.

14. He comes with all _____ and _____ and

    _____. 2:9

15. He comes with all deceivableness of unrighteousness in them that _____. 2:10
16. These people perish because they _____ _____ the _____ of the _____. 2:10
17. What does God send these people because of their attitude? 2:11. _____ _____.
18. God sends these, "that they should _____ a _____." 2:11.
19. In what did these people who were deceived by the Man of sin take pleasure? 2:12. _____.
20. Paul was bound (obligated) to give thanks for the Thessalonians, "because God hath from the beginning _____ _____ you to _____." 2:13
21. Through what two things had God chosen them to salvation? 2:13. _____ _____; _____ _____.
22. By what were the Thessalonians called? 2:14. _____ _____.
23. To what had God called them? 2:14. _____ _____ _____ _____
24. "Therefore, brethren, _____ _____, and hold the _____ which ye have been taught." 2:15.
25. By what two means had they been taught? 2:15. _____; _____.
26. Unto whom did Paul pray? 2:16. (2 answers) _____ _____; _____.
27. What has God given us through grace? 2:16. (2 answers) _____ _____; _____.
28. Paul prayed that God would "_____ your _____, and _____ you in every good _____ and _____." 2:17.
29. Memorize II Thess. 2:3, 14.

II THESSALONIANS, CHAPTER TWO
Chapter Topic, *"The Man of Sin"*
Outline

I. Paul's entreaty about the Lord's coming; 2:1-3a.
  1. Matters involved; 2:1
    a. The coming of our Lord.
    b. Our gathering together unto him.
  2. Be not shaken or troubled; 2:2
    a. Things by which they might have been shaken;
      (1) Spirit.
      (2) Word.
      (3) Letter as from us
    b. The idea that left them shaken—Belief that the day of Christ had come.
  3. Certain events must precede the coming; 2:3a
    a. A falling away.
    b. Revelation of the man of sin.

II. The Man of sin; 2:3b-12
  1. He is the son of perdition; 2:3b
  2. He opposes and exalts himself; 2:4
  3. He will sit in the temple of God; 2:4
  4. Paul had warned them about him; 2:5
  5. He was being withheld; 2:6-7
    a. The mystery of iniquity was already working; 2:7
    b. One now hindered his appearance; 2:7
  6. He shall be revealed; 2:8
  7. The Lord shall destroy him; 2:8
  8. His coming is after the working of Satan; 2:9-12
    a. With all power, and signs, and wonders; 2:9
    b. With all deceivableness; 2:10
    c. He comes "in them that perish;" 2:10-12
      (1) They received not the love of the truth; 2:10
      (2) Gods sends them strong delusion; 2:10-11
        (a) So that they should believe a lie; 2:11
        (b) That they might be damned; 2:12
      (3) They had pleasure in unrighteousness; 2:12

III. Thanksgiving for God's choosing the Thessalonians; 2:13-15
  1. Chosen through sanctification of spirit; 2:13
  2. Chosen through belief of the truth; 2:13
  3. Called by the gospel; 2:14
  4. Therefore, stand fast; 2:15

IV. Prayer that they be comforted and stablished; 2:16-17

Text (2:1-2)

1 Now we beseech you, brethren, touching the coming of our Lord Jesus Christ, and our gathering together unto him; 2 to the end that ye be not quickly shaken from your mind, nor yet be troubled, either by spirit, or by word, or by epistle as from us, as that the day of the Lord is just at hand;

Translation and Paraphrase

1. But (now) we (must) beseech you, brethren, concerning the (second) coming of our Lord Jesus Christ, and our gathering together unto him (in the air).

2. (We beseech you) that you not (allow yourselves to) be quickly (blown about like waves and) shaken from your senses; neither (should you) be alarmed; (Do) not (be misled) by (anyone who says he has a revelation of the) Spirit, nor by (any) word (which you may have heard from us or anyone else), nor by (any) letter (which may be represented) as (coming) from us, (giving out the idea) as (if it were a fact) that the day of the Lord has already come.

Notes (2:1-2)

1. No Scriptural teaching has been more frequently abused than the teaching about the Lord's second coming. Men have spent enormous amounts of time trying to determine exactly when the Lord will return, even after the Lord has made it very plain that we have NOT been given that information. But when men have made predictions concerning exactly when the Lord is going to come, they have usually been successful in getting a group of deluded followers, who forsake the work they should be doing, and all of them go out to some isolated spot to meet the Lord, only to be disappointed when nothing happens.

2. The Thessalonians had likewise become greatly agitated about the Lord's coming. In fact some of them thought that the day of the Lord *had already come.* This certainly shows that they had a poor knowledge of what was going to happen at that time.

3. Our English text says that they were not to be shaken—"as that the day of Christ is *at hand.*" We might assume from this that they only thought that Christ's coming was very near. Actually the phrase "at hand" means "has already come." This translation (or a similar one) is given in the New English Bible, Moffatt, Goodspeed, Rotherham, Amplified New Testament, Revised Standard, etc.

(The Gr. verb is *enesteken,* a 3rd pers. sing. perf. ind. of *enistemi. Enistemi* occurs only seven times in the N.T. In six of those occurrences it is in some perf. form. A check of those references will show that *enistemi* in the perf. does not mean "near at hand," but it means "already present." See I Cor. 7:26; Heb. 9:9; Rom. 8:38; I Cor. 3:22; Gal. 1:4.)

4. This second chapter of II Thessalonians was written to remove misapprehensions on the subject of the Lord's coming. It reveals that the Lord is not to come until certain events have taken place first. These are:

    (1) A falling away (or apostasy) from the truth; 2:3

    (2) The removal of some power which hindered the manifestation of the man of sin; 2:6-7

    (3) The manifestation of the man of sin; 2:8

5. Note that in the outline chapter two is entitled, "The man of sin." By remembering that topic you will be able to recall what is in the chapter.

6. Notice that Paul entreated us "BY" the coming of our Lord Jesus Christ, and BY our gathering together unto him. (King James version). The word *by* in this verse is a very poor translation. The Greek word *(huper)* means "concerning" or "in behalf of." Paul besought the Thessalonians *concerning* the coming of the Lord, not *by* it.

    The reader who compares "beseech by" in II Thess. 2:1 with that in Rom. 12:1 (where the word is *dia,* not *huper*) will be led astray.

7. Notice carefully the two things about which Paul besought us:

    (1) The coming of our Lord Jesus Christ.

    (2) Our gathering together unto him.

    Observe that he associates these two things with the "day of Christ" (or the "day of the Lord," as it is given in the best manuscripts).

    Notice further that the Lord's coming and our gathering together unto Him are not to occur until there has been a falling away and the man of sin has been revealed. II Thess. 2:3.

    All of this leads us to say that the idea that the man of sin is to appear AFTER the church has been gathered out of the world cannot be true. Strangely this is a rather popular idea. But please observe carefully that our gathering together unto the Lord, etc. is not to happen until the falling away and the revelation of the man of sin have occurred FIRST.

8. Concerning the manner in which we shall be gathered unto the Lord, see notes on I Thess. 4:17. Also Matt. 24:31 and Mark 13:27.

9. It is quite evident from Paul's words in II Thess. 2:2 that the Thessalonians (or at least some of them) were highly wrought up about this matter of the Lord's coming. Paul urges them not to be "shaken" or "troubled." These are strong words. "Shaken" (*saleuo*) sometimes refers to the motion of winds, storms, waves. It is used in Acts 16:26 to tell how the prison was shaken. "Troubled" (*throeo*) is also a strong word, meaning "to frighten, alarm, trouble." (Thayer). It is the same word as the Lord used in Matt. 24:6, warning the disciples not to be troubled about wars and rumors of wars.

10. Paul mentions three possible sources of this wrong teaching that the day of the Lord had already come:

(1) Spirit—This probably refers to some person who claimed to have a revelation of the Spirit. There were men with spiritual gifts such as prophecy in the Thessalonian church. I Thess 5:19-20. Compare I John 4:1.

(2) Word—This could refer to many things, such as a misinterpretation of something Christ Himself or Paul had said.

(3) Letter as from us—Some suppose that this refers to a forged letter represented as coming from Paul. Some think it refers to a misunderstanding of what Paul had said in his earlier letter.

The fact that Paul closes this letter (3:17) with the notation, "The salutation of Paul with mine own hand, which is the token in every epistle: so I write," rather hints that there may have been a false letter pretending to have come from Paul.

However, McGarvey thinks that the "letter as from us" was only a misapplication of what Paul said in his first epistle. He argues that it is unlikely that Paul would have failed to rebuke such a forgery if one existed. Paul even scolded them for forgetting what he had said before. II Thess. 2:5. How much more would he have exposed a forgery.

Probably the truth of the matter is that Paul himself was not sure what was the source of this idea that the day of the Lord was already come. If he were not certain about the source of this idea, how can we be?

11. Some interpreters try to make a distinction between "the day of Christ" (as some ancient manuscripts word this verse) and the "day of the Lord" (as others give it). Surely this is a distinction without a difference, since Christ himself is the Lord. (For more concerning "the day of the Lord," see notes on I Thess. 5:2, par. 5.)

Text (2:3)

3 let no man beguile you in any wise; for *it will not be*, except the falling away come first, and the man of sin be revealed, the son of perdition,

Translation and Paraphrase

3. Let no one deceive you (about this) by any method, because (that day shall not come) except (or until) the apostasy (a departure from the faith) come first, and the man of lawlessness be revealed, (he who is) the son of perdition (the man devoted to eternal misery).

Notes (2:3)

1. Have these two things—the falling away, and the man of sin—yet happened? If they have not, then the Lord cannot come until they do. If they have already appeared, then we can look for the Lord at any time. We believe that these two things have long ago appeared.

2. Paul's teaching in this verse does NOT indicate that he had changed his mind about the Lord's coming from views he had once held. Some allege that Paul had earlier said that Christ's coming was near, but that he had changed his mind by the time he wrote this to think that the second coming was far off. In II Thess. 2:5 Paul reminds them that even when he was with them he had told them the same things that he here writes about. Paul had not changed his teachings. The Thessalonians had simply forgotten what he said, or perhaps it never penetrated their minds in the first place.

3. This "falling away" (Gr., *apostasia*) refers undoubtedly to a religious falling away. Another word for "falling away" is "apostasy." *Apostasia* is always used in the Greek Old Testament (Septuagint) in the sense of a religious falling away. See Josh.

190

22:22. II Chronicles 29:19; 33:19; Jer. 2:19. Thayer defines *apostasia* as a "falling away, defection, apostasy." The word is found elsewhere in the N.T. only in Acts 21:21, where it might be rendered "apostasy from Moses." All of this causes us to think that the "falling away" predicted by Paul is a falling away from the faith as taught by Christ and the apostles.

4. This verse speaks not of *a* falling away, but of *the* falling away. It is a particular apostasy which Paul has in mind.

Matthew 24:10-12 tells of a falling away which was to precede the destruction of Jerusalem by the Romans. See Matt. 24:15-16. But it is not the same apostasy to which Paul refers in II Thess. 2:3. We mention Matt. 24, because when some people read that chapter, they fail to observe carefully when Jesus spoke about the destruction of Jerusalem and when he talked about the end of the world. Because of this careless interpretation, they often take passages that clearly pertained to the destruction of Jerusalem (such as 24:6-12) and apply them to the conditions at the end of the world.

5. The identification of the man of sin is probably as controversial a matter as anything in the Bible. Paul had given the Thessalonians teaching about the man of sin which we have not heard, and the matter may have been much clearer to them than to us.

6. We prefer to call the man of sin "the man of lawlessness," in accordance with the reading of the Greek text of both Nestle and Westcott and Hort. Both of these have *anomia* (lawlessness) in the text and *hamartia* (sin) in the margin.

The name, "man of lawlessness," matches up with the phrase, "mystery of lawlessness," in II Thess. 2:7. The "man of lawlessness" (Gr., *anomia*) is obviously the crowning height of the "mystery of lawlessness" (or "mystery of iniquity" as the King James text gives it).

7. A "man of lawlessness" would be a man who was not subject to any law. The American Standard version of I John 3:4 says, "Sin is lawlessness." This well describes the mind of the sinner. He refuses to be subject to any law, human or divine. Thus "the man of lawlessness" will be that person who, above all others, is not subject to the law of God, but obeys only his own desires.

8. The expression, "son of perdition," means (according to Thayer) "a man doomed to eternal misery." This same description is ap-

191

plied to Judas in John 17:12. "Perdition" *(apoleia)* means "destruction" or "waste" (as in Mark 14:4). Like the word *olethros* used in II Thess. 1:9, it does not imply annihilation.

9. When we speak of the "man of lawlessness," our minds frequently connect him with "antichrist" mentioned in I John 2:18, 22; 4:3; II John 7. However, the Bible does not specifically connect them, and any connection that we might make between the two would have to be regarded as only speculation. We hear lots of preaching about THE antichrist. But John makes it rather clear that antichrist is not one supremely evil person, but that anyone who denies that Jesus is the Christ or that He came in the flesh is antichrist. There were antichrists even in John's time. Many modernist preachers and scholars who deny our Lord's deity should rightfully be called antichrist. But we stand on very shaky support when we teach that there will be some one particularly terrible ANTICHRIST in the future.

10. There are several general schools of interpretation concerning what the "falling away," "the man of sin," and "that which hinders" are.

   a. Some just frankly disregard the whole business. In the *Interpreter's Bible,* in the exposition of this section, the view is given that as dwellers in the twentieth century, with its deliverance from much theological ignorance and medieval superstition, we feel superior to any such conception of antichrist as possessed Paul and the Thessalonians. Those who believe that Paul was an inspired apostle of Christ can not, of course, have any such opinions as this.

   b. Some think the man of sin is the papacy

   c. Some think the man of sin is the Roman emperor and the mystery of lawlessness is the Roman empire. It is a fact that some of the Roman emperors demanded worship and exalted themselves just as the man of sin was to do. II Thess. 2:4. Caligula in 39 or 40 A.D. tried to set up his statue in the temple in Jerusalem as an object of worship. But none of the Roman emperors perfectly fulfilled Paul's description of the man of sin. Hence, this interpretation does not seem to be the right one.

   d. Some think that the mystery of lawlessness is Judaism,

192

and that the man of sin is some leader in that faith. By this view that which hinders would be the Roman empire.

    e. Some think that the man of sin is Antichrist, a future world dictator who will rule during a brief period between the taking of the saints out of the world and the thousand years of Rev. 20:3-4. We shall discuss this view more fully in the notes that follow.

    f. Some say he is (or was) Hitler, Stalin, Khrushchev, or some other person.

11. The two interpretations held by most Bible-believers are the futurist (or pre-millenial) view and the historical view. We want to discuss these interpretations more fully.

I. THE FUTURIST (or pre-millenial) view.

(This view is held by many devout Christians in our times.)

    A. View summarized.

        1. The *falling away* refers to the ungodly conditions to exist in the world shortly before the Lord returns. Many people consider that present world conditions are the fulfillment of this prophecy of the "falling away."

        2. The *man of sin* is the Antichrist, one individual, who is to be a world dictator and rule AFTER Christ has taken the church out of the world at the "rapture." He will be almost an incarnation of Satan. Some think he will be a Jew (basing this idea on Daniel 11:37, although the meaning of that verse is far from certain). He will supposedly rule the world during the great tribulation to last seven years after Christ had taken the church to himself.

        3. *That which hinders* the appearance of the man of sin is the Holy Spirit. It is argued that the Holy Spirit is he who restrains evil in this world, and that when Christ takes the church out of the world at the rapture that the Holy Spirit will no longer be in the world in the degree in which He is during the church age, and that evil will run almost unrestrained, and incredible suffering will result to mankind.

B. Arguments for this view

    1. "The fathers of the early church, for at least three centuries after the apostolic age, while differing on some minor details, seemed unanimous in understanding that the *man of sin* was not a system of deceit and wickedness, or a succession of individuals at the head of such a system, but some one man, the living personal Antichrist, the incarnation of Satan craft and energy, who should put forth his power to weaken and destroy the church." (Preacher's Homiletic Com.)

    2. We certainly are living in perilous times, a time when men have fallen away from the old-fashioned faith and virtues, a time like those described by Paul in II Tim. 3:-5 where he describes the "last days." In our times atheistic communism is laboring to the utmost to rule the world, by force if possible, and by subversion, infiltration, and propaganda if force cannot be used. As this book is written Communist governments rule nearly half of the world's population, and no country on earth has escaped the poison of Communist influence.

    Religiously the world is also in a desperate state. Men have religions of every kind, but deny the power of true faith. Churchmen seem more interested in federating denominations than in the faith. They are more interested in this present life than in men's eternal salvation. The World Council of churches seems to be working toward forming a powerful super-church to include everyone who is religious, regardless of what he believes. Some think that this religious monster will join forces with Antichrist. Old-fashioned Bible believers are mocked in many churches and theological seminaries. But I am still proud to be one.

    Christians must keep themselves informed about these things that are going on. Only if Christians *know* what is going on and *stand up* for Christ and his kingdom will our country, or even civilization, endure. Christians, God shall bruise Satan *under your feet* shortly. But if you don't know anything about

Satan's activities, and don't stand for anything, God won't be able to use you to bruise Satan. Romans 16:20.

C. This view is not absolutely the only possible one.

1. What we have said about world conditions is only a speck of the mountain of dirt that we could sweep up about our times. But it is still hotly debatable that conditions in our times are worse than they were in the early centuries of Christianity. Moral conditions were as bad then, or worse, than now. (See our notes on I Thess. 4:1-3, and Introductory Section VI, par. 11.). Christianity was persecuted as much or more in the early centuries as it is now.

2. Also the ungodly conditions which Paul said would exist in the "last days" (II Tim. 3:1-5) have existed ever since Paul wrote those words. For we have been living in the "last days," or last dispensation, ever since the day of Pentecost. (Acts 2:17.)

3. Also it is not necessary to interpret the "man of sin" and the "falling away" as being events which are limited to a short period immediately before (and after) Christ returns. Certain Scriptures and facts almost compel me to think that the "falling away" and the "man of sin" have both been with us for a long time already.

II. THE HISTORICAL view.

(This view is the one favored by the author of this book.)

A. View summarized.

1. The *falling away* refers to that corruption of the apostles' teaching by heathenism which occurred during the early centuries of the church and resulted in the development of the Roman Catholic religion. This apostasy is still in progress, as Rome is still adding new doctrines to its creed. And the false doctrines developed during the falling away have been adopted by many Protestants, as well as by the Roman church.

2. The *man of sin* probably refers to the papacy, the visible, personal head of the "falling away."

3. *"That which hinders"* the appearance of the man of sin (II Thess. 2:6-7) probably was the Roman gov-

ernment. For several centuries the Roman government held in check the attempts of power-hungry Roman bishops to take control of both the spiritual affairs of men and the political authority as well.

We do not expect you to accept our opinions about these matters just because we have stated them bluntly. But we do ask you to study seriously the reasons for holding these views.

B. Arguments for this view.

1. The "mystery of lawlessness" (2:7) which resulted in the falling away and the appearance of the man of sin, was *already at work* in Paul's time.

That being so, surely then Paul could not have been referring to things that would not happen until the nineteenth and twentieth centuries when he spoke of the "falling away."

There are numerous references in the New Testament which show that false doctrines, unauthorized power grabs, etc. were already developing. See Jude 4, III John 9, Acts 20:29-30, II Pet. 2:1, Col. 2:8. These seem to be a part of the developing "mystery of lawlessness."

2. In I Tim. 4:1-3 Paul told how some would depart from the faith. They would forbid to marry, and command to abstain from meats, etc. This is a clear prophecy of such things as the Roman church practices when it forbids its priests and nuns to marry and forbids its members to eat meat at certain times.

In describing this departure from the faith, Paul used the verb form *apostesontai*. This is a form very similar to the word *apostasia*, the word translated "falling away" in II Thess. 2:3. This similarity of language causes us to associate the "falling away" with Romanism and not with twentieth century Communism or other evils of our times.

3. In Daniel chapter two, Daniel prophesied about four great world empires—the Babylonian, Persian, Grecian, and Roman. After those empires the God of heaven would set up a kingdom (which we understand

to be the church. See Special Study V.) Gods kingdom would never be destroyed, nor should the sovereignty of it be left to another people. (Dan. 2:44 R.V.)

It appears to us that if some Antichrist is going to rule the world, that Daniel's prophecy would have to be wrong in indicating that there would only be four empires before God's kingdom should prevail and fill the earth. (Dan. 2:35)

4. Note that the "falling away" and the "man of sin" are associated with the *"mystery* of iniquity" in 2:7. The use of this term *mystery* suggests that there may be a connection with Rev. 17:5, where the great harlot is given the name "MYSTERY." This mystery woman in Revelation is ROME. For she is identified as that city that sits on seven mountains (or hills) and rules over the kings of the earth. Rev. 17:9, 18). Rome is the only city on earth that fulfills those descriptions.

5. The "falling away" which occurred over the years and produced the Roman Catholic religion is the greatest "falling away" of all ages. We list here a *few* of the many departures from the New Testament faith, which, when all taken together, surely must be THE falling away:

  (1) Bishops take authority over elders (Presbyters) Second century.

  (2) Infant "baptism" first mentioned—About 150 A.D.

  (3) Many heathen rituals—candles, incense, robes, etc.—added to Christian worship—third century.

  (4) First human creed (Nicene)—325 A.D.

  (5) Christianity made the sole state religion—394 A.D.

  (6) Mary entitled "Mother of God"—431 A.D.

  (7) Confession of sins to a human priest—About 457 A.D. Made compulsory in 1215 A.D.

  (8) Lord's supper became a mass (sacrifice) and masses for the dead became frequent—Sixth century.

  (9) The pope gains universal authority—About 606 A.D.

      (10) Transubstantiation—1215 A.D.

      (11) Indulgences—About 1164 A.D.

      (12) Adoration of images legalized—About 800 A.D.

      (13) Tradition made equal to the Scriptures—About 1545 A.D.

      (14) Apocryphal books added to Bible—1546 A.D.

      (15) Purgatory—Originated in the tenth century. Made official 1438.

      (16) People deprived of the cup in communion— About 1414.

      (17) Celibacy promoted (405 A.D.) and enforced (1123 A.D.)

      (18) Sprinkling authorized—1311.

      (19) Immaculate conception of Mary—1854.

      (20) Infallibility of the pope—1870.

      (21) Assumption of Mary into heaven—1950.

6. The papacy fulfills the descriptions of the man of sin. He sits in the temple of God, showing himself that he is God. The papacy consists of one official man. He came into power as a result of the falling away from the New Testament faith. (For more about how the papacy fulfills the description of the man of sin, see notes on the verses that follow, II Thess. 2:4-7.)

Text (2:4)

4 he that opposeth and exalteth himself against all that is called God or that is worshipped; so that he sitteth in the temple of God, setting himself forth as God.

Translation and Paraphrase

4. (The man of lawlessness will be a man) who (both) opposes and exalts himself above all that is called divine or that is religiously honored, so that he (shall) sit in the temple of God, exhibiting himself (as if it were true) that he is God.

Notes (2:4)

(For the general discussion of the falling away and the man of sin, see notes on 2:3.)

1. Here is a summary of the descriptions of the man of sin:

    (1) He opposes all that is called God.

    (2) He exalts himself above all that is called God or that is worshipped.

198

(3) He is to sit in the temple of God.

(4) He exhibits himself as if he were God.

(5) His appearance was hindered by some force that already existed in Paul's time. 2:6-7.

(6) The mystery of iniquity, which led to his appearance, was already working in Paul's time. 2:7.

(7) He will continue in existence till the Lord Jesus comes. 2:8.

(8) The Lord shall destroy him with the brightness of his coming. 2:8.

(9) He shows power, signs, and lying wonders (false miracles). 2:9.

(10) He comes with all deceivableness of unrighteousness. 2:10.

2. Both of the verbs—"opposeth" and "exalteth"—have as their object "all that is called God, or that is worshipped." The man of sin opposes the true God and His Christ, and exalts himself above them.

3. "All that is called God" refers to anything, or anyone, who is divine and is of God—to heaven, to God Himself, to the Lord Jesus, to the word of God, the Holy Spirit, etc.

4. The expression, "that is worshipped," comes from the Greek *sebasma.* From this word came Sebastus, or Augustus (the Worshipful), which was the title of the Roman emperors. "A man of that age could hardly see this word in such a connection without thinking that Paul meant to convey the idea that the antichrist would arrogate to himself all the reverence then claimed by the great civil lords of the earth such as emperors, kings, etc." (McGarvey). Today men bow down before the pope in the same manner that men used to bow down before kings.

5. What is the *temple* of God in which the man of sin is to sit? Some say that this refers to the temple of God which was in Jerusalem. However, no such great pretender as the "man of sin" ever sat in the temple in Jerusalem before it was destroyed by the Romans in 70 A.D.

It seems to us that the temple of God to which Paul refers must be the church. The term *temple* is a favorite name of Paul's for the church. Notice I Cor. 3:17; II Cor. 6:16; Ephesians 2:12.

If the temple of God is the church, then the Roman popes very fully fulfill the description of the man of sin. For they sit in the church and are religious lords.

It is hard to see how the man of sin could be an atheistic communist, and still sit in the temple of God and represent himself as God.

6. Numerous men in the history of the world have taken to themselves the honor of being as great as God.

The heart of the prince of Tyre was lifted up, and he said, "I am a God; I sit in the seat of God." Ezekiel 28:2.

King Herod (Agrippa) set himself forth and accepted acclamation of being God. Acts 12:22.

The popes have called themselves by titles as great (or greater) than those of God. Note this title which has been used: "Our Lord God the Pope, another God on earth——doeth whatsoever he listeth, even things unlawful, and is more than God."

Text (2:5)

5 Remember ye not, that, when I was yet with you, I told you these things?

Translation and Paraphrase

5. Don't you remember (how) that when I was still with you, I kept telling you these (very) things?

Notes (2:5)

1. This little verse has surely been included in the sacred Scriptures to blast forever out of existence any idea that Paul at one time said that the Lord was going to come very quickly, and then that he later decided that the Lord was not going to come for a long time.

2. It is a serious thing to charge that Paul changed his mind and wrote one teaching in one place in his letters and another teaching in another place. If Paul changed his mind, he could not have been writing a message that God revealed to him. For God does not change. Malachi 3:6. If Paul did not write the message that Christ revealed to him, then much of our Christian faith rests on nothing but the quicksand of human wisdom. For much of our Christian doctrine rests on the writings of Paul.

3. While Paul had been with the Thessalonians, he "kept telling" them these very things about the coming of the man of sin and the falling away. (The imperfect tense here indicates repeated action in the past.)

Text (2:6-7)

6 And now ye know that which restraineth, to the end that he may be revealed in his own season. 7 For the mystery of lawlessness doth already work: only *there is* one that restraineth now, until he be taken out of the way.

Translation and Paraphrase

6. And now you (Thessalonians) know what it is that is hindering (the appearance of the man of lawlessness, and is causing things to work out) so that he may be revealed in his own (divinely appointed) time.

7. (It should be obvious to you that such a man of lawlessness is coming) for the hidden scheme (and program) of lawlessness is already at work. Only, he who alone is now hindering (the appearance of the man of lawlessness will continue to hinder) until he be (gone) out of the midst (of us).

Notes (2:6-7)

1. There was some force in existence in Paul's time which was hindering the appearance of the man of sin. Phillips translation puts it this way: "You will probably also remember how I used to talk about a 'restraining power' which would operate until the time should come for emergence of this man."

2. The word "withholdeth" in 2:6 is the same Greek word which is translated "let" in 2:7. This is a bad rendering for modern readers. The words is both instances mean "to hinder, hold back, restrain." (Note our translation and paraphrase for this meaning.)

3. The Thessalonians probably knew a lot more clearly that we do what was "withholding" the appearance of the man of sin. Paul had told them more clearly than it has been told to us. But while we do not have the information they had, we do have much history behind us, by which we can often see the manner of God's dealings.

4. If something in Paul's time was withholding the coming of the man of sin, surely the man of sin could not be some twentieth century individual.

5. It is noteworthy that in verse six the restraining power is described as *neuter*. But in verse seven, it is *masculine*, "*he* who alone is now hindering."

   This probably indicates that the restraining power is *both* an abstract force and a personal figure. The restraining authority would be neuter, but the personal force masculine, indicating two aspects of the same power and authority.

6. Note that God had a specific time designated on His divine calendar of events in which He would permit the appearance of the man of sin. Nothing happens by accident in this world. God may let some men run pretty wild, but He still holds the reins, and no one can get so far out of hand as to defeat His program.

7. The "mystery of iniquity" (or "mystery of lawlessness") refers to the hidden programs and scheme of the devil and lawless men.

   This mystery of iniquity was already at work in Paul's time. Many New Testament references indicate that a falling away from the truth was already developing in apostolic times. See I John 4:1,3; Jude 3; I John 2:18-19; II John 7, etc.

8. The "mystery of lawlessness" in 2:7 is evidently a part of the same ungodly system that produced the "man of lawlessness," mentioned in 2:3. The mystery of lawlessness seems to be the antithesis of God's saving mystery in Christ. Eph. 3:3,9.

9. The King James version says, "Until he be *taken* out of the way." The word *taken* is not actually in the Greek text. It is probably better to render it as in our paraphrase, "Until he be (gone) out of the midst (of us)." The Scripture does not say that God himself was going to *take* out the restraining power, but that eventually it would be out by some means or other.

10. What is this force that restrained the appearance of the man of sin. For some ideas about this, see notes on 2:3, par. 10.

    Some interpreters feel that the Holy Spirit is He who hinders the appearance of the man of sin. Isa. 59:19 is quoted to support this view. However, it is pure speculation to say that the influence of the Holy Spirit is to be withdrawn out of the earth as long as it shall stand. No Scripture actually says this. Also we wonder why the Holy Spirit should restrain this particular evil, that is, the appearance of the man of sin. Evil in many forms is rampant now, and certainly needs to be hindered.

11. We prefer the view (as stated in our notes on 2:3) that the restraining power was the *Roman empire*.

    During the first three hundred years of the history of Christianity it was a persecuted illegal religion. This fact hindered any power-hungry "Christian" bishop from assuming a lot of authority.

    In the years that followed the adoption of Christianity as the state religion (325 A.D.), emperors like Constantine and Theodosius considered themselves not only to be head of the state, but head of the church as well. For example, Constantine called the council of Nicea to settle the dispute about the nature of Christ.

    In the fourth century as the barbarians began to invade the Roman empire, it became weaker and weaker, and its emperors became less and less strong.

In those times many of the bishops of Rome were strong-willed, capable men. Gradually the Roman bishops came to have more power and the. emperors less. The Roman bishops were further strengthened when the capital of the Roman empire was transferred to Constantinople in the East.

Leo the Great, bishop of Rome 440-461 A.D., greatly strengthened the authority of his office. On two occasions he saved Rome from being sacked, first by Atilla the Hun, and secondly by Genseric the Vandal. In return for such services the Roman emperor gave Leo authority over the bishops and churches in every province.

The Western Roman Empire fell in 486 A.D., and this gave the Roman bishops almost a free hand in Europe.

Bishop Gelasius (492-496) contended that although the king rules over men in the world, yet he is duty bound in spiritual things to submit to his religious prelates.

Later Roman bishops, such as Gregory the Great (590-604) formed alliances with civil rulers in the West, as well as emperors in the East.

While some strong emperors occasionally resisted the popes for many centuries, the popes became so strong that kings (such as Charlemagne) received their crowns from the hands of popes, and the popes sometimes commanded people in various countries to disobey their kings when the kings would not submit to the authority of the Roman church.

12. Maybe we are wrong, but all of this history which we have mentioned, and a lot more like it, sounds to us like a description of what Paul was talking about when he prophesied about the appearance of the man of sin after the power that hindered him had gone.

13. McGarvey lists nine ways in which the papacy fulfills the prophecy about the falling away and the appearance of the man of sin:

   (1) It has one official man at its head, and the arrogancy of its claims are centered in him.

   (2) That man came with, and out of, an apostasy, the very kind of an apostasy such as Paul describes elsewhere. II Tim. 3:1-9; I Tim. 4:1-3.

   (3) The spiritual pride, lawlessness, and desire for power which worked in Paul's day was curbed by the Roman civil government which dominated and persecuted.

(4) When the bishop of Rome began to assert power, he was in conflict with the civil government.

(5) When the Roman empire collapsed, the Roman church became all-powerful.

(6) The same apostasy has been preserved carefully. The line of popes has been preserved, and will apparently be continued until Christ returns.

(7) The papacy exalts itself against God and Christ, taking unto itself titles which God alone has the right to wear.

(8) The popes sit in the temple of God.

(9) The papacy proves its claims by fraudulent miracles, signs, and wonders, cures effected by relics and shrines. See notes on II Thess. 2:9, par. 3.

Text (2:8)

8 And then shall be revealed the lawless one, whom the Lord Jesus shall slay with the breath of his mouth, and bring to nought by the manifestation of his coming;

Translation and Paraphrase

8. And then the lawless one shall be revealed, whom the Lord Jesus shall take away by the spirit (or blast) of his mouth, and do away with by the (shining) appearance of his coming.

Notes (2:8)

1. The man of sin will suffer a complete ruin at the coming of the Lord. With all the evil and false religion that there is in this world, Christians would be very disheartened if it were not for their confidence in the Lord's return.

2. The Wicked one (or man of sin) was to be revealed when the one that had been hindering his appearance was taken out of the way. See the notes on II Thess. 2:6-7.

3. The Lord Jesus will destroy the Wicked one with the spirit of his mouth. The expression, "spirit (or breath, or blast) of his mouth," refers to the power of the presence of Jesus. It does not mean that Jesus shall destroy the man of sin by converting his followers. The word "breath" does not signify God's truth or instruction, but the execution of his judgment. (See Special Study VI, question 3.)

Numerous references in the Bible contain the expression, "breath of his mouth," or similar phrases. Isa. 11:4: "With the breath of his lips shall he slay the wicked." See also Job 4:9; II Sam. 22:16; Isa. 30:27-28, 33. They all describe the execution of God's judgment.

4. The word "Jesus" in our translation of 2:8 is included on quite

strong evidence in the ancient manuscripts. Nestle's Greek and numerous English versions include it.

5. Apparently the Wicked one will continue to exist until the Lord comes, for the Lord shall destroy him with the brightness of his coming. Chapter eighteen of Revelation tells how the great city Babylon (or Rome) will be destroyed. While we do not long to see men perish, nor do we long for vengeance on anyone, we do long to see God's truth be victorious.

6. This verse speaks of the "brightness of his (the Lord's) coming." Rotherham translates this phrase, "the forthshining of his Presence."

   Certainly, since the Lord is going to be revealed from heaven in flaming fire (II Thess. 1:7-8), and in great glory (Matt. 24:30), His coming will be bright and overpowering.

   The same word which is translated "brightness" here *(epiphaneia)*, is translated "glorious appearing" in Titus 2:13: "looking for . . . the glorious appearing of the great God and our Saviour, Jesus Christ." See also I Tim. 6:14.

7. Again in this verse we have the word *parousia*. (See notes on I Thess. 2:19, par. 7 for its meaning.) Here the Lord's parousia (presence or coming) is connected with the destruction of the man of sin. In I Thess. 4:15 the parousia is connected with the resurrection and taking up of the saints.

   All of this leads us to repeat once more that the Thessalonian epistles rule out the idea that Christ is coming one time to take his church out of the world, and then will come again (a third time) with his church to punish sinners, and set up His kingdom. There is only one parousia of the Lord, and at the parousia the saints will be resurrected and caught up and the man of sin will be destroyed.

Text (2:9)

9 *even he,* **whose coming is according to the working of Satan with all power and signs and lying wonders,**

Translation and Paraphrase

9. (This one whom the Lord Jesus shall do away with is he) whose coming corresponds to the activity of Satan (who does his work) with every (kind of) power, and signs, and false miracles (wonders of deceit).

Notes (2:9)

1. There is nothing more plainly taught in all the Bible than that Satan does miracles. Miracles in themselves do not prove that the miracle-worker is doing God's will.

    a. The magicians in Egypt did miracles and changed their rods into serpents. Exodus 7:11-12; II Tim. 3:8. Undoubtedly these were miracles of Satan.

    b. Deut. 13:1,3: "If there arise among you a prophet or a dreamer of dreams, and giveth thee a sign of a wonder . . . thou shalt not hearken unto the words of that prophet."

    c. Matt. 24:24: "For there shall arise false Christs and false prophets, and shall shew great signs and wonders, insomuch that, if it were possible, they shall deceive the very elect."

    d. Matt. 7:22: "Many will say to me in that day, Lord, Lord, have we not . . . in thy name done many wonderful works? And then will I profess unto them, I never knew you: depart from me, ye that work iniquity."

    e. See also Rev. 18:23; 13:13; 19:20.

2. Think of all the religions that try to prove they are of God by the miracles they claim to do—Roman Catholic, Christian Science, Pentecostal, etc. They teach doctrines that contradict one another, but all try to prove they are of God by working (or claiming to work) miracles. But the miracles in themselves just do NOT prove that they are of the truth.

3. Since we have set forth the view that the falling away and the man of sin (mentioned in 2:3) are connected with the Roman Catholic religion, it is interesting to note how the Roman church is almost built on claims of miracles. Every time a dead man is proclaimed a "saint," there must be evidence (?) brought forth that he (or she) did at least two miracles. The shrines of Romanism (such as the one at Lourdes, France) attract thousands of pilgrams, many of whom go away saying they are healed. We read about Catholics who have spontaneously bleeding wounds (stigmata) in the places where Christ was wounded on the cross. We are told that the bread and wine miraculously change into the very flesh and blood of Christ during the mass. But why say more? Remember the apostle of Jesus Christ, Paul, warned us about "power and signs and lying wonders."

4. Of course the miracles of Christ and his apostles were genuine, even if Satan works false miracles. Acts 2:22; II Cor. 12:12.

5. There is little difference in meaning between the words, "signs" and "wonders." The term "wonders" (Gr., *teras*) is always in the plural in the N.T. and always joined with the word "sign."

6. Both the American Standard Version and the King James correctly assume that the "coming" referred to in 2:9 is the coming of the Wicked one, and not the same as the "coming" mentioned in 2:8, which is Christ's coming.

7. It is Satan's delight to counterfeit the things of God. Thus the man of sin is a counterfeit of Christ. They have several points of resemblance and contrast.

JESUS	THE MAN OF SIN
1. Has a "coming." I Thess. 2:19	1. Has a "coming." II Thess. 2:9
2. Did miracles. Acts 2:22	2. Does miracles. II Thess. 2:9
3. Is God. Heb. 1:8	3. Sets himself forth as God. II Thess. 2:4
4. Is over the house (or temple) of God. Heb. 3:6	4. Sits in the temple of God (as a usurper). II Thess. 2:4
5. Shall be glorified. II Thess. 1:10	5. Shall be destroyed. II Thess. 2:8

Text (2:10)

10 and with all deceit of unrighteousness for them that perish; because they received not the love of the truth, that they might be saved.

Translation and Paraphrase

10. And (his manner of coming is just what you might expect. It is in keeping) with every (form of) deceit (that is within the ability) of unrighteousness. (He comes particularly) to the lost, because they have not (welcomed nor) received the love of the truth that they might be saved (and therefore they are easily deceived by the doctrines of the man of sin).

Notes (2:10)

1. Two things are stated about the "coming" of the Wicked one, the man of sin:
   (1) He comes with all power, and signs, and lying wonders. 2:9.
   (2) He comes with all deceivableness of unrighteousness. 2:10.

2. We have talked to numerous people who have gone off into some cult or strange doctrine. Many of these people have told us, "I had been a member of several churches, and I tried to understand the Bible, but I just never was satisfied unto I went into my present belief."

3. Perhaps the reason that they were not satisfied was that they

207

had been fed on denominational teaching, rather than actually on what the Bible says. Such doctrines as (1) that we are saved by faith *alone,* or (2) that "one church is just as good as another," or (3) that "everybody is going to heaven; we are just going there by different routes," are enough to make anybody dissatisfied if he has studied the Scriptures with understanding.

A person will surely be more than satisfied with his faith, if he will do these things:

(1) Believe in Jesus as God's son and your only Lord and savior.

(2) Take the Bible as your only authority.

(3) Repent and be baptized (immersed) for the remission of sins, as the Holy Spirit commanded. Acts 2:38.

(4) Call yourself a Christian, or a disciple of Christ, but don't wear any denominational names invented by men.

(5) Consider yourself a member of ONLY that divine church to which the Lord adds all saved people. Acts 2:47. If Paul and the early Christians could be members of the Lord's church without belonging to any denomination, we also can do it and should.

(6) Be faithful in worship, telling others about your faith, giving your money, prayer, and the study of God's word.

4. Still there are people who have known the truth, but are restless and desire to know things that God has not revealed. They are always looking for something novel and spectacular, something that will make them feel that they are superior to their brethren. They long to be the "enlightened ones," the gnostics. This is a dangerous attitude of mind, and often causes them to accept some outlandish doctrine.

We should have an attitude such as David had when he said, "Lord, my heart is not haughty, nor mine eyes lofty: neither do I exercise myself in great matters, or in things too high for me." Psalm 131:1.

5. The "deceivableness of unrighteousness" means "the deceit which unrighteousness uses." Unrighteousness will use any trick to win followers. Unrighteousness uses half-truths, the pressure of business and friends, appeals to pride, brainwashing, and any other method that will obtain our support.

Because Christians are harmless as doves, they sometimes mistakenly assume that others have the same straight-forward, good-intentioned spirit that they themselves have. Unfortunately that is not the case. Hence we must not only be as harmless as doves, but as wise as serpents. Matt. 10:16.

6. This verse mentions "them that perish." These people are also called "them that are lost." (The word here translated "perish" *(apollumi)* in the middle voice means "to be lost.")

Thus we read in II Cor. 4:3-4 that, "If our gospel be hid, it is hid to them that are *lost:* in whom the God of this world (Satan) hath blinded the minds. . ."

Text (2:11-12)

11 And for this cause God sendeth them a working of error, that they should believe a lie: 12 that they all might be judged who believed not the truth, but had pleasure in unrighteousness.

Translation and Paraphrase

11. And on account of this (attitude) God sends to them (through the working of Satan some) activity of error to cause them to believe the lie (that what the man of sin says is true, and many other lies also).

12. (And thus being led to believe the lie that they actually wanted to believe, things are worked out) so that they all may be condemned, (those dissatisfied souls) who did not believe the truth, but (on the contrary) were well pleased with unrighteousness.

Notes (2:11-12)

1. This thought may astound some people, but the Scriptures actually teach that when men refuse to accept what God plainly says, that God sends delusion to them, that they may believe a lie and be condemned.

2. There are numerous examples of this in the Bible.

   (1) God hardened Pharaoh's heart and caused him to suffer many plagues, because Pharaoh first hardened his own heart. Exodus 3:19; 5:1-2; 7:3, 13.

   (2) God hardened the hearts of the wicked inhabitants of Canaan, so that they would fight Joshua and be destroyed. Joshua 11:20.

   (3) God sent a lying spirit to the prophets of Ahab, so that Ahab would go into battle and be killed. I Kings 22:19-23. (Of course, Ahab had long before rejected Jehovah.)

   (4) God turned the Gentiles who refused to honor Him as God, over to a reprobate mind, to do those things which were horribly evil and self-destructive. Romans 1:28.

   (5) Likewise now the lie of the man of sin comes to those who will not receive the love of the truth. Beware.

3. These verses bring out the point that when people believe a lie, they will be damned. How then can anyone dare to say, "It makes no difference what you believe as long as you are sincere"?

209

4. Those who reject the gospel of Christ, His miracles, and His coming, often end by adopting superstition and believing some strange and unproven system of doctrine. He who refuses to receive the truth will at last believe lies. This is an unalterable reality. Almost any minister can tell of cases in his own experience where people rejected the gospel, and then later were taken in by some cult or sect.

5. The exceeding wickedness of sin is often not appreciated by the sincere child of God. He judges the feelings of others by his own nature which has been sanctified by the Spirit of God. But we must not permit ourselves to live in a dream world. Sin is very ugly, and very strong, and very deeply rooted. What it can do to the nature of a man is astounding.

   The practice of sin even causes men to take pleasure in unrighteousness. They are proud to be wicked. Their glory is in their shame. Such people deserve to be damned.

   They refuse to have God in their knowledge and try to suppress God's truth by unrighteousness. They know the judgment of God, that people who do such things are worthy of death. But they not only do those things, but take pleasure in associating with others who do them, and in encouraging others to practice them. Romans 1:18, 28, 32.

6. One group of men who refused to believe the truth was the Jews. They could never refute Paul's preaching, but they refused to obey it, and even forbade Paul to preach to the Gentiles so that they might be saved. I Thess. 2:16.

   Paul told Timothy that men would turn away their ears from the truth, and be turned unto fables. II Tim. 4:4. Such people often end up following some strange doctrine.

7. While sinners may have pleasure in unrighteousness, love rejoices not in unrighteousness, but rejoices in the truth. I Cor. 13:6. Christians are ruled by love.

STUDY SUGGESTION

Turn ahead now to the "Did You Learn?" questions following the notes on this chapter, and see if you can answer questions 1 to 45.

Text (2:13)

13 But we are bound to give thanks to God always for you, brethren beloved of the Lord, for that God chose you from the beginning unto salvation in sanctification of the Spirit and belief of the truth:

Translation and Paraphrase

13. But we are obligated to give thanks to God always for you,
brethren beloved by the Lord, because (you have received the
love of the truth and escaped the strong delusions, and) God
has chosen you (from the beginning to be) firstfruits unto salvation, by means of the sanctification of (our) spirit (which is
done by the Holy Spirit), and (by) belief of the truth.

Notes (2:13)

1. This verse is much consolation to us. In the preceding paragraph we considered the terrors of the man of sin, and the strong
delusions that are sent to those who will not believe the truth.
Now Paul reassures the Thessalonians, and all other true Christians, that they are beloved of the Lord, and that God has
chosen them unto salvation. They are not deceived by delusions.
They are beloved by the Lord.

2. In our outline we have called this brief paragraph "Thanksgiving for God's choosing the Thessalonians." (2:13-15).

3. From the beginning God has chosen and foreordained that some
of the Gentiles should be saved. God chose the Gentiles who accepted Christ as his people. See Ephesians 1:4; 3:5-6; Romans
9:24-26. See also the notes on I Thess. 1:4.

4. This verse begins much like II Thess. 1:3: "We are bound (that
is, obligated or indebted) to give thanks always to God for you."
See notes on II Thess. 1:3 for further comment.

5. Note that we are chosen unto *salvation*. Oh, the joy of that
word. It means safety, deliverance, and security.

6. Two means are set forth as being the cause of our being chosen:
    (1) Sanctification of spirit.
    (2) Belief of the truth.

7. There is a bit of uncertainty about the Greek text of this verse.
The phrase, "from the beginning" (Gr., *ap' arches*), is given as
"firstfruits" (Gr., *aparchen*) in Nestle's Gr. text. Westcott and
Hort's Gr. text has "from the beginning" in the text and "firstfruits" in the margin. As you can tell, there is only one letter
of difference in the two renderings. The division between the
words proves nothing, as in the old Greek manuscripts there
were no breaks between any of the words.

   I find no English version (except Moffatt) inserting the word
"firstfruits" into the text, although several have it in the margin. On the whole I think we are justified in saying that the

King James version is as accurate as any in rendering it "from the beginning."

8. What is "sanctification of the Spirit"?

This phrase is also used in I Peter 1:2: "Elect according to the foreknowledge of God the Father, through *sanctification of the Spirit,* unto obedience and sprinkling of the blood of Jesus Christ."

The word "sanctification" itself means "a making holy, consecration, purification." See notes on I Thess. 4:3.

Let us note first of all that the Greek text does not say, "Sanctification of *the* Spirit." The word "the" is not included. However, by common consent of scholars the omission of the *the* does not rule out the possibility that the spirit referred to is the Holy Spirit. But the absence of the article does make it possible that the spirit may *not* be the Holy Spirit.

Thus there are two possible interpretations of the phrase "sanctification of the Spirit:"

   (1) A sanctification wrought by the Holy Spirit. (Subjective genitive). This is the view of Thayer and A. T. Robertson.

   (2) A sanctification of our human spirit. (Objective genitive). This view is favored by Moffatt and Lenski. Moffatt translates the phrase, "By the consecration of your spirit."

Lenski objects to the idea of the subjective genitive ("sanctification by the Holy Spirit") and says that the fact that God, i.e. his Spirit, does the sanctifying work need not be stated, for this lies in the word "sanctification," which is in itself a term that expresses action. It is our "spirit" that God sanctifies, just as it is "truth" that our faith trusts.

According to either interpretation, it is the Holy Spirit that does the sanctifying. But we personally favor the view that it is our spirit that is sanctified (the objective genitive). II Cor. 7:1 lends support to this view. "Let us cleanse ourselves of all filthiness of flesh and *spirit.*" Obviously the human spirit is meant there. So also I Thess. 5:23, where Paul prayed that our whole *spirit* and soul and body would be sanctified.

Text (2:14)

14 whereunto he called you through our gospel, to the obtaining of the glory of our Lord Jesus Christ.

Translation and Paraphrase

14. Unto which (salvation) he (has) called you by our gospel
(which we preach), to (bring you unto that glorious day when
we shall rejoice in) the obtaining of the glory of our Lord Jesus
Christ (as our bodies are resurrected and transformed to become like his glorious body).

Notes (2:14)

1. What is it "whereunto" God has called us? He has called us
unto the whole program of being saved through sanctification of
spirit and belief of the truth. (The genders of the Greek words
indicate that no specific antecedent is in mind.)

2. Often people speak about being *called* by God through various
means. The Scriptural method of being called is to be called *by
the gospel*. Compare Romans 8:29-30.

3. The goal to which God has called us is that we may obtain the
glory of our Lord Jesus Christ.

     a. We become like Christ as we live the Christian life. II Cor.
        3:18: "But we all, with open face beholding as in a glass
        the glory of the Lord, are changed into the same image
        from glory to glory, even as by the Spirit of the Lord."

        As a man and woman who are married for many years
        come to resemble one another, so we come to resemble
        Christ as we live with Him.

     b. When the dead are resurrected, we shall be transformed to
        be like God and Christ, and our worthless bodies shall be
        made anew like Christ's glorious body.

        Phil. 3:21: Christ "shall change our vile body, that it
        may be fashioned like unto his glorious body."

        I John 3:2: "We know that he shall appear, we shall be
        like him: for we shall see him as he is."

        Romans 8:21 tells how the whole creation longs for the
        manifestation of the sons of God (the Christians), for the
        creation itself shall be then delivered from the bondage of
        corruption into the glorious liberty of the children of God.

        Romans 8:17: "If we suffer with him, we shall also be
        glorified with him."

3. If you have ever admired and marvelled at Christ (as I'm sure
you have), rejoice that you may share His glory.'

Text (2:15)

**15 So then, brethren, stand fast, and hold the traditions which ye were
taught, whether by word, or by epistle of ours.**

Translation and Paraphrase

15. Therefore then, brethren, stand (solidly) and hold fast the teachings which ye were taught, whether by (our spoken) word or by our letter.

Notes (2:15)

1. If the Thessalonians did not stand fast in the traditions that they had been taught, they would soon be in the condition of those who loved not the truth, and were deceived by delusion. See 2:10-12.

   We likewise must stand fast in what we have been taught. We cannot be revamping the gospel message in each generation to suit ourselves.

2. We must mention again the use of that beautiful term, "brethren." Christians ought to address one another as "brother" or "sister."

3. The command, "Stand fast," is very emphatic. It enjoins us stand firm, persist and persevere. Compare I Cor. 16:13; Gal. 5:1.

4. The reference to "traditions" in this verse might give some people the idea that the church today should have spoken traditions as a guide as well as the written word. This is the Roman Catholic position.

   A Catholic booklet entitled "A Catechism For Inquirers" says, "Where is God's revelation to man contained?" The answer given is that "God's Revelation to man is contained in the Bible and in Tradition." It asks another question: "Where else, then, is God's Revelation contained?" Answer: "It is contained in Tradition, i.e. in the living word of Christ and His apostles, which was not written down by them." (The booklet here refers to II John 1:12 and II Thess. 2:14 as proof of their statement.) Another question from the same book asks, "Where is this Tradition to be found?" Answer: "This Tradition is to be found chiefly in the writings of the Fathers of the Church of the first centuries of Christianity, in the decrees of the Church Councils, in the decisions of the Popes, and in the ceremonial of the Church."

5. It is a fact that the early church depended partly on oral teaching. But it is a mistake to allege that the gift of inspired oral teaching has been preserved by the "Church." By the close of Paul's life he wrote to Timothy and said, "All Scripture is given by inspiration of God . . . that the man of God may be *perfect*,

throughly furnished unto *all* good works." II Tim. 3:16-17. If the Scriptures alone can make us perfect, and thoroughly furnished unto ALL good works, we do not need any other traditions.

6. Furthermore, there is a grave danger that we may fall into the same condemnation that the Jews received because they added human traditions to the laws of God. Jesus said, "In vain do they worship me, teaching for doctrines the commandments of men." Matt. 15:9. Also note Mark 7:9: "Full well ye reject the commandment of God, that ye may keep your own tradition."

7. The only apostolic traditions we now have are those in the Scriptures. This was not true of the Thessalonians. They had oral information, and at the time Paul wrote to them very few of the New Testament books had been written.

8. Paul declared that if anyone preached a gospel different from what he preached, he was to be accursed. Gal. 1:8-9. Paul told us that when we *read,* we may understand his knowledge of the mystery of Christ. Eph. 3:4. Let no one be misled or intimidated by people who claim to know more of God's will than the apostles have left for us in the New Testament. Often we see things practiced by people who follow their traditions that are contrary to what we read in the Bible. Surely any tradition that contradicts what the New Testament says cannot be a tradition approved by God.

9. Let us stand fast, and hold the apostolic traditions as we have been taught. The Thessalonians had been taught by word of mouth. We haven't. Both we and the Thessalonians have been taught by Paul's letters. Let us hold fast to these teachings.

Text (2:16-17)

16 Now our Lord Jesus Christ himself, and God our Father who loved us and gave us eternal comfort and good hope through grace, 17 comfort your hearts and establish them in every good work and word.

Translation and Paraphrase

16. Now may our Lord Jesus Christ himself, and God our father, who has loved us and given (us) everlasting consolation and good hope by (his) favor,

17. May he comfort your hearts and strengthen (you) in every good work and word.

Notes (2:16-17)

1. There is quite a contrast between the eternal destruction awaiting the sinner (II Thess. 1:9), and the everlasting consolation

which the Christian has. God's consolations are eternal in their effects.

2. These verses form the second of the prayers that close every chapter in II Thessalonians. In our outline, we call this a prayer that they be comforted and stablished.

3. There is no thought in the gospel message more precious than the thought that God loves us. Rev. 1:5: "Unto him that *loved* us and washed us from our sins in his own blood." I John 4:19: "We love him, because he first loved us."

4. Notice the close relation of God and Jesus. Both of them give us everlasting consolation. Both of them are asked to comfort and stablish the Thessalonians. Paul addresses his prayer to both. We do not honor God by placing Jesus second. They rank together. See John 5:23.

5. We so often need spiritual consolation. Paul prayed, "The Lord . . . comfort your hearts."

6. We have good hope from God, and our hope comes through His *grace*, that is, His favor. Our hope does not rest on our own works or our own merit. Because our hope rests on His favor, and because His favor is as high as the heavens, our hope is very sure.

7. In this prayer we sense Paul's anxiety for the Thessalonians. He was burdened greatly, desiring that they would become established firmly in the faith. "Stablish" means to make stable, set firmly, set fast, strengthen, make firm. (Thayer)

8. An anxious spirit, such as Paul's finds relief and comfort in prayer. Every minister must emphatically be a man of prayer.

9. We notice that both our words and our works must be established. What we say and what we do must both be right in the sight of God. "By thy words thou shalt be justified and by thy words thou shalt be condemned." Matthew 12:3.

STUDY SUGGESTION

Turn now to the "Did You Learn?" questions that follow, and see if you can answer questions 46 to 63.

DID YOU LEARN?
(Questions over II Thessalonians, chapter 2)

1. What is the topic of II Thessalonians, chapter 2?
2. What idea had greatly excited the Thessalonians? (2:2)
3. Concerning what two things did Paul beseech the Thessalonians? (2:1)

4. Did the Thessalonians think that the day of the Lord was near or already here? (2:2)

5. What three events were to precede the day of the Lord? (2:1-2)

6. What three sources of misinformation does Paul list as possibly causing the excitement? (2:1-2)

7. Explain what each of these three sources of misinformation may refer to.

8. What is another word for "falling away"? (2:3)

9. From what would people fall away? (2:3)

10. Did Paul predict "the" falling away or "a" falling away? (2:3)

11. The man of sin is also called the man of _____
    _____. (2:3)

12. What does the phrase "son of perdition" mean? (2:3)

13. Who is called the "son of perdition" in the gospels? (2:3)

14. Does the Bible specifically connect the man of sin and antichrist? (2:3)

15. According to the futurist (or pre-millenial) view, what is (1) the falling away, (2) the man of sin, and (3) that which hinders the appearance of the man of sin? (2:3)

16. Did the early church fathers regard the man of sin as being one man, or a succession of men at the head of a system? (2:3)

17. Are moral conditions in the world worse now than they were in Paul's time? (2:3)

18. How long have we been living in the "last days"? (2:3)

19. According to the historical view (favored in this book), what is (1) the falling away, (2) the man of sin, and (3) that which hindered the appearance of the "man of sin"? (2:3)

20. True or false (circle which)—The mystery of lawlessness was already working in Paul's time. (2:3,7)

21. Mention several departures from the New Testament faith which might be part of the "falling away." (2:3)

22. What two things does the man of sin do toward all that is called God? (2:4)

23. Where shall the man of sin sit? (2:4)

24. What does he exhibit himself to be? (2:4)

25. What is the "temple of God" where the man of sin sits? (2:4)

26. Name some people who have exhibited themselves as if they were God. (2:4)

27. How do you know that Paul did not once tell the Thessalonians that Christ's coming was very near, and then later say that certain things had to happen first? (2:5)

28. What kept the man of sin from appearing long before he did appear? (2:6)

29. What is the relationship between the word "withholdeth" in 2:6 and "let" in 2:7? What do these words mean?

30. Is the force that restrained the man of sin an abstract force or a personal figure? (2:6-7)

31. Explain the phrase "mystery of iniquity." (2:7)

32. What is the restraining power, according to the view favored in this book? (2:7)

33. Explain how this restraining power hindered the appearance of the man of sin. (2:7)

34. List four ways in which the papacy fulfills the descriptions of the man of sin. (2:7)

35. How will the wicked one be destroyed? (2:8)

36. Is there one parousia of the Lord when He takes his church out of the world, and then another parousia when He will destroy the wicked one? (2:8)

37. Does miracle-working power prove that a man is pleasing to God? (2:9)

38. The coming of the Wicked one is after the working of whom? (2:9)

39. Was the man of sin to work miracles? (2:9)

40. What does the phrase "deceivableness of unrighteousness" mean? (2:10)

41. Unto (or "in") what people does the Wicked one come? (2:10)

42. What do these people refuse to receive? (2:10)

43. What does God send to people who will not receive the love of the truth? (2:11)

44. Give two examples where God sent delusions to people so that they might believe a lie and be damned. (2:11-12)

45. In what did the people who did not believe the truth take pleasure? (2:12)

46. Had the Thessalonians received the strong delusions and believed a lie? (2:13)

47. What is the brief paragraph, 2:13-15, called in the outline? (2:13)

CHAPTER TWO

48. Unto what had God chosen the Thessalonians and the other Gentile Christians? (2:13)

49. What are the two possible interpretations of the phrase "sanctification of the Spirit"? (2:13)

50. Through what other means (besides sanctification of spirit) had God chosen the Thessalonians? (2:13)

51. By what means had God called the Thessalonians? (2:14)

52. What is the goal to which God has called us? (2:14)

53. Which were the Thessalonians to do: (1) Stand fast; or (2) Search out the will of God for their own generation? (2:15)

54. What were the Thessalonians to hold fast? (2:15)

55. By what two means had they been taught? (2:15)

56. Why do we believe that the church now has no oral traditions that should be added to the writings of the apostles? (2:15)

57. In the outline what is the prayer in 2:16-17 called?

58. To what two people is this prayer addressed? (2:16)

59. God has given us everlasting _____
_____. (2:16)

60. Through what have we been given good hope? (2:16)

61. Did Paul feel that the Thessalonians were established firmly in the faith? (2:17)

62. In what two things did Paul pray that they would be established? (2:17)

63. Quote or write out from memory II Thess. 2:3, 14. 2:3 begins, "Let no man——." 2:14 begins, "Whereunto he——."

II THESSALONIANS, CHAPTER THREE

Chapter Topic:

Withdraw from Idlers

"Withdraw yourselves from every brother that walketh disorderly
——for——there are some——working not at all." II Thess.
3:6, 11

THINKING THROUGH THESSALONIANS
Chapter Topic: "Withdraw From Idlers"

1. Paul asked for prayer that the word of the Lord might do what? (3:1) (Two answers) _____
   _____ ; _____ .

2. Paul requested prayer that he might be delivered from _____
   _____ and _____ men. (3:2)

3. Who is always faithful? (3:3) _____ .

4. What will the Lord do for us? (3:3) (two answers) _____
   _____ ; _____
   _____ .

5. True or false (circle which)—Paul had confidence that the Thessalonians would do what he commanded them. (3:4)

6. Into what two things did Paul pray that God would direct the hearts of the Thessalonians? (3:5) _____
   _____ ; _____
   _____ .

7. What did Paul command the Thessalonians to do toward disorderly brethren? (3:6) _____ .

8. The disorderly brethren did not walk after (or according to) the _____ which they received of Paul. (3:6)

9. Whose example should the Thessalonians have followed? (3:7)
   _____ .

10. Paul did not eat any man's bread _____
    _____ . (3:8)

11. When did Paul work, so that he might not be chargeable to any of them? (3:8) _____ .

12. Yes or No (circle which)—Paul had power (or authority) to ask the Thessalonian Christians to support him, so that he would not have to support himself. (3:9)

13. Why did Paul labor as he did? (3:9) _____
    _____ .

14. What had Paul commanded them? (3:10) _____
    _____
    _____ .

15. The disorderly brethren among the Thessalonians were _____
    _____ not at all, but were _____
    _____ . (3:11)

16. Paul commanded the disorderly that with quietness they _____ _____ and _____ their _____ _____. (3:12)
17. "Brethren, be not _____ in _____ _____ _____." (3:13)
18. Paul told the Thessalonians that if any man would not obey this epistle to "note that man and _____ _____ _____ _____ with him." (3:14)
19. Why were they to do this? (3:14) _____ _____.
20. Nonetheless, they were not to count him as an _____ _____. (3:15)
21. Paul calls the Lord, "The Lord of _____." (3:16)
22. What did Paul pray that the Lord would give them? (3:16) _____.
23. Who personally wrote the salutation of this epistle? (3:17) _____.
24. What was the taken of every genuine epistle of Paul's? (3:17) _____ _____.
25. What did Paul pray would be with all of them? (3:18) _____ _____ _____.
26. Memorize II Thess. 3:1,3,10.

II THESSALONIANS, CHAPTER THREE
Chapter Topic, *"Withdraw From Idlers"*

Outline

I. Request for prayer; 3:1-2
   1. That the word may run and be glorified; 3-1
   2. That they may be delivered; 3:2
II. Expressions of confidence; 3:3-5
   1. In the Lord; 3:3,5
      a. He is faithful; 3:3
      b. He will stablish you.
      c. He will keep you from evil.
      d. Prayer that the Lord would direct them; 3:5
         (1) Into the love of God.
         (2) Into the patience of Christ.
   2. In the Thessalonians; 3:4

III. Withdraw from idlers; 3:6-15
    1. The command; 3:6
    2. Paul's example of working; 3:7-9
       a. Behaved not disorderly; 3:7
       b. Worked night and day; 3:8-9
    3. This command taught previously; 3:10
    4. The report concerning idlers; 3:11
    5. Idlers commanded to work; 3:12
    6. Be not weary in well doing; 3:13
    7. Withdrawal to produce shame; 3:14-15
IV. Prayer for peace; 3:16
Conclusion; 3:17-18
    1. Paul's own salutation; 3:17
    2. Benediction of grace; 3:18

Text (3:1)

**1 Finally, brethren, pray for us, that the word of the Lord may run
and be glorified, even as also** *it is* **with you;**

Translation and Paraphrase

1. (Finally) brethren, for the future (please) be praying for us,
that the message of the Lord may run (without ceasing) and be
glorified (in the lives of many people) just as (it) also (does)
among you.

Notes (3:1)

1. How often Paul asked for prayer. (See notes on I Thess. 5:25,
par. 1.) Do you ever pray for preachers and missionaries? They
are only men. They need your prayers.
2. Notice how unselfish Paul's prayer was. He did not ask for
prayers for his own ease, but only that the word of God may
make progress.
3. Please recall now the chapter topic of chapter three, "Withdraw
from idlers," and recall point I in the outline of chapter 3, "Request for prayer" (3:1-2).
4. The word "finally" does not necessarily indicate a conclusion,
but only a new phase of discussion which does happen here to
be the closing one. (The Greek is *to loipon,* "for the future,"
"what remains," "hereafter," "henceforth," "for the rest.")
5. Note that the gospel is the "word of the Lord," and not the
"wisdom of men."
6. Paul speaks here of the word of the Lord as living and moving.
Compare Heb. 4:12. Also Psalm 147:15. The word of God is
not a dead writing, but a dynamic living power.

7. The gospel needs free course. It can be hindered by opposition and sometimes almost stopped altogether. A runner could not make very good time running in a junk yard. Satan likewise makes the path of the gospel a real obstacle course. But prayer can clear out the obstacles.

8. How different this verse sounds from popular denominational expressions. Men say, "Pray for a great moving of the Spirit." Paul said, "Pray that the word of the Lord may run and be glorified." (Amer. Stan. Vers.)

9. Paul compliments the Thessalonians by indicating that the word of the Lord had free course in their hearts. This was a deserved compliment. But it is one that can easily be lost. We cannot rest on past laurels. The word of God must continue its course in our hearts without letup.

Text (3:2)

2 and that we may be delivered from unreasonable and evil men; for all have not faith.

Translation and Paraphrase

2. And (please pray also) that we may be delivered from perverse (men, such as are out of their divinely appointed place and manner of life) and (from) evil men. For (it goes without saying that) the faith is NOT (held) by all (people. And these unbelieving men would hinder us if they could).

Notes (3:2)

1. Paul did not ask for prayer merely to escape hardship and persecution. Compare II Thess. 3:1. He wanted to be delivered from the restraint that wicked men would impose on his preaching.

2. Everywhere Paul went he faced "unreasonable and wicked men," such as he described here. In fact he was facing such men in Corinth at the time this letter was written. See Acts 18:6, 12.

3. The word translated "unreasonable" (Gr., *atopos*) means "out of place, not befitting, unbecoming, improper, wicked unrighteous." (Thayer). The Amplified New Testament renders it "perverse" and the New English Bible as "wrong-headed." (We like that rendering.)

4. It has always been true that "all men have not faith." Those without faith are not to be relied on without caution. They often plot and persecute in an attempt to hinder the preaching of the gospel. Even Jesus would not commit himself to men, because he knew all men, and knew what was in man. John 2:24-25.

225

5. Some people will never believe, no matter how clearly and tenderly the gospel is preached to them. We can only pray that we may be delivered from such men.

Text (3:3-4)

3 But the Lord is faithful, who shall establish you, and guard you from the evil *one*. 4 And we have confidence in the Lord touching you, that ye both do and will do the things which we command.

Translation and Paraphrase

3. But (though there are many men who have no faith,) the Lord is (always) faithful. (It is he) who will strengthen (and make) you (firm in the faith) and (will) keep you from (Satan) the evil one.

4. And we have confidence in the Lord concerning you (knowing that the Lord works within us all,) that you both (now) do and will (continue to) do the things which we command you.

Notes (3:3-4)

1. Men may be naturally wicked and actively engaged in evil against us, but the Lord is faithful. He will keep us from evil (or from the evil one). He that is within us is greater than he that is in the world. I John 4:4.

2. Paul prayed in II Thess. 2:17 that God would stablish them. Now in this verse he expresses confidence that God would do that very thing. (See notes on II Thess. 2:16-17 for more about being "stablished".)

3. Many verses in the New Testament teach us that the Lord will keep Christians from evil. These are precious promises.
   a. Jude 24: "Now unto him that is able to keep you from falling."
   b. I Pet. 1:5: You "who are kept by the power of God."
   c. II Pet. 2:9: "The Lord knoweth how to deliver the godly out of temptation."
   d. John 17:15: "I pray not that thou shouldest take them out of the world, but that thou shouldest keep them from the evil."
   e. See also I Cor. 10:13.

4. However, many verses also warn us that we can refuse to avail ourselves of God's keeping power and thus we *can* fall away.
   a. Gal. 5:4: "Ye are fallen from grace."
   b. Heb. 3:12: "Take heed, brethren, lest there be in any of you an evil heart of unbelief, in departing from the living God."

c. Heb. 4:11: "Let us labor therefore to enter into that rest, lest any man fall after the same example of unbelief."

5. The power of God which can keep us from Satan is ours for the taking. But we ourselves have to do the taking, and when we have once taken it, we must hold it fast.

6. The thing that made Paul confident about what the Thessalonians would do was his confidence in what God would do for them. God's faithfulness inspires confidence in the faithfulness of God's children.

7. The things which Paul commanded the Thessalonians were undoubtedly those traditions which they had been taught, whether by word, or by this epistle. II Thess. 2:15.

8. Paul's confidence in his converts was a real joy to him. He had no confidence in what evil men might do. But he had confidence in what his Christian brethren would do. Compare II Cor. 7:16: "I rejoice therefore that I have confidence in you in all things."

Text (3:5)

5 And the Lord direct your hearts into the love of God, and into the patience of Christ.

Translation and Paraphrase

5. (We desire not merely that you perform those things which we command you,) but may the Lord (actually) guide your hearts (by a straight path) into (an attitude of mind in which you will truly possess) the love of God, and into the patience and steadfastness) of Christ. (These divine qualities are needed by us all.)

Notes (3:5)

1. Again the apostle is on his knees: His prayer in this verse expresses the longing so often stated in the Thessalonian letters that they might be made perfect and become like the Lord.

2. Our feelings toward all men should not be mere human feelings, but we should have within us the love of God and the patience of Christ. These were the feelings that Paul wanted the Thessalonians to have.

3. The word "direct" (*kateuthuno*) means to "make straight, guide, direct." (Thayer). In the N.T. it is found only here and in Luke 1:79. In the Gr. O.T. it is found in Solomon's prayer: *"Prepare* their (the people's) hearts unto thee."* I Chron. 29:18; II Chron 19:3. King Jehoshaphat *prepared* his heart to seek God.

Like a bee making a straight line to his hive, our hearts should be so prepared and directed by the divine nature within

227

us that they will go straight and without wavering into the will of God.

4. Paul prayed that the Lord would direct their hearts into two things:

    (1) *The love of God.* This does not mean that they should come to be loved by God, for they had already shared His love when they were saved. Rather it means that *they* should come to have so much of the love of God within them that it would shine forth out of them.

    (2) *The patience of Christ.* The word *patience (hupomone)* here means steadfastness or endurance. It is not limited to patiently waiting for Jesus to come back, but it signifies that we should have the same patient disposition that Christ had. "Let us run with *patience* the race that is set before us." Heb. 12:1.

Text (3:6)

6 Now we command you, brethren, in the name of our Lord Jesus Christ, that ye withdraw yourselves from every brother that walketh disorderly, and not after the tradition which they received of us.

Translation and Paraphrase

6. But we command you, brethren, by the name (and therefore by the authority) of the Lord Jesus Christ, that you (refuse to associate with and) withdraw yourselves from every brother (any Christian) who is walking (and conducting his daily life) in a disorderly manner (like a soldier out of the ranks,) and (is) not (walking) according to the traditions which ye received from us.

Notes (3:6)

1. In II Thess. 3:4 Paul expressed confidence that the Thessalonians would obey his commands. Now he gives one. "Don't associate with Christians who won't work."

2. "Walking disorderly" in this verse applies to a refusal to work. See II Thess. 3:11-12.

3. This command is not addressed to an evangelist, or bishop, or elder, but to the "brethren," the whole church.

4. The command is given in the name of Christ, that is, by His authority. Paul did not give this command on the authority of his own likes and dislikes.

5. There are several types of sinners mentioned in the New Testament, from whom we are to withdraw ourselves. In every case these are (professed) church members who do these things. We

can't withdraw ourselves from all the sinners in the world without going out of the world, but certain things are not to be tolerated if one who is called our "brother" (fellow-Christian) does them.

(1) Rom. 16:17—Avoid those which cause divisions and teach doctrine contrary to that which we have learned.

(2) I Cor. 5:11—Do not keep company with a Christian brother who is a fornicator, covetous, idolater, railer, drunkard, or extortioner.

(3) I Tim. 6:5—Withdraw from those who will not consent to the words of Christ, but dispute perversely, and think that godliness is a way of gain.

(4) II John 10—Receive not into your houses those who bring not the true doctrine about Christ.

(5) Matt. 18:15-17—Reject those who wrong you, if they will not make it right after you go and tell them.

(6) II Thess. 3:6, 10-12—Withdraw from church members who will not work. II Thess. 3:14.

6. The word "disorderly" means "out of the ranks" (often used to refer to soldiers out of the ranks), "disobedient to the prescribed order or rule," "irregular." The same word is used in II Thess. 3:11. In this chapter it refers to those who would not work but were busybodies, meddling in other people's business.

7. Notice carefully that we are only to withdraw from those who *walk* disorderly. *Walk* is a present participle, indicating a continuous manner of conduct. There is a great deal of difference between an occasional lapse in doing our duty to God and in *walking* that way consistently.

8. Concerning the *traditions* which Paul insisted that they obey, see the notes on II Thess. 2:15.

Text (3:7-8)

7 For yourselves know how ye ought to imitate us: for we behaved not ourselves disorderly among you; 8 neither did we eat bread for nought at any man's hand, but in labor and travail, working night and day, that we might not burden any of you:

Translation and Paraphrase

7. For you yourselves know how you ought to imitate us (in the way we lived), because we were not (like) disorderly (soldiers while we were) among you:

8. Neither did we eat (and get our) bread free gratis from anyone, but (we obtained our food) by (fatiguing) labor and (hard)

229

toil, working day and night, so that we would not (be a) burden (to) any of you.

Notes (3:7-8)

1. Often I have marvelled that Paul never hesitated to urge people to follow him. We are all aware of our own failings, and are therefore reluctant to tell people to imitate us. But the people in most churches will never rise higher than their leaders. So if the ministers and leaders do not set an example for the people to follow, the people will not rise to new spiritual heights. We should not boast about doing good, but we should not hesitate to be a visible and unashamed example.

2. Note these other Scriptures where Paul speaks about people "following" (or, more correctly, imitating) him: I Cor. 11:1; Phil. 3:17; I Thess. 1:6.

3. The Thessalonians were commanded to withdraw from every brother who walked disorderly and would not work. (See notes on II Thess. 3:6.) Paul could say without any hesitation that he himself had NOT walked disorderly among them as far as working was concerned. He had gone far beyond the demands of duty and necessity.

4. Eating bread "for nought" means eating free gratis, or at someone else's expense. (The Gr. is *dorean,* the accusative of *dorea,* used adverbially.)

5. Concerning how Paul worked night and day and labored and toiled, see notes on I Thess. 2:9.

6. Lest anyone think by this verse that ministers have no right to impose upon their people the burden of supporting them, read the next verse, II Thess. 3:9.

Text (3:9)

9 not because we have not the right, but to make ourselves an ensample unto you, that ye should imitate us.

Translation and Paraphrase

9. (Now we did) not (labor to support ourselves) because we do not have authority (to demand support from you), but so that we could (both be and) give ourselves (as) an example to you, so that you might imitate us (with confidence that you would be doing what is right).

Notes (3:9)

1. Numerous Scriptures indicates that ministers of the gospel have the right to receive support. See Matt. 10:10; I Cor. 9:14; I Tim. 5:17; Luke 10:7.

2. This verse repeats the thought of II Thess. 3:7 that Christian leaders should set an example for people to follow, if they expect the people to rise to greater heights in their service to Christ.

3. Concerning the word *ensample* (Gr., *tupos*) see notes on I Thess. 1:7, par. 2.

4. Concerning the matter of being followers (or imitators) of Paul, see notes on II Thess. 3:7-8, paragraphs 1 and 2.

5. Paul worked for three reasons.

    (1) To make himself an example of how every Christian should work.

    (2) To deprive his enemies of any opportunity of saying that he was preaching for money. See II Cor. 11:9,12.

    (3) Also Paul felt that preaching the gospel without charge was for him a bonus of service that he wanted to give. See I Cor. 9:14-18.

Text (3:10)

10 For even when we were with you, this we commanded you. If any will not work, neither let him eat.

Translation and Paraphrase

10. (We set you an example of how you ought to work and support yourselves. You must all do likewise.) Because even while we were (in Thessalonica) with you, we kept commanding you that if any (man) did not desire to be working (and wouldn't work), don't let him eat.

Notes (3:10)

1. The saying, "He who will not work shall not eat," is famous in American history. Captain John Smith of the Jamestown colony laid down that rule in Virginia.

2. However, the principle is much older than John Smith. Paul said practically the same words to the Thessalonians. And the principle goes clear back to the time of Adam when God said, "In the sweat of thy face shalt thou eat breat, till thou return unto the ground." (Gen. 3:19). He who is able to work and unwilling to do so shall not be fed. Compare Eph. 4:28; Rom. 12:11.

3. Christianity is a religion for working men. Jesus was a carpenter. (Mark 6:3). Peter was a fisherman. Paul was a tentmaker. (Acts 18:3).

4. In the first letter to the Thessalonians Paul wrote about this matter of people who would not work. There he besought and

exhorted them to, "Do your own business, and to work with your own hands, as we commanded you." I Thess. 4:10.

5. Evidently the loafers had not paid attention to Paul's exhortation in his first letter. So now in this letter, Paul states the matter as a command and puts some real teeth into it. No work, no eat.

6. The statement, "We commanded you," is in an imperfect tense, which indicates repeated action in past time. Therefore we have rendered it in our translation, "We kept commanding you."

Text (3:11)

11 For we hear of some that walk among you disorderly, that work not at all, but are busybodies.

Translation and Paraphrase

11. (We repeat our command about working,) for we keep hearing that some (among you) are walking disorderly (like the out-of-rank soldiers we mentioned), not working (at all), but going around (the) work, (bustling, and piddling around with trifling, useless matters).

Notes (3:11)

1. It seems to be a pet notion of some Bible interpreters to think that these people in the Thessalonion church who were not working were the people who thought that the Lord had come (or was coming very soon). Their idleness is assumed to have been caused by their faulty ideas about the Lord's coming.

   The Scripture makes absolutely no connection between the fact that these people were loafing and their faulty notions about the Lord's coming. The habit of idleness may have been part of their background, as many of the Greeks were not very ambitious about physical work. Compare Titus 1:12, and the notes on I Thess. 4:11-12.

2. Concerning this matter of walking *disorderly,* see the notes on II Thess. 3:6, paragraphs 2 and 6.

3. Paul had no doubt received frequent reports from people coming in and out of Corinth about things that were happening in Thessalonica. He kept hearing (imperfect tense) that some of them were not working.

4. There is a little play on words in this verse which is not apparent in English. We have tried to bring it out in our translation and paraphrase.

   Paul said that he heard that some were not working (Gr., *ergadzomai*), but were busybodies (Gr., *periergadzomai*). *Periergadzomai* has the meaning of going around the work (as if dodging it), or "bustling about uselessly, busying one's self with trifling, needless, useless matters." It is used to describe people who are meddlesome in the affairs of others. See I Tim. 5:13.

Moffatt renders the phrase cleverly: "Busybodies instead of being busy."

Text (3:12)

12 Now them that are such we command and exhort in the Lord Jesus Christ, that with quietness they work, and eat their own bread.

Translation and Paraphrase

12. But such as these (who are not working) we command and exhort in the Lord Jesus Christ (by His name and authority) that they, while working with quietness (and not meddling in the business of others), eat their own bread (which they have earned themselves).

Notes (3:12)

1. The idlers in the Thessalonian Church were restless and meddlesome, not quiet and industrious. It is usually true that people who have no business of their own try to meddle in the business of others.

2. The word "quietness" in this verse is from the same root as the word "quiet" in I Thess. 4:11, where Paul told them to study to be quiet. See notes on that verse.

3. Every Christian mechanic or professional man should know that he is expected to give his very best service in return for the pay he receives. When we serve our masters, we serve the Lord Christ.

4. Those who had been idle were to earn and eat THEIR OWN bread. The words, "their own," are emphatic.

Text (3:13)

13 But ye, brethren, be not weary in well-doing.

Translation and Paraphrase

13. But (we must say to all of) you, brethren, do not become weary in doing good.

Notes (3:13)

1. Life becomes tiresome, and boresome, and seems futile to all of us at times. But we should not get weary of the duties of life so as to desire idleness. Discharge all your duties faithfully, whether secular or religious. God's rest lies ahead of us. See Heb. 4:9 and Rev. 14:13.

2. Gal. 6:9: "And let us not be weary in well-doing: for in due season we shall reap, if we faint not."

I Cor. 15:88: "Be ye steadfast, unmovable, always abounding in the work of the Lord."

3. To become weary (Gr. *egkakeo*) means to lose courage, become weary, faint, flag. It is used in Eph. 3:13 where Paul urges "that ye *faint* not at my tribulations." Also in II Cor. 4:1, 16.

4. We like J. B. Phillips translation of this verse. "And the rest of you—don't get tired of honest work."

Text (3:14-15)

14 And if any man obeyeth not our word by this epistle, note that man, that ye have no company with him, to the end that he may be ashamed. 15 And *yet* count him not as an enemy, but admonish him as a brother.

Translation and Paraphrase

14. But if anyone (will) not obey our word (which we send) through (this) epistle, take not of this (person, and then be careful) not to keep company with (or get mixed up together with) him, so that he may be ashamed (and repent).

15. But (even while shunning him) do not consider him as (if he were) an enemy, but keep exhorting him as a brother (for such he still is, even though an erring one).

Notes (3:14-15)

1. Some people are just too stubborn and willful to be treated gently. They do not appreciate nor respond to kindness. But few people can bear the test of being left severely alone. Therefore Paul tells us that if any church member will not obey the instructions in this letter that his Christian brothers are to take notice of him and have no company with him. If he will not repent because the apostles of Christ have spoken, he must be made ashamed of his course by seeing that it is repudiated by the church.

2. Christians never should shun one of their sinning brethren because they desire to make him a laughing-stock, but so that, feeling ashamed, he may quickly make himself right with God and his brethren.

3. For a list of evil which are not to be tolerated, and from which we should withdraw, see notes on II Thess. 3:6, par. 5.

4. The command, "Have no company with him," (Gr., *sunanamignumi*) means not to get mixed up together with him, nor to keep company or be intimate with him.

5. The object of all church discipline is to save and not to punish.

234

We leave all punishing strictly in the hands of God. Note that even in I Cor. 5:5, where Paul told the church to put out the incestuous man, that this was done so that his fleshly instincts would be destroyed and his spirit saved in the day of the Lord Jesus.

6. We are not to hate the offending brother nor consider him as our enemy. Rather we should weep over him. Lev. 19:17: "Thou shalt not hate thy brother in thy heart; thou shalt surely rebuke thy neighbor, and not bear sin because of him." (Amer. Stan. Vers.)

Text (3:16)

16 Now the Lord of peace himself give you peace at all times in all ways. The Lord be with you all.

Translation and Paraphrase

16. Now may the Lord of peace himself give the peace (of heaven) unto you throughout everything (you do and) in every manner (that He can provide it). The Lord be with all of you.

Notes (3:16)

1. The church in Thessalonica had passed through stormy waters. The apostle prays that God may now give them peace in the harbor of His care.

2. In our outline, this prayer that closes chapter three is called (obviously enough), "Prayer for peace."

3. Although much of the third chapter of II Thessalonians contains strong words, it closes with sincere good wishes and a prayer for peace.

4. This peace is not a far-off peace, but a peace now, and by every possible means.

5. For the meaning of the title, "God of peace," see notes on I Thess. 5:23, par. 3.

6. Paul, like Jesus, gave his followers the benediction of peace. John 14:27. "Peace I leave with you, my peace I give unto you: not as the world giveth, give I unto you. Let not your heart be troubled, neither let it be afraid."

Text (3:17)

17 The salutation of me Paul with mine own hand, which is the token in every epistle: so I write.

Translation and Paraphrase

17. (I close with) the salutation of (myself,) Paul, in my own hand (writing). (Watch for this salutation,) which is (my) sign in every (true) epistle (of mine). Thus I write.

235

Notes (3:17)

1. Here Paul closed his epistle by adding the salutation in his own handwriting. The letter had thus far been written by one to whom he dictated, as was his custom, but now he adds this brief final salutation in his own handwriting. It was the proof that the epistle was truly from Paul. Perhaps their attention is called to this because of a false epistle. See notes on II Thess. 2:2, par. 10.

2. Certain other epistles close exactly as this one.

I Cor. 16:21—"The salutation of me Paul with mine own hand."

Col. 4:18—"The salutation by the hand of me Paul." (Actually the Greek of these two verses is identified with that in II Thess. 3:17.)

Gal. 6:11—"See with how large letters I write unto you with mine own hand."

Text (3:18)

18 The grace of our Lord Jesus Christ be with you all.

Translation and Paraphrase

18. May the favor of our Lord Jesus Christ be with all of you. (Amen)

Notes (3:18)

1. As in every one of Paul's epistles, he closes with the benediction of grace, or divine favor. We are saved by grace. We live by grace. We shall praise God's grace throughout the ages to come. Eph. 1:6.

2. The word "Amen" is omitted in Nestle's Greek text. (He does place it in the margin.) Also it is omitted by the American Standard Version and others. But it rests on fairly substantial authority, and we include it in our paraphrase. It seems so appropriate following the riches of this epistle. See notes on I Thess. 5:28.

STUDY SUGGESTIONS—

1. Review the outline of II Thessalonians, chapter 3.
2. See if you can answer the "Did You Learn?" questions that follow immediately.

DID YOU LEARN?

(Questions over II Thessalonians, chapter 3)

1. What is the chapter topic of II Thess., chapter 3?
2. What is the heading of the section, 3:1-2, in the outline?
3. For what two things in 3:1-2 did Paul request prayer?

4. What did Paul desire that the word of the Lord might have and be? (3:1)

5. From whom did Paul request prayers that he might be delivered? (3:2)

6. What do men without faith sometimes do that affects the preaching of the gospel? (3:2)

7. Though men may be without fault, who is always faithful? (3:3)

8. From what will God keep us? (3:3)

9. Will God's keeping power save us regardless of what we do? (3:3)

10. Paul's confidence in the Thessalonians was based on his confidence in whom? (3:4)

11. Paul was confident that the Thessalonians would do what? (3:4)

12. Into what two things did Paul pray that the Lord would direct their hearts? (3:5)

13. How were the Thessalonians to treat those who walked disorderly? (3:6)

14. To what does walking *disorderly* refer in this chapter? (3:6)

15. What is the idea implied in the expression, *"walking* disorderly"? (3:6)

16. Whom were the Thessalonians to follow (or imitate)? (3:7)

17. What does "eating bread *for nought*" mean? (3:8)

18. Does a minister have the right to receive support for his work? (3:9)

19. Why did Paul work to support himself? (3:9)

20. What had Paul commanded them while he was yet with them about working? (3:10)

21. What connection is there between the fact that some of the Thessalonians were not working and their faulty ideas about the Lord's coming? (3:11)

22. Some of the Thessalonians were "working not at all, but were _____." (3:11)

23. Whose bread were the idlers to eat? (3:12)

24. In what are we not to become weary? (3:13)

25. How were the Thessalonians to treat any man who would not obey the words of Paul's epistle? For what purpose were they to do this? (3:14)

26. Were the Thessalonians to regard a disobedient brother as an enemy? (3:15)

27. What did Paul ask the God of peace to give to the Thessalonians? (3:16)

28. What is the topic of the prayer that closes chapter three? (3:16)
29. How did Paul show that this epistle was a genuine epistle from him? (3:17)
30. What is the benediction of II Thessalonians? (3:18)
31. Quote, or write out, from memory II Thess. 3:1,3,10.
    3:1 starts, "Finally, brethren,————."
    3:3 starts, "But the Lord is————."
    3:10 starts, "For even when we were————."

Special Studies

I. THE COMING JUDGE
By Seth Wilson

When Jesus was riding into Jerusalem on a donkey, surrounded by the excited throng shouting His praise, the people of the city asked, "Who is this?" And some of the crowd answered, "This is the prophet Jesus, from Nazareth of Galilee."

How far short their description fell! How little they really understood who He was!

Today, far too many people are thinking of Jesus as only a teacher or prophet from Galilee in the days of long ago. They think that He has had some interesting and important effects upon society. They may respect somewhat His teaching and His following, but they only think that they know Jesus.

No one knows Jesus who thinks that He belongs to the past, or who considers that we have to do only with the moral and social application of His teaching.

He is far more than a prophet in the past. He is a power in the present. And He is the most certain and significant of all the prospects for the future!

Jesus is living and reigning today at the right hand of the Father in heaven, offering His covenant of mercy and the new birth of the Spirit to all who will receive, calling out of the world a people for His own possession. He is coming again to earth to consummate this age, to receive His redeemed ones unto Himself, to purify His kingdom, and to execute the righteous judgment of God upon all the living and the dead.

The gospel of Christ is a message of facts—facts of history, unchangeable as the past naturally is, and sure as historical records and testimony can make them. But they are not just ordinary facts such as might be found in every part of history. They are unique facts of men's experience with God when God came to men in human form in the person of Jesus Christ. They are the incomparable facts of His life and works, revealing His divine person and power and His eternal purpose for all men of every age. Thus the gospel is not merely a record of the past. It is even more than the truth regarding our present duty and welfare. It points inexorably to the future. It is most important as a preparation for and a promise of things to come. Predictions are an inseparable and most vital part of the gospel, giving meaning to its facts and purpose to its commandments. The promises and warnings of the Lord help to enlighten and to motivate every believer of His word.

The most important prospects for the future for you and me and everyone are not the prospects of national prosperity or depression or war or conquest of space, but the certain coming of Jesus to end this age and to institute a new order of things.

WE CAN BE SURE OF HIS COMING

That He is coming is sure because He said so. We, of course, cannot know it or prove it any other way, except to take His word for it. But we can trust Him completely because of the undeniable facts of His first coming which clearly proved His divine character. To anyone who believes in Him as the Son of God the predictions of His word are plain enough to make us very sure that He is coming back in person in visible form.

He said, "If I go . . . I will come again, and receive you unto myself" (John 14:3). "For the Son of man shall come in the glory of His Father with his angels; then he shall reward every man according to his works" (Matt. 16:27). "When the Son of man shall come in his glory, and all the holy angels with him, then shall he sit upon the throne of his glory" (Matt. 25:31). "They shall see the Son of man coming in the clouds of heaven with power and great glory" (Matt. 24:30b). Under oath in court, on trial for His life, Jesus said, "Hereafter shall ye see the Son of man sitting on the right hand of power, and coming of the clouds of heaven" (Matt. 26:64).

He made several parables for the purpose of emphasizing the importance of His coming and the need for being watchful and ready for it. "As in the days of Noah . . . . so shall the coming of the Son of man be" (Matt. 24:37-42; Luke 17:26-30). The householder and the thief; the faithful and the wicked servants (Matt. 24:43-51). The foolish virgins (Matt. 25:1-13). The parables of the talents (Matt. 25:14-30) and of the pounds (Luke 19:11-27).

239

Angels said, "This same Jesus, who was received up from you into heaven, shall so come in like manner as ye beheld him going into heaven" (Acts 1:11).

Those whom Jesus sent to preach the gospel He also inspired by His Spirit to guide them into all truth and to make known to them things to come (John 16:13-15). Throughout their preaching and their writings they taught that Jesus was coming again *in person*. "For the Lord himself shall descend from heaven with a shout, with the voice of the archangel, and with the trump of God: and the dead in Christ shall rise first" (I Thess. 4:16). See also Acts 3:20,21; I Per. 1:7; 5:4; II Pet. 3:3,4; James 5:7; Heb. 9:28; I John 2:28; Rev. 1:7; I Cor. 1:7; 4:5; 11:26; 15:23; Phil. 3:20, 21; Col. 3:4; I Thess. 1:10; 2:19; 3:13; 4:16-18; 5:1-4, 23; II Thess. 1:7-10; 2:1,8; I Tim. 6:14,15; II Tim. 4:1,8; Tit. 2:13. The apostolic writers not only speak plainly and directly of Christ's coming, but they also refer to His "appearing", "being manifested," His "presence," the "revelation" of Christ, and the "day of Christ." (e.g. Phil. 1:6,10; I Cor. 5:5; II Thess. 2:2; Heb. 10:25).

Some men say they count 318 times that His coming is mentioned in some manner in the 260 chapters of the New Testament. No doubt some of that number are obscure references, and of some it may be very doubtful whether they are interpreted correctly when they are applied to the second coming of Christ. But definite and plain predictions of that great event are made literally dozens of times such manner that they could not be fulfilled in the conversion or death of individuals, in the beginning of the church, the coming of the Holy Spirit, or the judgment upon Jerusalem. They emphatically predict things which have not happened yet and they could not point to a secret or "spiritual" or invisible coming.

WHEN? NO ONE KNOWS.

When He is coming, we do not know, because He has not told us that (Matt. 24:36). He has continually emphasized the need to be ready at all times because no one will know when He is to come (See Rev. 16:15; I Thess. 5:2,3; Matt. 24:27-51; 25:1-13). He will come as a thief in the sense that His coming will be unannounced, unexpected and sudden. In the same sense it will be as travail upon a woman with child.

But he has assured us that when He does come it will be evident to all, with power and great publicity, as the lightning in the east is seen unto the west, with a great shout and the sound of the trumpet (Rev. 1:7; Matt. 24:26,27,30,31; I Cor. 15:52; I Thess. 4:16).

WHY HE WANTS US TO KNOW OF THE FUTURE

Our Lord wants us to know some things about the future. He wants us to be warned and prepared for crisis that must come. He wants us to understand the nature of our salvation, and know that this world is not our hope or our permanent home. He wants us to look forward with hope and longing to His coming in glory and to our perfect union with Him whom we love. He wants us to realize that He Himself is our destiny and our exceeding great reward. He wants us to have assurance and comfort in the afflictions and sorrows of life.

He would have us all to be as strong and stedfast as Paul, by having his kind of faith in the "far more exceeding weight of eternal glory" and by looking with him "not at the things which are seen, but at the things which are not seen." Read II Cor. 4:16 to 5:11.

Daily consciousness of the imminent return of Christ will surely prompt more godly living, promote more sacrificial giving, produce more patience and even rejoicing under trials, and purify our motives in all that we do. We need to realize that we do not live our lives to be seen of men, or to "get by" in the world; but we do all our works under His watchful eye, and we shall soon stand before Him to give account.

The heart of Christianity is the vital power of faith, hope, and love—all centered upon Jesus Christ. Any one who does not believe His word enough to hope for His coming and to love His appearing will surely lack the personal force of Christ in his life.

The predictions of His coming should be even to the unbeliever an inducement to heed more seriously Christ's commands and claims, because His coming is a threat to the disobedient as well as a promise to the faithful.

WHAT WILL HAPPEN WHEN HE COMES?

The Lord has revealed only a few particulars and some things of the general nature of the great events which will take place when He comes. No doubt there are many things in store for us that we have not been told because we could not grasp and appreciate them now. Very likely some of the things predicted will not happen just as we imagine them. It is difficult, if not impossible, to tell in what order or how close together the following events will come to pass. But we are told that in connection with His coming or after it: the

241

dead will be raised (I Thess. 4:16; John 5:28,29); the saved will be with the Lord (John 14:3; I Thess. 4:17); the bodies of the redeemed will be changed into the likeness of the body of His glory (Phil. 3:21; I Cor. 15:52-54; Rom. 8:23-25); the world and the works therein will be burned up (II Pet. 3:11-13); a crown of glory will be given to the faithful (II Tim. 4:8; I Pet. 5:4); Christ will execute judgment upon all men (II Tim. 4:1; Jude 14,15; Acts 10:42; 17:31; John 5:22-29; II Cor. 5:10); He will reject many who thought they were saved (Matt. 7:21-23; 22:13,14; Luke 13:25-27; cf. Matt. 13:40-43 and 47-50); the door of salvation will be forever closed (Luke 13:25-28); there will be grief and terror in the hearts of many because they are unprepared to meet Him (Matt. 24:30,50,51; 25:30; Rev. 1:7; 6:14-17; Luke 13:28; I Thess. 5:3; II Thess. 1:7-9).

Whether or not all men are to be judged at one time, or whether there will be two judgments, or three or five, is relatively unimportant. Probably no man knows just how and when it will all be done, but the Lord will take care of it without our figuring it out. The important matter is to be ready for judgment by being in Christ, and to know that "We must all appear before the judgment seat of Christ; that every one may receive the things done in the body, according to what he hath done, whether it be good or bad" (II Cor. 5:10).

Let every sinner remember this fact, and contemplate what it will mean—our Savior will be our Judge! He who once served the sentence of death for us, who now makes intercession for us at the throne of God, who invites all to come unto Him and be saved—it is He who will come in flaming fire, rendering vengeance upon all that know not God and obey not the gospel!

II. A SECRET RAPTURE CONSIDERED
By Seth Wilson

I truly desire to see people awakened to the reality and tremendous significance of the second coming of our Lord. But to put all the emphasis upon a secret rapture and mysterious disappearance of the saved, as if that were certainly the nature of Christ's coming, is to teach as Bible truth what is at best a doubtful, speculative view of the implications of the Bible.

The Lord's coming is surely and clearly taught; so also is the separation of the saved from the unsaved, the resurrection of those in Christ, the transformation of the bodies of both the living and the resurrected saints, and their rising to meet Him, ever to be with Him. But after much restudy of the Scriptures, I agree with R.A. Torrey's statement: "The doctrine of the secret rapture of believers does not seem to have much support in Scripture."

I have seen the Baptista motion picture on the rapture and have heard the idea for years. I have had no particular reason to oppose it, and have no feeling against it, if that is what the Lord wants to do; but I just can't find that the Scripture teaches it. I have the MILLENIUM BIBLE by Biederwolf before me; and it makes the fullest study of all the implications which men have found in or read into every prophetic passage. It certainly favors a premillenial view with separate resurrections, a period of tribulation, etc.; but its comments on the rapture are divided, uncertain, and confused, not at all strong for a secret rapture.

I Thess. 4:13-17 does indeed teach that the saved (both living and resurrected) will be caught up to meet the Lord in the air at His coming, but there is no indication that it is silent and secret so that it leaves the rest of the world mystified by their absence. It says that the Lord will come with a shout, with the voice of the archangel, and the trumpet of God. How can we know that this coming to meet His saints is a different coming from that described in Rev. 1:7 where it says: "Every eye shall see him, and they also that pierced him"? He said that we should not believe it if one said, "He is in the secret chambers." "For as lightning cometh out of the east and shineth even unto the west, so shall the coming of the Son of man be." (Matt. 24:26,27; Luke 17:23,24).

Those who hold that Matt. 24:30—"They *shall see* the Son of man coming on the clouds of heaven with power and great glory"—refers to a third coming (or to a second phase of His coming) seven years after He has taken the saved out of the earth, run into serious difficulties. They must make verse 31 refer to a group called "his elect" who are not of the church or the redeemed at His coming. The parable of the ten virgins surely does not indicate that those who are unprepared at His coming will be gathered in later. I Thess. 5:3 indicates that the coming of the Lord which brings sudden destruction upon the wicked is to be in a time when they are saying, "Peace and safety," which hardly seems to be at the climax of seven years of terrible tribulations after all the righteous have disappeared.

The Scriptures most cited as teaching this seven years of tribulation are from Daniel and Matt. 24:21, 29, which in context refer to the Jews and the fall of Jerusalem. In Luke 17:22-37 Jesus told His disciples that they would desire to see one of the days of the Son of man, but would not be able to, until He comes upon both the godly and the ungodly by surprise when they are buying, selling, planting, and building, apparently unmindful of any impending judgments.

The Bible does not say that Jesus is coming once "for his saints" and again "with his saints." The passage in I Thess. 4:13-17, which is supposed to teach the former, says, "even so them also that are fallen asleep in Jesus will God bring with him." If "to be absent from the body is to be at home with the Lord" (see II Cor. 5:8; Phil. 1:21-23), then, when the Lord comes to unite the dead saints with the living ones and to transform the bodies of both (see I Cor. 15:51; Phil. 3:20, 21), why wouldn't He bring the saints with Him? Isn't it also possible that Jude 14—"The Lord came with ten thousands of His holy ones" (this is the American Standard Vers. and "saints" simply means "holy ones")—refers to the angels that come with Him, as stated in Matt. 25:31—"And all the holy angels with him" (see also Matt. 16:27)? Matt. 13:39-41 says He will send the angels to gather the wicked, and Matt. 24:31 also says that when He comes, He will with the sound of a great trumpet send forth His angels to gather His elect from all parts of the world.

The statements about one being taken and another left (Matt. 24:40, 41; Luke 17:34, 35) do not necessarily picture a secret rapture. The word which is translated "taken" in each of these verses is the same word exactly which is used in John 14:3—"I will come again and receive you unto myself." These verses may only say that of people who live and work together here, one will be received by the Lord and the other left out, when Jesus comes for His own.

When the Scripture says that His coming will be as a thief in the night, it explains that it means suddenly and unannounced upon those who are not looking for Him, but it never indicates that it means stealthily and unseen. (See I Thess. 5:1-3; Luke 12:39-46; Matt. 24:42-44; Rev. 16:15). In fact, Peter says: "But the day of the Lord shall come as a *thief*; in which the heavens shall pass away with a great noise; and the elements shall be dissolved with a fervent heat, and the earth and the works that are therein shall be burned up." All this comes "as a thief!"

There may be some time between events that are associated with the Lord's coming, the resurrection of the saved, the resurrection of the wicked, the judgments of men, destruction of the earth, establishment of a new heaven and new earth wherein dwelleth righteousness (II Pet. 3:13), etc. But the time tables which men offer on the "rapture," the "tribulation," the "revelation of Christ with the saints," the "millenium," the "judgment of the nations," etc., is all speculative. It is not found in the Scripture and the advocates of all these things cannot find grounds enough to agree among themselves concerning the order and timing of them.

Even the expression in I Thess. 4:16—"the dead in Christ shall rise first"—does not necessarily depict a second resurrection. The contrast which is stated in the context is between the living believers and the dead believers. The living will not precede the dead, because the dead will be raised first. Then (next) the living will be caught up with them to meet the Lord in the air. Nothing at all is said about the resurrection of the unbelievers in the entire chapter.

I know that Rev. 20:5 says, "The rest of the dead lived not until the thousand years should be finished. This is the first resurrection." I am not at all sure exactly what many verses of this chapter refer to, although their general intent is clear. But I do notice that it does not say, or even clearly imply, that the reigning with Christ for one thousand years to take place upon the earth. And it does not say, or even clearly imply, that the thousand years of reign begins at the second coming of Christ. It says that John saw the "souls" of martyrs and of undefiled worshippers of Jesus reigning with Him. Jesus is reigning even now, at the right hand of God, far above all rule, and authority, and power (Eph. 1:20-23). Long ago He told the church in a letter, that He had overcome and sat down on His Father's throne with him. (Rev. 3:21). Jesus said on earth that He was a king, and that His kingdom was not of this world (John 18:33-37). He also solemnly promised that the kingdom would come with power while many that heard Him speak were still alive (Mark 9:1). The apostles preached that the Christians of their day were in the kingdom of God's dear Son (Col. 1:13; Rom. 14:17), although they looked forward to the kingdom of the future also (II Pet. 1:11, and others). They considered that the universal gospel of their day fulfilled the prophecy of Amos 9:11, 12 about God's building again the tabernacle of David (Acts 15:15-18). Rev. 1:6 cites it as a fact in John's day that "He made us to be a kingdom and priests." They even speak (rather mystically) of the fact that He has raised us up with Christ and made us to sit with Him in the heavenly places (Eph. 2:6). The first resurrection of Rev. 20:5 could be the resurrection of the believer when he is "raised with him (Christ)" and "made alive together with him" (Col. 2:12,13; 3:1; Eph. 2:5). Or why couldn't it?

III. WHAT WILL HAPPEN WHEN JESUS COMES BACK?

By Wilbur Fields

1. Every eye will see him. Rev. 1:7
   a. He will come visibly. Matt. 24:27
   b. He will come with angels (Matt. 16:27), and with clouds, and power, and great glory. (Matt. 24:30)

2. He will come with a shout, and with the voice of the archangel (Michael; Jude 9), and the trumpet of God. I Thess. 4:16; Matt. 24:31; I Cor. 15:52

3. Many will wail when they see Him. Rev. 1:7

4. All who are in the graves will come forth. John 5:28-29
   a. Both the just and the unjust. Acts 24:15
   b. The dead are raised incorruptible. I Cor. 15:52
   c. The dead in Christ are resurrected first, before we that remain are caught up. I Thess. 4:16-17.

5. Our bodies shall be instantly changed to become immortal (I Cor. 15:52-53), powerful (I Cor. 15:43), and spiritual (I Cor. 15:44).

6. The saved shall be caught up into the clouds to meet the Lord in the air. I Thess. 4:17. Angels will gather together the Lord's chosen ones. Matt. 24:31.

7. There will be a separation on earth. The saved will be taken and the wicked left. Matt. 24:40-41; 13:49; Luke 17:34-36.

8. Angels shall gather the wicked, like reapers gather up tares. Matt. 13:40-41.

9. All nations shall be gathered before the judgment throne. Matt. 25:31-32.

10. The judgment will follow. Matt. 25:33-46; Rev. 20:11-13.
    a. Christ will be the judge. Matt. 25:31-32; Acts 10:42; John 5:22.
    b. At the judgment those who are saved will face no condemnation, and have no sins to give account for. But they

will be judged to determine the reward of their works. John 5:24. Romans 8:1; Hebrews 8:12; I Corinthians 3:14; II Cor. 5:10.

11. The wicked shall be cast into the lake of fire. Rev. 20:15; Matt. 25:46; Mark 9:43-48.

12. The present earth and heaven shall be pass away. II Peter 3:10, 12; Rev. 20:11; Hebrews 12:26-27.

13. A new heaven and new earth will be revealed. II Peter 3:13; Rev. 21:1.

14. Christ will deliver the kingdom (the church) to the Father. I Cor. 15:24.

15. The saints will enter into the city, New Jerusalem. Rev. 22:14.

16. The New Jerusalem will come down out of heaven. Rev. 21:2, 10. (Presumably it will come down to the new earth. Note Rev. 21:24-26.)

17. The saints will serve God in the new heaven and earth forever and ever. Rev. 22:3; 21:24-26.

"Therefore, be ye also ready; for in an hour that ye think not the Son of Man cometh." Matt. 24:44.

IV. THE COMING OF THE LORD WITH ALL HIS "SAINTS"
By Wilbur Fields

In our notes on I Thess. 3:13 we stated our opinion that the *saints* who will come with Jesus from heaven will be the angels, his "holy ones."

While this teaching has been held by most Bible interpreters throughout the centuries, it is now regarded almost as modernism by some people.

As a sample of the teaching now popular among some people, we quote here from a widely circulated series of prophecy lessons:

"We need to ever keep in mind that there will be a 'second coming' and a 'third coming' of Christ, which some writers prefer to speak of as the first and second phase of Christ's return." "He will return 'FOR his saints,' and he will also return 'with His saints.' When He returns FOR His saints, then it is that He comes only in the clouds. But when He returns with his saints, then it is that His feet will once again stand on the Mt. of Olives."

According to this system of interpretation, the following series of events will occur when Christ comes:

(1) He will come FOR His saints in the clouds.

(2) The dead in Christ will be resurrected.

(3) The resurrected and the living saints will be taken up out of the world to be with Christ, leaving the unsaved behind. (This taking up of the saints is usually called the "rapture," a term not found anywhere in the Scriptures. See brother Seth Wilson's fine article, "A Secret Rapture Considered," in this book.)

(4) Following the "rapture" there will (supposedly) be a period of 7 (or 3½) years, during which the Antichrist will rule the world, and a Great Tribulation will occur.

(5) Then Christ is to return WITH his saints to punish sinners and reign for a thousand years (the millenium).

May we offer three objections to this system of interpretation.

(1) We observe first of all that the Scripture in NO place makes any distinction between Christ's coming FOR His saints, and his coming WITH His saints. It does not even use the expression, "coming FOR His saints." We would be the first to acknowledge that Christ is coming to take up His saints to be with Him, but to make a distinction between that coming and the coming WITH His saints is to make a distinction where the Scriptures make none.

(2) I Thess. 3:13 almost utterly rules out the possibility that Christ is coming back with his people, after having taken them out of the earth previously.

In that verse Paul prayed that the Thessalonian Christians might be established unblameable in holiness *at the coming* of our Lord Jesus with all His saints.

Now surely no one could say that saints who had been resurrected and transformed in body, and taken up to be with Jesus would need to be further established unblameable in holiness. Only if they were here on earth would they need to be established in holiness when the Lord comes.

Unless the saints (referring to the people) could be in two places at once, we cannot interpret the phrase, "with all his saints," to mean "with all his *people*."

They would have to be on earth where they needed to be established unblameable in holiness. And they would have to be with the Lord coming down from heaven at the same time, if the idea is true that the Lord is coming with all his people.

(3) Thirdly, the word "saints" is frequently applied to angels as well as people.

The word "saint" means "holy one." Note these references where it refers to angels:

(a) Deut. 33:2—"And he came with ten thousands of *saints*." (This describes how the Lord came down on Mt. Sinai.)

(b) Dan. 4:13—"I saw in the visions of my head upon my bed, and behold, a watcher and an *holy one* came down from heaven." See also Dan. 4:23. The word here translated "holy one," is the same word as is elsewhere translated "saint."

(c) Daniel 8:13—"Then I heard one *saint* (or holy one) speaking, and another *saint* said unto that certain *saint* which spake." These *saints* were the angels that revealed to Daniel the visions.

(d) Psalm 89:5-7—"And the heavens shall praise thy wonders O Lord: thy faithfulness also in the congregation of the *saints* (holy ones). For who in the heaven can be compared unto the Lord? Who among the sons of the mighty can be likened unto the Lord? God is greatly to be feared in the assembly of the *saints* (holy ones), and to be had in reverence of all them that are about him."

(e) Luke 9:26—"For whosoever shall be ashamed of me and of my words, of him shall the Son of man be ashamed, when he shall come in his own glory, and in his Father's, and of the *holy angels*." See also Mark 8:38 and Rev. 14:10. The word translated "holy" in all of these verses is the same word that is translated *saints* in many other places.

Many verses teach plainly that Christ is coming back with the angels. See II Thess. 1:7; I Thess. 4:16; Mark 8:38; Matt. 16:27; 25:31; Luke 9:26. But the only way that men can "prove" that *people* will be WITH Christ when He comes back is to interpret dogmatically the word *saints* to mean "people," when it does not necessarily refer to people at all.

The view that the "saints" (or holy ones) who will come with Jesus are angels adds light to the following verses:

(1) Zechariah 14:5—"And the Lord my God shall come, and all the *saints* with thee." (The American Stan. Vers. renders this verse: "And all the holy ones with thee.")

(2) Jude 14—"And Enoch also, the seventh from Adam, prophesied of these saying, Behold, the Lord cometh with ten thousands of his saints, to execute judgment——." (Amer. Stan. Vers. has "with ten thousands of his holy ones.")

We agree with R. C. Foster in his statement: "We do not read of two comings of Christ at the end of time, but one great coming on the clouds of heaven even as He ascended, and then the judgment of all the world." (THE FINAL WEEK, p. 114).

V. "THE THRONE OF HIS FATHER DAVID"

By Wilbur Fields

"The Lord God shall give unto him the throne of his father David." Luke 1:32

These words were spoken by the angel Gabriel to Mary, when he told her that she would conceive and bring forth a son, Jesus.

Many people feel that this prophecy has not yet been fulfilled, and that Jesus has not yet received the throne of his father David. They look forward to a time when Jesus will sit on the throne of David in Jerusalem, and reign for a thousand years.

Sometimes the question is asked, "Who is now sitting on the throne of David?" The answer that is sought in many cases is, "No one."

However, we think that Jesus Christ IS now ruling from the throne of David. Please let us give you five reasons why we think this:

I. *The throne of David is the same as the throne of God.*

    a. Exodus 19:3-6—When the Israelites were constituted into a nation, they became a "kingdom of priests and a holy nation." God was their king.

    b. I Sam. 8:7—When the Israelites demanded that they have a king to rule over them, God said, "They have rejected *me,* that I should not reign over them."

    c. II Sam. 3:10—This is one of many passages that uses the expression "throne of David."

    d. I Chronicles 29:23—"Then Solomon sat on the *throne of the Lord* as king instead of David his father."

    e. Jeremiah 22:30—God spoke of King Jehoiachin (Coniah) in this manner: "For no man of his seed shall prosper, sitting upon the throne of David, and ruling any more in Judah."

    f. These Scriptures point out that God was the original king of Israel. But the Israelites rejected God from being king over them, and chose a king of their own. God permitted this, and the throne of God was to that degree moved from heaven to earth. Thus we find the throne of David being called the throne of the Lord. David's throne was God's throne. After the time of Coniah and the destruction of Jerusalem, the kingdom was withdrawn from Jerusalem and Judah. The throne of David, the throne of God, was gone from the earth.

II. *Christ was to receive his kingdom in heaven, not on earth.*

 a. Daniel 7:13, 14—"I saw in the night visions, and behold, one like the Son of man came with the clouds of heaven, and came to the Ancient of days (who is God), and they brought him near before him. And there was given him dominion, and glory, and a kingdom, that all people, nations, and languages should serve him." (Notice that Christ received his kingdom when he was before God in heaven.)

 b. Luke 19:11-12—This Scripture tells how Christ, as he drew near to Jerusalem for His last visit, told a parable, because some thought that the kingdom of God should immediately appear. In his parable He told how a nobleman had to go into a far country to receive for himself a kingdom. The nobleman represents Christ himself. Christ had to go into a far country, heaven, to receive his kingship, and this He did when he ascended back into heaven. He is king there now. And, as in the parable, He will return, not so much to reign (for He is already doing that now), but to judge his servants. Luke 19:15

 c. Christ said, "My kingdom is not of this world." John 18:36. We do not look for a worldly, material manifestation of Christ's kingdom.

III. *The time for the establishment of the Lord's kingdom is long since past.* If Christ is not king by now, and isn't ruling from David's throne, then the word of God has come to nought.

 a. Daniel 2:44—The kingdom of God was to be established in the days of the fourth world empire, the Roman. The kingdom of God was to be established "in the days of these kings." The Roman empire fell in 486 A.D. If Christ's kingdom were not established before then, the word of God has come to nought.

 (Incidentally, the four empires of which Daniel prophesied were the Babylonian, Persian, Macedonian, and Roman.)

b. The kingdom was nigh (or near) in the time of John the baptist. Matt. 3:2.

c. The kingdom was to be established during the lifetime of those living while Christ was still on earth. Mark 9:1. Surely Christ told the truth. Surely his kingdom was established, and he sits upon the throne.

IV. *After the day of Pentecost, when the church was established, the kingdom of Christ is always spoken of as being in existence.*

a. Before Pentecost, the kingdom is spoken of as future. See Mark 15:43; Acts 1:6.

b. After Pentecost, it is spoken of as existing.

(1) Col. 1:13—"And hath translated us into the kingdom of his dear Son."

Note—The kingdom of Christ is also the kingdom of God. See Eph. 5:5.

(2) Rev. 1:9—"I John, who also am your brother, and companion in tribulation, and in the kingdom and patience of Jesus Christ, was in the isle that is called Patmos."

(3) Hebrews 12:28—"Wherefore we receiving a kingdom which cannot be moved——."

(4) Acts 8:12—"But when they believed Philip preaching the things concerning the kingdom of God, and the name of Jesus Christ——."

V. *The Scriptures indicate that Christ is now ruling on the throne.*

a. Rev. 3:21—"To him that overcometh will I (Jesus) grant to sit with me in my throne, even as I also overcame, and am set down with my Father in his throne." (Remember that the throne of David and the throne of God were the same throne.)

b. I Cor. 15:25-26—"For he (Christ) must reign till he hath put all enemies under his feet. The last enemy that shall be destroyed is death." (Of course Christ will destroy death by the resurrection of the dead.) These verses indicate that Christ's reign is to *end* when the dead are raised, instead of just beginning following the resurrection, as some teach.

c. Mark 16:19—"So then after the Lord had spoken unto them, he was received up into heaven, and sat on the right hand of God."

d. Psalm 110:1-2—"The Lord said unto my Lord, Sit thou at my right hand, until I make thine enemies thy footstool. The Lord shall send the rod of thy strength out of Zion: *rule* thou in the midst of thine enemies." (This is a clear prophecy about Jesus. See Heb. 1:13. Note that Jesus is to *rule* while he is at the right hand of God in heaven. He is sitting in his Father's throne, which is also the throne of David. How can anyone say that no one is now sitting on the throne of David?)

e. Acts 10:36—"Jesus Christ: (he is *Lord* of all:)"

"Hail to the *King* we love so well!
Hail! Immanuel!
Glory and honor and majesty,
Wisdom and power be unto thee,
Now and evermore;——
King of Kings and Lord of Lords,
All hail, Immanuel!
(D. R. Van Sickle)

VI. QUESTIONS ABOUT "SPIRIT" AND "SOUL"

By Wilbur Fields

1. Is there any difference between *spirit* and *soul*?
2. What are the words which are translated as *spirit* and *soul*?
3. What does the word *spirit* mean and refer to?
4. Does man have a *spirit*?
5. Can the spirit of man exist apart from his body?
6. What does the word *soul* mean?
7. What is the relation of soul to spirit?
8. Is the soul immortal?

Question 1—Is there any difference between *spirit* and *soul*? Or are they two names for the same thing?

There surely is a difference between them. Otherwise Paul could not have written in I Thessalonians 5:23: "Your whole *spirit* and *soul* and body be preserved blameless at the coming of our Lord Jesus Christ." Neither could he have written in Hebrews 4:12 that the word of God pierces even to the dividing asunder of soul and spirit.

Question 2—What are the words which are translated as *spirit* and *soul*?

Words translated *spirit* are *ruach* (a Hebrew word in the Old Testament), and *pneuma* (a Greek word in the New Testament.)

These two words have almost identical meanings. (Another Hebrew word which is translated *spirit* a few times is *neshamah,* which means "breathing" or "breath.")

Words translated *soul* are *nephesh* (Hebrew), and *psuche* (Greek). These words also have almost identical significance.

Don't let these Greek and Hebrew words scare you. Wherever they may be used in the remaining questions, they will be explained.

Question 3—What does the word *spirit* mean and refer to?
   a. The word "spirit" (in both Greek and Hebrew) means "wind" or "breath." See Gen. 8:1 and John 3:8 for examples of this.
   b. Then sometimes it signifies anger or fury, as in the expression, "the *blast* of thy nostrils." (Job 4:9). It is used this way in II Thess. 2:8.
   c. Then *spirit* refers to mental or moral qualities in general, as in Ex. 28:3, "spirit of wisdom," and Ezek. 11:9, "a new spirit."
   d. The word "spirit" is applied to apparitions (or ghosts). See Luke 24:37.
   e. The word applies to the life-principle, applying alike to God, who is spirit (John 4:24), to angels who are ministering spirits (Heb. 1:14), and to man's life-principle.

Question 4—Does man have a "spirit"?
   Emphatically he does.
   a. Zechariah 12:1—"The Lord formeth the *spirit* of man within him."
   b. Numbers 16:22—"O God, the God of the *spirits* of all flesh."
   c. James 2:26—"As the body without the *spirit* is dead."
   d. Job 32:8—"There is a *spirit* in man: and the inspiration of the almighty gives them understanding."
   e. Man is a creature to whom life has been imparted by God's spirit. Our life is only a result of God's breath (spirit) upon us. Our spirit and breath is God's breath. Job 34:14—"If he (God) set his heart upon man to gather unto himself his *spirit* and his breath, all flesh shall perish together, and man shall turn again unto dust." See also Isa. 2:22.

Question 5—Can the spirit of a man exist apart from his body?
   Yes.
   a. Hebrews 12:23—Ye are come to the "*spirits* of just men made perfect." (Even Paul the apostle never considered he was perfect on earth. Phil. 3:12. But Christians have come into fellowship with the spirits of saints who are dead to earth, but made perfect before God.)

b. I Pet. 3:19—"He (Christ) went and preached unto the *spirits in prison*." (These "spirits in prison" were the people who had been disobedient to the word of God in the time of Noah.)

c. Acts 7:59—"Lord Jesus, receive my spirit." (Stephen was dying as he spoke these words.)

d. Ecclesiastes 12:7—At death, "then shall the dust (our bodies) return to the earth as it was: and the *spirit* shall return unto God who gave it." (There is something within man that the gravedigger cannot bury. It is the spirit of man.)

e. Numerous other Scriptures go along with this teaching that the real person can exist apart from his body. Note II Peter 1:13-14: "As long as I am in this *body*, knowing that shortly, *I* must put off this tabernacle (or body)." Also II Cor. 5:9, "We labor, that whether present or *absent* (from the body) we may be accepted of him." (There is more on this subject under question 8 in this article.)

Question 6—What does the word *soul* mean?

This word has many meanings and applications. It cannot be adequately defined by just one definition, unless a very broad definition is given.

The Hebrew word *nephesh* (translateld "soul") is found 754 times in the Old Testament (according to Young's Concordance), and is translated 35 different ways. It is translated "soul" 428 times (in the King James version), "life" 119 times, "person" 30 times, "self" 19 times, "heart" 15 times, "mind" 15 times, "creature" 9 times, "dead body" 8 times, and 27 other ways not more than five times each. In one place (Isa. 19:10) it is even rendered (and obviously well) as "fish."

It is a common error to take a meaning of *nephesh* which it has in some references, and then to argue that that is its meaning always. For example, some say that *nephesh* just means the "person himself." One writer arguing for this view says that when God created man, the combination of the body and the breath of life BECAME a living soul. "Only as these are brought together do we have a living breathing being or person. The Bible use of the word "soul" makes it clear that this, and *only* this, is its meaning." We agree that the Bible uses the word *nephesh* (or soul) to mean the "person himself." But it is just plain wrong to say that that is its only meaning.

Likewise some say that the *soul* is the animal life which is in the blood. It is a fact that the word *nephesh* (soul) has this meaning in many references. But this is NOT its only meaning.

Some interpreters (especially those who believe in soul sleeping and annihilation) refer to the references (there are very few of them) where the word *nephesh* (soul) refers to a dead body, and then try to imply that that is what the word "soul" means in other references.

In an effort to determine what the word *nephesh* (or soul) refers to in the Bible, I have gone over all its occurrences, plus the 103 occurrences of *psuche* (soul) in the New Testament. In most cases we can tell by the context what the word refers to. For example if a Scripture passage speaks about laying up words in your heart and *soul,* we naturally interpret the word soul to mean "mind" in that reference, as indeed it does in several references.

My survey of all the occurrences of *nephesh* and *psuche* leads me to this conclusion: *Nephesh* (soul) *refers to any and all of the manifestations of life, both human and animal, material, mental, or emotional, both in the body and out of the body.* (That is a broad definition, if you ever read one.)

I do not claim my analysis is infallible. For in many cases the word *nephesh* can have more than one significance in one reference. But here is a list of some of the most frequent applications of the word *nephesh,* as they appeared to me:

(1) Approximately 215 times in the O.T. *nephesh* refers to a person or the person himself. Certainly a whole person is a manifestation of life. Deut. 10:22; Gen. 12:5. Compare Acts 2:41.

(2) Approximately 195 times it refers to the animal life which is in the blood, or just to "life." See Gen. 19:20; Lev. 17:11; Deut. 12:23. Animals have *nephesh* as well as humans. Prov. 12:10; Gen. 1:20, 30. Note—If the *nephesh* is *in* the blood, manifestly it cannot always mean "the person himself."

(3) Approximately 115 times it refers to man's deep innermost nature. Ps. 103:1: "Bless the Lord, O my soul." See also Deut. 11:13; Song 1:7.

(4) Approximately 53 times *nephesh* apparently means emotions or feelings. I Sam. 30:6; I Sam. 2:33 (where it is rendered "heart"); Zech 11:8.

256

(5) About 18 times it means "mind" (and is translated that way 15 times). Deut. 11:18; Gen. 23:8.

(6) About 17 times it means "appetite." Prov. 23:2; Deut. 12:15; Micah 7:1.

(7) Fourteen or more times it refers to God's nature, being, and feelings. Lev. 26:11; Ps. 11:5; Gen. 1:21.

(8) It means "creature" at least 12 times. Gen. 1:21.

(9) It means "affection" approximately 9 times. Ezekiel 23:18; Gen. 34:3.

(10) In eight references it is rendered "dead body." Lev. 21:11; Num. 6:6; 9:6,7,10; 19:11, 13. Haggai 2:13. The fact that a dead body could be called *nephesh* would seem to be due to the fact that the body becomes so closely identified with the person, that the body itself comes to be spoken of as the person. We still today speak about burying people when they die, although we do not mean to imply that we have buried the person's spirit, mind, feelings, etc.

(11) In contrast to the use of *nephesh* to describe a dead body, in several references it refers to the life-principle, or spirit, which can depart from the body and exist apart from the body. In such references the word *soul* is almost synonomous with *spirit*. Note these references:

> Gen. 35:18—"And it came to pass as her *soul* was in departing———."
>
> I Kings 17:21,22—"Elijah cried unto the Lord, and said, O Lord, my God, I pray thee, let this child's *soul* come unto him again———and the *soul* of the child came into him again." (If the soul cannot exist apart from the body, how could it have come back into him again?)
>
> Prov. 23:14—"Thou shalt beat him (thy son) with the rod and shalt deliver his *soul* from hell." (The word "hell" in this reference refers to Sheol, the unseen world, the abode of the dead.) Punishing a child will not save him from dying and going into the unseen world. Hence this verse must refer to some place besides the grave where the soul can go into a place of security, if he has been chastised as a youth and directed to live in the right way.
>
> See also Psalm 16:10 and Isa. 38:17.

257

(12) *Nephesh* means "pleasure" in about 4 cases. Ps. 105:22.

There are a few other meanings of the word *nephesh* in the O.T., each used only a few times.

A study of the 103 occurrences of *psuche* (soul) in the New Testament indicates that it has a significance practically identical with *nephesh* in the O.T. *Psuche* is translated as "soul" 58 times, "life" 40 times, "mind" 3 times, "heart" once, and "heartily" once.

Besides the references in the Old Testament which show that the *soul* can live on after death and does not require a body to have identity, these New Testament references confirm the same:

(1) Matt. 10:28—"Fear not them which can kill the body, but are not able to kill the *soul*." This verse could have no meaning if the soul ceased to exist at physical death.

(2) Luke 12:20—"This night thy *soul* shall be required of thee."

(3) Rev. 6:9; 20:4—In these verses John tells about seeing the *souls* of them that had been slain.

(4) Rev. 18:13—"merchandise——of slaves and souls of men." Manifestly the word "soul" in this verse does not mean "persons, " for it is contrasted with slaves, who are living beings up for sale.

(5) See also Acts 2:27, 31, where Christ's soul is said not to have been left in Hades. His *soul* here is almost synonomous with his *spirit*, which he commended unto God when he died. Luke 23:46.

(6) I Peter 4:19.

In summing up the meaning of "soul," let us repeat again. The word *soul* refers to any and all of the manifestations of life, both human and animal, material, mental, or emotional, both in the body and out of the body. It is a very inclusive word.

Question 7—What is the relation of soul to spirit?

(1) Sometimes the two words mean practically the same thing. The *spirit* can be called soul because the soul is the manifestation of the life produced by the spirit. Thus it is used in Acts 2:27; Rev. 6:9; 20:4; I Kings 17:21-22; Luke 12:20.

Don DeWelt correctly says, "The *soul*, or *life* in the blood of man is never called *spirit*. But the eternal invisible *spirit* is sometimes called *soul* or *life*." (From YOU AND ME AND GOD.)

(2) Man IS not a spirit (as God is), but he HAS a spirit. Man both IS and HAS a soul, which can be surrendered, as Elijah said in I Kings. 19:4, "O Lord, take away my life (nephesh)."

(3) When the word *soul* refers to animal creatures, or to the life which is in the blood, it has little or no relation to *spirit*.

(4) The soul, or life manifested, is the result of the inbreathing of the divine spirit. The soul is the sum of all the personal manifestations of the life which springs from the spirit. It it our personal identity, and will be preserved at the coming of the Lord Jesus.

Question 8—Is the soul immortal?

As you can understand by what has been said in this article, if by *soul* we refer to animal life or something similar, of course the soul is not immortal and can die. The word soul often means "the person himself," and when used with this meaning, anyone would admit that the soul will die.

However, in those references where the word *soul* is practically synonomous with *spirit*, we would expect to find the soul continuing a conscious existence after physical death, and we do find just that.

We have avoided using the term "immortal soul" because the Scriptures do not use that particular expression, and we desire to speak where the Scriptures speak and be silent where they are silent.

However, this does not cancel out the precious hope of the child of God that when is absent from the body, he will be at home with the Lord. II Cor. 5:8-9. This cannot refer to our existence after the resurrection, for we shall have a body then. I Cor. 15:44. At death our spirit leaves the body. Then while we are *absent from the body*, we may be present with the Lord (if we have been saved by accepting Christ).

A similar thought is given in Phil. 1:23, where Paul expressed himself as being in a strait (or quandry), desiring both to remain on earth so he could help the Philippians develop in their faith, and a "desire to *depart and to be with Christ*, which is far better." If there is no conscious existence after physical death until the resurrection, this verse does not make much sense. If that were the case, Paul just as well have been patient, for no one will see Christ until the resurrection, and we shall all see Him at the same time.

We prefer to hold the belief that Stephen evidently held. When Stephen was being stoned to death, he saw the heavens opened, and Jesus standing at the right hand of God. Stephen prayed, "Lord Jesus, receive my spirit." He expected to go where Jesus was, and so do I. Acts 7:55-59.

The Scriptural teaching that we may depart and be with the Lord is one of the greatest comforts of the gospels to the Christian. We thrill to know that we are only two or three heartbeats away from the Lord.

Besides this hope of the future life, there is the ever-present hope that the Lord Jesus may come this day, even before we die.

Both of these hopes are most precious to those who have accepted the Lord Jesus Christ, "who died for us, that whether we wake or sleep, we should live together with him." I Thess. 5:10.

(For information, write Wilbur Fields, Box 356, Oregon, Missouri.)